BURT'S

ILLUSTRATED GUIDE

OF THE

CONNECTICUT VALLEY,

CONTAINING DESCRIPTIONS OF

MOUNT HOLYOKE, MOUNT MANSFIELD, WHITE MOUNTAINS,
LAKE MEMPHREMAGOG, LAKE WILLOUGHBY,
MONTREAL, QUEBEC, &c.

BY HENRY M. BURT.

NORTHAMPTON:
NEW ENGLAND PUBLISHING COMPANY.
1867.

CASE, LOCKWOOD & CO.,
PRINTERS AND BOOKBINDERS,
HARTFORD, CONN.

LOCKWOOD & MANDEVILLE,
Electrotypers,
HARTFORD, CONN.

THE EDITOR'S APOLOGY.

In presenting this book to the public, it has been the aim of the Editor to awaken an increased interest in New England's fairest and loveliest regions, and to assist the seeker after pleasure to obtain a more perfect knowledge of the grandeur and beauty of Connecticut Valley scenery and that bordering on it. He has aimed to discard glittering generalities for solid substance, stopping by the way only long enough to point out the piquant condiments that each may flavor to his own taste. He has also endeavored to present briefly and tersely each object of interest from its own standpoint, so that the traveler, whether in pursuit of business or pleasure, can find something suited to his wants.

Every town and mountain of importance on the entire route, from the Ocean to the St. Lawrence, has been visited, and the statements made concerning them in this volume are from original and reliable sources, and not from hasty glances and antiquated gazetteers, as is too frequently the case with many of the guide books that have been published.

In preparing the Guide the Editor has kept in view the wants of the public, and has bestowed commendation only upon such places and persons as he conscientiously believed to be worthy, avoiding in every instance that which might tend to vex and mislead.

An occasional anecdote and reminiscence, many of them never before in print, have been culled from the way-side and are here presented, to enliven and relieve the monotony of description, as too much of a good thing is apt to weary the best of tastes.

The Guide is at your service, Reader, and it is hoped you will find in it a help to your enjoyment of a tour through the Connecticut Valley, where it is confidently believed you can find increased health and a pleasant life-long remembrance.

CONTENTS.

PASSENGER FARES FOR 1867.

PASSENGER RATES.	From Philadelphia.	From New York.	New Haven.	Hartford.	Springfield.	Northampton.	Greenfield.	Brattleboro.
To Montreal, via Connecticut River Line and Vermont Central Railroad,	$19.25	$12.50	$12.50	$12.00	$11.50	$10.85	$10.15	$9.20
To Montreal, via White Mountains, Lake Memphremagog, and Quebec,	35.50	29.75	29.75	28.65	27.75	27.10	26.40	25.45
Montreal, via Lake Memphremagog,	21.75	16.00	16.00	14.90	14.00	13.35	12.65	11.70
Quebec, via Lake Memphremagog,	21.50	15.75	15.75	14.65	13.75	13.10	12.40	11.45
Crawford House, White Mountains,	16.00	13.00	13.00	11.90	11.00	10.35	9.65	8.70
Profile House, White Mountains,	14.50	11.50	11.50	10.40	9.50	8.85	8.15	7.20
Newport, (Lake Memphremagog,)	14.05	11.05	11.05	9.95	9.05	8.40	7.70	6.75
Mount Mansfield House at Stowe,	13.35	10.35	10.30	9.25	8.35	7.70	7.00	6.05

SUMMER TIME TABLES FOR 1867, COMMENCING JULY 2nd.

CONDENSED TIME TABLE

FROM NEW YORK TO MONTREAL, WHITE MOUNTAINS, AND LAKE MEMPHREMAGOG.

GOING NORTH. LEAVE	Express.	Montreal Express.	Express.	Steamb't from Peck Slip.	Express.
	A. M.	P. M.	P. M.	P. M.	P. M.
New York, - - - -	8.00	12.15	3.00	3.15	8.00
Bridgeport, - - -	10.15	2.30	5.14		10.33
New Haven, - - - -	11.00	3.20	6.00	8.15	11.20
Hartford, - - - -	P. M. 12.23	4.47	7.15	9.42	A. M. 12.40
Springfield, - { Arrive,	1.10	A. 6.00	A. 8.10	10.46	A. 1.40
Springfield, - { Leave,	2.00	L. 6.30	A. M. L. 7.45	A. M. L. 7.45	A. M. L. 7.45
Northampton, - -	2.53	7.20	8.35		
Greenfield, - - -	3.43	8.04	9.23		
South Vernon, - -	4.17	8.33	10.00		
Brattleboro, - - -	4.45	8.57	10.30		
Bellows Falls, - -	5.40	10.00	11.40		
Windsor, - - - - -	8.00	11.10	P. M. 12.45		
White River Junction, - {	9.00	11.47	A. 1.15		
	A. M. 8.20	A. M. 8.20	L. 1.45		
Wells River, - - -	10.15	10.15	3.38		
Lttleton, - - - -	11.15	11.15	4.40		
"Profile House," - -	P. M. 1.00	P. M. 1.00	6.30		
"Crawford House," -	4.00	4.00	9.30		
St. Johnsbury, - - -	A. M. 11.10	A. M. 11.10	4.34		
Newport and Lake Memphremagog, - - -	P. M. 1.00	P. M. 1.00	6.30		
White River Junction, -		11.47	1.20		
Montpelier, - - -		A. M. 3.00	3.45		
Waterbury, - - - -		3.22	4.03		
Leave Waterbury by Stage for Stowe and Mansfield House,	A. M. 9.00	P. M. 4.00	5.30		
Essex Junction, - -		4.30	5.00		
Burlington, - - - -		5.05	5.35		
St. Albans, - - -		5.40	6.00		
St. Johns, - - - -		8.00	8.00		
Montreal, - - - -		9.30	10.55		

R. A. DEMING, Agent at Crawford House.

CONDENSED TIME TABLE

FROM MONTREAL, WHITE MOUNTAINS, AND LAKE MEMPHREMAGOG TO NEW YORK.

GOING SOUTH. LEAVE	Morning Express.	Night Express.	Morning Express.	Steamb't Train.
Montreal,		P. M. 4.00		
St. Johns,		5.05		
St. Albans,	A. M. 6.40	7.20	Mixed to Bellows Falls,—then Express.	
Burlington,	7.15	8.00		
Essex Junction,	7.50	8.45		
Mansfield House, (Stowe,)	6.30	2.00		
Waterbury,	8.50	9.48		
Montpelier,	9.05	10.05		
White River Junction,	M. A 12.00	A. M. 1.25		
Newport, Lake Memphremagog,	A. M. 7.15	P. M. 7.00		
St. Johnsbury,	9.18	9.00		
"Crawford House,"	4.30	12.30		
"Profile House,"	7.00	3.00		
Littleton,	9.00	5.00		
Wells River,	10.13	10.00		
White River Junction,	A 11.55 P. M. L 12.25	A 11.34 A. M. L 1.25	A. M. 4.00	
Windsor,	1.05	2.05	5.05	
Bellows Falls,	2.25	3.32	7.50	
Brattleboro,	3.15	4.27	8.50	
South Vernon,	3.45	4.46	9.23	
Greenfield,	4.14	5.15	9.59	
Northampton,	5.08	5.54	10.54	P. M. 7.30
Springfield,	6.00	A 6.30 L 7.00	A 11.30 M. L 12.00	8.20
Hartford,	6.50	8.10	P. M. 12.50	9.30
New Haven,	8.00	9.45	2.05	11.00
Bridgeport,	8.35	10.22	2.40	
New York,	10.45	P. M. 12.30	4.45	A. M. 5.30

J. C. STEVENS, Agent at Profile House.

NEW YORK AND NEW HAVEN RAILROAD.

NEW HAVEN TO NEW YORK.

Fares.	Distance.	STATIONS.	Boston Express.	Accommo-dation.	Boston Express.	Norwalk Special,	Boston Express.	Accommo-dation.	Express.	Stamford Special.	Local Express.	Accommo-dation.	Norwalk Special.	P. Chester Special.	Mail Train.
	Miles.		P. M.	P. M.	P. M.	P. M.	P. M.	P. M.	P. M.	A. M.	A. M.	A. M.	A. M.	A. M.	A. M.
		Arr. N. Y. 27th St. Dep.	10.50	8.10	7.20	5.20	4.55	1.20	12.45	9.50	9 25	8.50	8.00	6 35	5.00
	1	Dep. 42d Street.	10 42	8.04	7.14	5.14	4.47	1 12	12.37	9.40	9.18	8.42	7.52	6 28	4.54
	6	Harlem.													
	12	Williams' Bridge.		7.35		4.44		12.43		9.10		8.13	7.22	5.58	
$0.45	15	Mount Vernon.		7.29		4.38		12.35		9.04		8.06	7.14	5.50	
.55	18	New Rochelle.		7.21		4.29		12 26		8 55		7.56	7.06	5 41	
.65	22	Mamaroneck.		7.12		4 20		12.16		8.46		7.46	6.57	5.33	
.75	25	Rye.		7.03		4 11		12.06		8.36		7 36	6.48	5.25	
.80	27	Port Chester.		6 58		4.06		12.01		8.31		7.31	6.43	5 20	
1.00	29	Greenwich.		6.51		3.59		A. M. 11.53		8.24		7.23	6.36	5 14	
1.05	30	Cos Cob.		6.46		3.55				8.19		7 17	6.31	5.09	
														5 00	
1.15	35	Stamford	9.26	6.37	5.58	3.37	3.32	11.40	A. M. 11.15	8.10	8.03	7.08	6 21		3.39
1.25		Noroton.				3.34						6.56	6.12		
1.25	39	Darien.		6.25		3.31		11.27			7.53	6.53	6.09		
1.30	43	Norwalk.	9.07	6.17	5.39	3.25	3.12	11.19	10.55		7.45	6.45	6.00		3.20
1.40	46	Westport.		6.08				11 09			7.36	6.37			
1.60	50	Southport.		5.58				10.59			7.25	6.27			
1.65	52	Fairfield.		5.53				10.54			7.20	6.22			
1.70	57	Bridgeport.	8.35	5.40	5.05		2.40	10.40	10.22		7.08	6.08			2.50
1.80	60	Stratford.		5.32				10.31			7.00	6.00			
	62	Naugatuck R. R. Junc.		5.27				10.26							
2.05	65	Milford.		5.19				10.19			6.49	5.48			
2.25	70	West Haven.													
2.25	74	Dep. New Haven. Arr.	8.00	5.00	4.30		2.05	10.00	9.45		6.30	5.30			2.15

Read upward.

NEW YORK AND NEW HAVEN RAILROAD.

NEW YORK TO NEW HAVEN.

Fares.	Distance.	STATIONS	Accommo-dation.	Boston Express.	Norwalk Special.	Accommo-dation.	Boston Express.	Stamford Special.	Boston Express.	Accommo-dation.	Local Express.	Norwalk Special.	Stamford Special.	P. Chester Special.	Mail Train.
	Miles.		A. M.	A. M.	A. M.	A. M.	P. M.	P. M.	P. M.	P. M.	P. M.	P. M.	P. M.	P. M.	P. M.
		N. Y. 27th St. Dep.	7.00	8.00	9.00	11.30	12.15	2.15	3.00	3.45	4.30	5.30	6 30		8 00
	1	42d Street.	7.08	8.08	9.08	11.40	12.23	2.25	3.10	3.55	4.40	5.40	6.38		8.08
	6	Harlem.				P. M.									
	12	Williams Bridge.	7.37		9.39	12.09		2 54		4.25		6.10	7.09		
$0.45	15	Mount Vernon.	7.45		9.46	12 16		3.02		4.32		6.17	7.17		
.55	18	New Rochelle.	7.54		9.54	12.24		3.12		4 42		6.28	7.26		
.65	22	Mamaroneck.	8.03		10 03	12.34		3.22		4.52		6.38	7.36		
.75	25	Rye.	8.12		10.12	12.44		3.32		5.02		6.48	7.45		
.80	27	Port Chester.	8.17		10.07	12.49		3.37		5.07		6.53	7.50		
1.00	29	Greenwich.	8.24		10.24	12.56		3 45		5.15		7.01	7.57	Stam. Spec'l.	
1.05	30	Cos Cob.	8.29		10.30	1.01		3.51		5.21		7.07	8.02	A. M.	
1.15	35	Stamford,	8.39	9.24	10.41	1 11	1.39	4.00	4.26	5.32	5.52	7.17	8.10	6.15	9.30
1.25		Noroton.			10.50	1.20					6.01	7.26		6.23	
1.25	39	Darien.	8.50		10.53	1.23				5.44	6.04	7 29		6.25	
1.30	43	Norwalk.	8.58	9.42	11.00	1.31	1.57		4.44	5.52	6.12	7.37		6.32	9.49
1.40	46	Westport.	9.08			1 40				6.01				6.39	
1.60	50	Southport.	9.18			1.50				6.11				6 48	
1.65	52	Fairfield.	9.23			1 55				6.16				6.51	
1.70	57	Bridgeport.	9 37	10.15		2.09	2.32		5.20	6.30	6.50			7.02	10.33
1.80	60	Stratford.	9.45			2.17				6.38				7.10	
	62	Naugatuck R. R. June.	9.52			2.29				6.50				7.16	
2.05	65	Milford.	10.00											7.24	
2.25	70	West Haven.												7.40	
2.25	74	New Haven. Arr.	10.20	10.50		2.50	3.10		6.00	7.10	7.30			7.45	11.10

Read upward.

NEW HAVEN, HARTFORD AND SPRINGFIELD RAILROAD.

NEW HAVEN TO SPRINGFIELD.

Fares.	Distance	STATIONS (LEAVE.)	Train from Hartford to Spring.	First Pass'nr Train.	Second Pass'nr Express Train.	Train from Hartford to Spring.	Third Passn'r Train.	Fourth Passn'r Express Train.	Steam-boat Train.	Night Express Train.	Sunday Mail Train.
		Springfield,	A. M. 7.08	A. M. 10.35	P. M. 1.10	P. M. 3.10	P. M. 5.55	P. M. 8.19	P. M. 10.46	P. M. 1.40	P. M. 10.02
$ .25	4	Longmeadow,	6.57	10.25		3.00	5 44		10.36		9.54
.35	8 5-8	Thompsonville,	6.46	10.15		2.48	5.33		10.27		9.46
.45	12 1-2	Warehousepoint,	6.34	10.04		2.36	5.22		10.16		9.40
.50	14	Windsor Locks,	6.29	9.58		2 30	5.15		10.09		9.35
.55	19 5-8	Windsor,	6.16	9.46		2.16	5.03		9.57		9.25
.95	26	HARTFORD,	6.00	9.31	12.23	2.00	4.49	7.30	9.42	12.40	9.12
1.10	31	Newington,		9.13			4.31		9 24		8 57
1.25	35 5-8	Berlin,		9.04	A. M. 11.57		4.21	7.05	9.13		8.48
1.45	44	Meriden,		8.47	11.37		4 04	6.47	8.56	A. M. 11.57	8.30
	46 1-2	Yalesville,		8 37			3.54		8.47		8.23
1.70	50	Wallingford,		8.29			3.48		8.41		8.18
1.90	55 1-8	North Haven,		8.16			3.34		8.25		8.08
2.05	66	NEW HAVEN,		8.05	11.00		3.20	6.10	8.15	11.20	7.55

NEW HAVEN, HARTFORD AND SPRINGFIELD RAILROAD.

SPRINGFIELD TO NEW HAVEN.

Fares.	Distance	STATIONS. (LEAVE.)	First Pass'nr Train.	Train from Spring. to Hartford	Second Pass'nr Express Train.	Third Pass'nr Train.	Train from Spring. to Hartford	Fourth Pass'nr Express Train.	Steam-boat Train.	Night Express Train.	Sunday Mail Train.
		SPRINGFIELD,	A. M. 7.00	A. M. 10.40	M. 12.00	P. M. 2.20	P. M. 5.10	P. M. 6.00	P. M. 8.20	A. M. 12.00	P. M. 10.25
$ .25	4	Longmeadow,	7.09	10.49	P. M.	2.29	5.19		8.29		10.32
.35	8 5-8	Thompsonville,	7.18	10 58		2.38	5.27		8.38		10.39
.45	12 1-2	Warehousepoint,	7.29	11.09		2.49	5.37		8.49		10.45
.50	14	Windsor Locks,	7.36	11.15		2 56	5.43		8.56		10.51
.55	19 5-8	Windsor,	7.50	11.29		3.10	5.57		9.10		11.03
.95	26	HARTFORD.	8.10	11.45	12.50	3.30	6.26	6.50	9 30	12.58	11.19
1.10	31	Newington,	8.23			3.42			9.43		11.28
1.25	35 5-8	Berlin,	8.35		1.12	3.54		7.11	9.55		11.37
1.45	44	Meriden,	8 55		1.30	4.15		7.29	10.16	1.35	11.54
	46 1-2	Yalesville,	9.02			4.21			10.22		11.59
1.70	50	Wallingford,	9.10			4.29			10.30		A. M. 12.04
1.90	55 1-8	North Haven,	9.23			4.41			10.42		12.15
2.05	66	NEW HAVEN,	9.41		2.05	4.58		8.00	11.00	2.15	12.28

CONNECTICUT RIVER RAILROAD.

TRAINS MOVING NORTH.									TRAINS MOVING SOUTH.					
Passen-ger.	Mixed.	Passen-ger.	Passen-ger.	Night Express.	Passen-ger.	Fares.	Distance	STATIONS. (LEAVE.)	Night Express.	Passen-ger.	Passen-ger.	Passen-ger.	Passen-ger.	Passen-ger.
A. M. 7 50	A. M. 8.55	P. M. 12.00	P. M. 2.00	P. M. 6.30	P. M. 8.50			SPRINGFIELD,	A. M. 6.30	A. M. 6.45	A. M. 11.28	P. M. 2.15	P. M. 5.51	P. M. 8.15
8 00	9.05	12 10	2.09	6.40	9.00	$.15	3½	BRANCH. { Chicopee Junc'n,		6.35	11.19	2.05	5.42	8.06
							4	BRANCH. { Chicopee Center,						
						.20	6	BRANCH. { Chicopee Falls,						
8.09	9 15	12.20	2.18	6.49	9.10	.30	7	Willimansett,		6.25	11.10	1.57	5.33	7.57
8 13	9.20	12.25	2.22	6 53	9.14	.35	8	HOLYOKE,		6 21	11.07	1.53	5.30	7.53
8.26		12.40	2.35	7.06	9.27	.55	13	Smith's Ferry,		6.08	10.54	1 40	5.17	7.40
8 39		12.50	2.48	7.19	9.37	.70	17	NORTHAMPTON,	5.53	5.58	10.46	1.30	5.08	7.30
8.49			2.59	7.29		.85	21	Hatfield,			10 33		4.56	Steamboat Train.
9.00			3.11	7.40		1.05	26	Whately,			10.21		4.45	
9.05			3.17	7.45		1.15	28	SO. DEERFIELD,	5.31		10.16		4.40	
9.16			3.28	7.56		1.30	33	Deerfield,			10.06		4.29	
9.26			3-40	8.06		1.40	36	GREENFIELD,	5.15		9.56		4.19	
9.42			3 57	8.21		1.70	43	Bernardston,			9.42		4.02	
10.00			4.12	8.35		1.95	50	South Vernon,	4.46		9.23		3.45	

☞ Discount of 5 cents to those purchasing Tickets at the Stations.

Vermont Central, Vt. & Canada, Sullivan, and Montreal & Vermont Junction Railroads.

GOING NORTH.

Miles.	STATIONS.	Day Express.	Mixed.	Mail.	Montreal Night Express.
		A. M.	P. M.	P. M.	P. M.
	Bellows Falls,	11.45	5.50		10.00
4	South Charlestown,	11.54	6.05		10.10
8	Charlestown,	12.04	6.30		10.21
13	North Charlestown,	12.15	6.53		10.38
18	Claremont,	12.25	7.15		10.46
26	Windsor,	12.45	8.00		11.10
30	Hartland,	12.54	8.10		11.21
34	North Hartland,	1.03	8.38		11.32
40	White River Junct'n, { Arr. / Lev.	Arr. 1.15 / Lev. 1.20	9.00	2.05	Arr. 11.47 / Lev. 11.55
41	White River Village,	1.23		2.10	12.01
43	Woodstock,	1.27		2.15	12.07
47	West Hartford,	1.35		2.24	12.18
53	Sharon,	1.46		2.37	12.35
58	South Royalton,	1.56		2.52	12.46
60	Royalton,	2.03		3.00	12.51
65	Bethel,	2.13		3.13	1.05
72	Randolph,	2.32		3.32	1.26
78	Braintree,	2.43		3.50	1.43
86	Roxbury,	3.00		4.12	2.07
93	Northfield,	3.15		4.30	2.25
	Montpelier Junction,	3.35		4.50	2.50
103	Montpelier,	3.45		4.40	3.10
104	Middlesex,	3.50		5.04	3.06
108	Waterbury,	4.03		5.20	3.22
120	Bolton,	4.20		5.40	3.45
123	Jonesville,	4.27		5 48	3.55
126	Richmond,	4.35		5.56	4.05
132	Williston,	4.50		6.10	4.20
136	Essex Junction,	5.00		6.25	4.31
141	Winooski,	5.27		6 28	4.55
144	Burlington,	5.35		7.00	5.15
140	Colchester,	5.18		6.34	4.55
147	Milton,	5.33		6 54	5.15
150	Georgia,	5.40		7.02	5.24
160	St. Albans,	6.00		7.25	6 10
	Alburgh Springs,	8.30			6.47
	Rouse's Point,	9.00			7.20
	Highgate Springs,	6.47			6.45
	St. John's,	8.00			8.05

GOING SOUTH.

Fares.	Miles.	STATIONS.	Express.	Day Express.	Night Express.
			A. M.	A. M.	P. M.
		St. Johns,		10.00	4.40
		Highgate,		11.12	6.05
		Rouse's Point,	4.30	10.45	5.40
		Alburgh Springs,	4.58	11.05	6.08
			Mail.		
		St. Albans,	6.30	12.00	7.25
.40	9	Georgia,	6.55	12.22	7.50
.55	13	Milton,	7.05	12.32	7.59
.85	20	Colchester,	7.25	12.50	8.20
1.30	32	Burlington,	7.00	1.35	8.00
	29	Winooski,	7.08	1.27	8.16
1.00	24	Essex Junction,	7.40	1.10	8.40
1.15	28	Williston,	7.50	1.20	8.50
1.35	33	Richmond,	8.05	1.33	9.05
1.50	37	Jonesville,	8.13	1.41	9.14
1.60	39	Bolton,	8.22	1.49	9.23
1.90	47	Waterbury,	8.42	2.10	9.48
2.10	52	Middlesex,	8.57	2.25	10.03
2.35	58	Montpelier,	9.20	2.50	10.05
	57	Montpelier Junction,	9.10	2.42	10.17
2.75	66	Northfield,	9.30	3.15	10.37
3.00	73	Roxbury,	9.50	3.30	11.00
3.35	82	Braintree,	10.14	3.50	11.25
3.55	88	Randolph,	10.30	4.02	11.40
3.85	95	Bethel,	10.48	4.19	12.00
4.05	100	Royalton,	11.00	4.27	12.13
4.15	102	South Royalton,	11.10	4.31	12.30
4.35	107	Sharon,	11.22	4.41	12.35
4.55	112	West Hartford,	11.36	4.52	12.50
4.75	117	Woodstock,	11.48	5.00	1.00
4.80	118	White River Village,	11.52	5.05	1.05
4.85	120	White River Junction,	Arr. 11.55 Lv. 12.25	5.10	Ar. 1.10 Lv. 1.25
4.90	125	North Hartland,	12.40		1.40
5.05	129	Hartland,	12.54		1.53
5.20	134	Windsor,	1.05		2.05
5.30	142	Claremont,	1.25		2.35
	146	North Charlestown,	1.40		2.45
5.45	152	Charlestown,	1.58		3.00
	156	South Charlestown,	2.10		3.10
5.60	160	Bellows Falls,	2.20		3.20

Vermont Central Railroad Line

CONNECTING AT BELLOWS FALLS, WITH

Connecticut River Railroad Line, for Springfield, New York, &c., forming

THE DIRECT RAILROAD LINE,

BETWEEN

New York, New Haven, Hartford, Springfield, &c., and the White and Franconia Mountains. Mount Mansfield, Montreal and Ogdensburg.

CONNECTIONS SURE, AND NO CHANGE OF CARS

BETWEEN

SPRINGFIELD and ST. ALBANS, and SPRINGFIELD and WELLS RIVER.

SLEEPING CARS are run on all night Passenger Trains

CONNECTICUT AND PASSUMPSIC RIVERS RAILROAD.

NEWPORT TO WHITE RIVER JUNCTION.					WHITE RIVER JUNC TO NEWPORT.		
Fares.	Distance.	Mail.	Express.	STATIONS.	Mail.	Express.	Sunday Express.
	Miles.	7.00 A. M.	6.45 P. M.	Derby.	6.45 P. M.	1.24 P. M.	
$0.25	5	7.15	7.00	Newport.	6.31	1.11	6.05 A. M.
.50	10	7.27	7.12	Coventry.	6.19	12.59	5 50
.75	14	7.40	7.25	Barton Landing.	6.07	12.46	5.38
1.00	20	7.59	7.44	Barton.	5.49	12 28	5 11
1.15	24	8.12	7.57	South Barton.	5 35	12.11 P. M	4.57
1.50	33	8 32	8.17	West Burke.	5.14	11.53	4.36
1.75	40			Folsom's.			
1.85	42	8 56	8.41	Lyndon.	4.54	11.30	4.16
2.00	6	9.06	8.51	St. Johnsbury Center.	4.41	11.17	4.03
2.10	9	9.18	9.00	St. Johnsbury.	4.32	11 13	3.56
2.20	52	9.25	9.07	Passumpsic.	4.21	10.59	3.46
2.35	6			McLerans.			
2.50	9	9.46	9.28	Barnet.	4.00	10.38	3.25
2.60	64	9.51	9.33	McIndoe's.	3.55	10.32	3.19
2.75	66			Ryegate.			
		4.30	12.30	Crawford House.	9.30	4.00	
		7.00	3.00	Profile House.	6.30	1.00	
		9.00	5.00	Littleton.	4.40	11.15	
2.90	70	10.13	9.54	Wells River.	3 37	10.16	3.02
3.05	4	10 28	10.04	Newbury.	3.20	9 55	2.50
3.15	7	10.35	10.11	South Newbury.	3 08	9 43	2.38
3.30	81	10.45	10.21	Bradford.	2.57	9.32	2.27
3 55	8	11 02	10.39	Fairlee.	2.41	9.16	2.11
3.75	93	11.16	10.51	North Thetford.	2.29	9.04	1.59
3.85	95	11.24	11.00	Thetford.	2.20	8.55	1.50
4.05	100	11.35	11.09	Pompenosuc.	2.09	8.44	1.39
4.25	5	11.50	11.26	Norwich.	1.55	8.30	1.25
4.40	10	12.00	11.36	White River Junction.	1.45 P. M.	8 20 A. M.	1.15 A. M.

Read downwards. Read upwards.

RAILROAD CONNECTIONS.

At Wells River with White Mountains Railroad for Littleton, and Boston, Concord and Montreal Railroad for Concord; at White River Junction with Northern Railroad for Concord, Manchester, Nashua, Lowell, Worcester, Boston; also with Vermont Central Railroad for Waterbury, Montpelier, Burlington, Saratoga, via Lake Champlain, Ogdensburgh and Montreal; also with Connecticut River Line for Bellows Falls, Saratoga, via Rutland, Brattleboro, Springfield, Hartford, New Haven, New York, and southern cities; also for New London Northern R. R., Amherst, Palmer, Willimantic, Norwich, New London and New York.

STAGE CONNECTIONS.

Stages leave Norwich for Hanover. Pompanoosuc for Union Village and Strafford. Thetford for West Fairlee, Vershire and Chelsea. Bradford for Corinth, Topsham, Washington, Orange, Montpelier and Barre. Wells River for Groton. Barnet for Peacham. St. Johnsbury for Danville, Walden, Hardwick, Cabot, Montpelier, West Concord, Lunenburg, Guildhall, Lancaster and Littleton. Lyndon for Wheelock, Sheffield and Island Pond. West Burke for Willoughby Lake. Barton for Glover and Craftsbury. Barton Landing for Irasburg. Newport for Troy, Derby for Derby Line, Stanstead, and eastern townships of Canada.

IRON STEAMER ORFORD.

Steamer Orford leaves Newport daily at 7.30 A. M., connecting with coaches for Sherbrooke—Grand Trunk Railroad—arriving at Montreal or Quebec the same evening. Returning, leaves Magog at 2.00 P. M., arriving at Newport to connect with 7.00 P. M. train for New York, Boston, and Burlington.

☞SMOKING CARS ON ALL TRAINS.☜

Luxuriously furnished "Ladies Cars" run daily between Springfield and Lake Memphremagog.

NO CHANGE OF CARS

between Boston (Lowell Depot) and Lake Memphremagog, or Springfield and Lake Memphremagog.

THROUGH TICKETS

sold at all the principal railroad stations for Profile House, (Franconia Mountains,) Crawford House, (White Mountains,) and Newport, (Lake Memphremagog.) Also at Profile House and Crawford House for Boston, New York, Saratoga, Montreal, Quebec, and intermediate stations.

☞ASK FOR TICKETS VIA PASSUMPSIC RAILROAD.☜

A. H. PERRY, Superintendent.

GUIDE BOOK.

INTRODUCTORY.

THE fertility and beauty of the Connecticut Valley have long been known to the favored few, and poets and artists have given the world glimpses of its salient points, but it was not until quite a recent period that its charming and matchless characteristics became known to the many. The extension of more rapid and comfortable modes of travel has opened the doors to this elysian field, and thousands come with the recurring period of foliage and flowers, to worship at the shrine of beauty found in lofty mountains, broad meadows and a majestic river. While the noble Connecticut is the Rhine of New England, the region of its source is the Switzerland of America, and year by year the pilgrims to this favored land journey thither in search of rest and inspiration.

There is hardly a town, mountain, or lake, along the entire route, that is not of interest to the tourist, but those which have attracted the most attention within the last few years, are New Haven, Hartford, Springfield, Northampton, Mt. Holyoke, Sugar Loaf Mountain, Greenfield, Brattleboro', Bellows Falls, White Mountains, Lake Willoughby, Lake Memphremagog, Quebec, Montreal, St. Albans, Burlington, and Mt. Mansfield.

From New York to Springfield there is a double track railroad, and the express trains stop only at Stamford, Norwalk, Bridgeport, New Haven, Meriden, Berlin Junction, and Hartford, running 136 miles in five hours. At Springfield the tourist will have 50 minutes for dinner. The Massasoit House is situated within a hundred feet of the eastern end, (south side) of the depot. A porter is always in attendance to take your baggage to the hotel.

In proceeding to the White Mountains, Lake Memphremagog, Quebec, Montreal, Mt. Mansfield, or intermediate points, you will take the cars of the Connecticut River Railroad, in Springfield, on the north side of the depot. If you are unacquainted with the route, you will do well to remember that the cars going either north or south, enter and leave the Springfield depot at its western end.

Between Springfield and Lake Memphremagog there is no change of cars. An elegantly furnished ladies' car runs through both ways on the morning trains. Going north on the train which leaves Springfield at 7.50 A. M., you stop about 20 minutes at Bellows Falls, where you can take dinner at the refreshment room, or wait until the arrival of the train at White River Junction at 1.15 P. M. At this place you have half an hour for dinner, either in going or returning from the White Mountains. Adjoining the refreshment room there is a dining hall, where you will find a neatly spread table and a good dinner. At Wells River, 40 miles from White River Junction, you change cars in going to the White Mountains. From there to Littleton the distance by the White Mountains Railroad is 20 miles. From Littleton you proceed by stage to Profile House, 12 miles, and to Crawford House, 22 miles.

The tourist should bear in mind that the Crawford House is in the White Mountains, and the Profile House in the Franconia Mountains. If you call for a ticket for the White Mountains, the agent will give you one to the Crawford House. You will find it to your advantage to purchase one to the Profile House, as this will save you 13 miles of staging the same day. If you leave White River Junction at 8.20 A. M., you reach the Profile House at 1, and the Crawford House at 4, P. M. If you leave at 1.45 P. M., (the morning train from

Springfield,) you arrive at the Profile House at 6.30, and at Crawford House at 9.30.

At Lake Memphremagog, 105 miles from White River Junction and 229 from Springfield, the cars stop at the door of the Memphremagog House, on the shore of the lake. Leaving Springfield at 7.45, A. M., you arrive there at 6.30, P. M. The next morning you can leave with Capt. Fogg on the steamer Mountain Maid, for a trip through the lake, which is 30 miles in length. You can stop at the Mountain House, 12 miles from the Memphremagog House, and ascend Owl's Head, which is nearly 3,000 feet above the lake, or proceed to Magog, at the outlet. From Magog you can stage it 16 miles to the Grand Trunk Railway, at Sherbrook, and proceed thence to Quebec or Montreal.

While the route from New York to the White Mountains and Quebec, through the Connecticut Valley, is far the most interesting, it is *seventy miles* shorter than any other.

In leaving New York, the tourist, if he prefers, can take the night boat to New Haven, spend a few hours the next morning in the city, and then proceed north.

In going to Mount Mansfield, you proceed to Waterbury, on the Vermont Central Railroad, where you take the stage for Stowe, 10 miles further north. At Stowe there is a first class hotel, capable of holding 300 guests. This is 8 miles from the summit, where there is another hotel, which will accommodate about 100 persons. Coaches run from Stowe to the Half-way House, 3 miles from the Summit House. The remainder of the distance is accomplished on horse back.

In going to Montreal, business men, especially, will find the route through the Connecticut Valley a desirable one. The train leaves New York at 12.15, P. M., arriving at Springfield at 6 o'clock. Here you have half an hour for supper. From Springfield to St. Albans, sleeping cars are run on all night trains, going through without change. You take breakfast at

St. Albans at 6, A. M., and arrive at Montreal at 9.30, A. M. Returning, you leave Montreal at 3.30, P. M., take supper at St. Albans, breakfast at Springfield, and dinner in New York, making this a pleasant and expeditious route between Canada and New York.

Having given this brief summary of the facilities for a tour through the heart of New England, a land not only overflowing with goodness and beauty, but rich in historical incident, the care-worn toiler is invited to green fields and shady nooks, where he will not only find rest, but lessons in the stones and running brooks.

THE ROUTE.

The ride over the New York and New Haven Railroad, a distance of 74 miles, is one of the most agreeable that can be taken by rail. Elegant private residences crown the hill-tops on every hand, evidences of wealth and refinement, while the views of the Sound at various points, dotted with the sails of busy commerce, and of the shores of Long Island in the distance, give pleasing variety to the scene. Many places along the route are of historic interest, where were enacted in the Revolution deeds that will be ever memorable. These villages have been built, or greatly improved, by persons doing business in New York, who have sought homes in quiet and rural places near the great city. The beautiful groves and lawns that are passed are in refreshing contrast with the paved and dirty streets just left behind.

Leaving the station at 27th Street, which is reached from the Astor House by horse cars and the public carriages, the train, drawn by horses, passes through the tunnel, and thence to 42d Street, where the engine is attached.

CENTRAL PARK.

As you proceed northward the eastern boundary of Central Park will be noticed on the left, a quarter of a mile from the railroad. It embraces nearly a thousand acres and in time will be one of the best parks in the world. Its lawns, walks, drives, lakes and fountains make it very attractive. At four o'clock every Saturday afternoon during the summer public concerts are given at the expense of the city, free to all, and thousands are attracted thither to listen to the music and stroll about the Park. In autumn, after the return of city tourists from the country the gathering is immense, and the display of elegant carriages and spirited horses has no equal at any other time or place in this country.

HIGH BRIDGE.

Five miles north of 42d Street is Harlem, once a suburban village, but now part of the Great Metropolis. Before crossing Harlem River,the northern limits of Manhattan Island, the western end of High Bridge is visible. This is one of the greatest triumphs ever made in the art of bridge building. It was built across Harlem River for the purpose of conveying the water flowing into Croton Aqueduct, to the receiving reservoir in New York. It is 1450 feet in length, 114 feet above tide and was built of cut stone. It has fifteen arches, eight of which are 80 feet span, and the whole cost of the bridge exceeded a million of dollars. A little steamer makes hourly trips during the summer from Harlem to the bridge, affording an excellent opportunity for strangers to visit it.

Crossing Harlem River the villages of Morrissania, Mott Haven, Mount Vernon and Fordham are passed before reaching Williams' Bridge, where the Harlem Railroad branches to the left and pursues a northerly route through the country, parallel with the Hudson River.

NEW ROCHELLE,

Nearly eighteen miles from New York, was settled by Huguenots from Rochellê, in France. For several years it was the residence of Thomas Paine, who died in 1809. He was buried here upon what was formerly a part of his own estate. The monument erected to his memory, bears the following inscription, in accordance with his own request: "Thomas Paine, author of Common Sense, died June 8, 1809, aged 72 years."

Paine was the son of an English Quaker, and coming to this

country in 1774 he settled in Philadelphia. In 1776 he wrote a pamphlet entitled Common Sense, in which he urged the separation of the colonies from the mother country. It met with universal favor and more than any one thing, brought the people to the point of resisting British tyranny. The pamphlet won him the friendship of Washington, Franklin, Dr. Rush and other distinguished American leaders, and Congress acknowledged his services by appointing him Secretary to the Committee on Foreign Affairs. He was the author of the often quoted line, "These are the times that try men's souls," which appeared in the Crisis, another Revolutionary pamphlet published by him. In 1787 he visited France, went from there to England, and returned to the United States in 1802, settling in New York. The Quakers refusing him a place of interment in their grounds, which favor he requested before his death, he was buried on his farm in New Rochelle. William Cobbett, the English reformer, who visited this country and wrote a biography of Paine, disinterred his remains and took them to England. The monument erected to his memory, stands within a few feet of where he was first buried.

THE STATE LINE.

The stations of Mamaroneck, Rye and Port Chester, are passed before reaching the boundary line between New York and Connecticut. The latter place is situated at the mouth of Bryam River where the tourist after crossing it enters the Nutmeg State.

GREENWICH.—THE SCENE OF GEN. PUTNAM'S DARING EXPLOIT.

Soon after passing Port Chester, and 31 miles from New York, will be seen the village of Greenwich, situated on a hill, about a mile north of the railroad. It contains some elegant residences and two large churches, Congregational and Episcopal, built of stone. The Congregational church stands in a conspicuous place and its spire can be seen for several miles on either side of the village. The Episcopal church stands almost on the brow of the hill further to the east. The view of the Sound and Long Island from the village is extensive and picturesque.

OLD PUT RIDING DOWN THE ROCKS.

This place was made famous by one of those daring exploits of Gen. Israel Putnam in the Revolution, which so distinguished him for bravery. Putnam was stationed here with 150 men and two cannon, which were without drag ropes or horses, to check the advance of the British, under Tryon, who was making an incursion into Connecticut with 1500 men. Tryon sent a party of dragoons, supported by infantry, to charge up the hill and dislodge Putnam's little band. A spirited firing was kept up until Putnam, seeing it would be useless to make further resistance, ordered his men to retreat into the swamp on the east beyond the reach of the cavalry. He kept his position until his men were safely away, and then, just as the British troopers were riding down upon him from the west, sure of their coveted prize, Putnam put spurs to his fleet horse and rode at break-neck speed to the east, down the stone steps that had been constructed for the use of the people who ascended the hill to attend church. When the British came to the spot Putnam had just left, their horses stopped with fright and the intrepid hero made good his escape. A volley was fired at him and one bullet passed through his hat. The General, still unharmed, kept on to Stamford where he raised a larger force and returned and fell upon Tryon's rear, then on retreat, and captured 38 prisoners and considerable amunition. The next day he made an exchange of prisoners with Tryon, who sent him a new suit of clothes, including a hat, to take the place of the one that had been pierced with bullets, a compliment for his bravery and hu-

manity. A man who stood near Putnam, says the historian, when he made the fearful plunge down the rocks, said he was "cursing the British terribly." The hill at this place is a hundred feet high and quite steep. A public road has been cut through the rocks just north of where this daring exploit occurred, leading to Coscob. A little way east of the

Greenwich depot the railroad passes through the same ledge and the locality can be seen from the cars. A few rods east of the Episcopal church, on the brow of the hill will be noticed a large, square white house. This stands about ten rods north of where the stone steps were located. They have been removed but the place still bears the name of "Put's Hill."

Soon after leaving Greenwich the road crosses Mianus River upon a draw bridge, forty feet above the water, where the trains stop in compliance with a law of the State. The village of Coscob will be noticed a mile north of the railroad.

STAMFORD.

Distance from New York, 35 miles; Montreal, 411; White Mountains, 297; Lake Memphremagog, 330; Quebec, 503.

Crossing Stamford River the express trains make their first stop out of New York, at the beautiful town of Stamford, one of the neatest on the whole line. This place is noted for its wide and shady streets, elegant private residences and great wealth. Over 150 people live here who do business in New York, going and returning by railroad. In summer from 1,000 to 1,500 New York people come here to spend the warm season. There are four public parks in the town, and the drives over the summits north and east of the village, from which an extensive view is had, are unsurpassed. There are eight churches in the town —one Congregational, Presbyterian, two Episcopal, Baptist, Universalist, Methodist, and one Catholic. Considerable business is done in manufacturing woolen goods, Olmstead's patent oiler, friction pulleys, well curbs, extracts of logwood, machinery, &c. There are three boarding schools for young ladies, and four for boys in the town. Among the residents are Brown Brothers, brokers in New York, Hoyt Brothers, leather merchants in New York, Thomas G. Rich, lawyer in New York, James H. Hoyt, Superintendent of the New York and New Haven Railroad, Geo. A. Hoyt, Treasurer Pennsylvania Coal Company, Rev. E. B. Huntington, author of the Huntington Memorial, and History of Stamford, and Capt. Wm. Skiddy, an extensive ship builder. The population of the town is 8,000 and that of the village about 4,000.

The next way station is Darien, a small and quiet village, situated upon a stream that falls into the Sound.

NORWALK.

Distance from New York, 43 miles; Montreal, 403: White Mountains, 289; Lake Memphremagog, 322; Quebec, 495.

Norwalk, the second stopping place for express trains leaving New York, and eight miles from Stamford, is celebrated for its oysters and hats. Some three to five hundred hands are employed in the oyster business and it is estimated that nearly $500,000 annually are received for the sale of oysters that are sent to other parts of the country. There is no other town on the Sound so extensively engaged in this business, Fair Haven standing next. The manufacture of hats is quite extensive and a large number of hands are employed. The straw hat factory employs about 2000, but not all of them reside in the town. The shirt factory, employing 400 hands, is the next most extensive manufacturing establishment. The village at the depot is known as South Norwalk, and has been built since the completion of the railroad; the old village, or Norwalk proper, is located about a mile and a half north of the railroad and is connected with the south village by a horse railroad built by LeGrand Lockwood, a wealthy broker doing business in New York but residing in Norwalk, of which town he is a native. Mr. Lockwood is building a magnificent residence of stone between the two villages, which can be seen from the cars. The streets are wide and the large shade trees and elegant residences give the appearance of neatness and comfort. There are nine churches in the two villages. The hills on the west, north and east, afford excellent sites for dwellings, and on many of them are extensive and costly edifices. Norwalk was almost totally destroyed by the British and Tories, who burnt it July 11th

1779. The loss, estimated by a committee appointed by the General Assembly, exceeded $116,000. The population of the town is upward of 8,000. The Danbury and Norwalk Railroad extends from the south village to Danbury, a distance of 24 miles.

Leaving Norwalk the railroad crosses the draw bridge forty feet above the water, where that sad disaster occurred to the express train, which run into the open draw, several years since, killing a large number of passengers. Great precaution has since been taken to prevent a repetition of such accidents.

Before reaching the next station for express trains, the beautiful towns of Westport, Southport and Fairfield are passed. North of Southport station is the Pequot swamp, where that once great and powerful tribe of Indians, in 1637, made their last stand against Connecticut and Massachusetts troops. Fairfield, was burnt July 7, 1779 by Gov. Tryon, who sailed the previous day from New Haven. This was one of the most destructive conflagrations occasioned by the British, during the Revolution. Two hundred houses were burnt just at night, by the order of Tryon. A thunder storm overspread the heavens soon after the village was set on fire, and the whole scene was one of terrible grandeur.

BRIDGEPORT.

Distance from New York, 59 miles; Montreal, 387; White Mountains, 273; Lake Memphremagog, 306; Quebec, 479.

Bridgeport, the third town at which express trains stop, and 14 miles from Norwalk, is a thriving city of 17,000 inhabitants. At the close of the Revolution there were less than a dozen houses where the city now stands. A horse railroad has been built from Division Street to Pembroke Lake, east of Wheeler & Wilson's sewing machine factory. An extensive business is done in manufacturing by Wheeler & Wilson and the Howe Sewing Machine Companies, the New Haven Arms Company, and by Hotchkiss & Sons, the latter manufacturers of hardware, &c.

There are 15 churches in the city. The South church, which was built in 1861, will seat 1,000 persons, and its spire is 209 feet high.

Washington Park in East Bridgeport, contains several acres and has a grove of native trees. Sea Side Park, situated on the beach south of the city, which has just been laid out at a cost of $20,000 and containing 16 acres of land, will be one of the finest pleasure resorts in the country. The beach is claimed to be the finest on the Sound and ample accommodations for bathing have been fitted up.

Elias Howe, the inventor of Howe's sewing machine, and the sewing machine needle, purchased P. T. Barnum's grounds at Iranistan, after his dwelling burnt, several years since, and is about to build a magnificent residence. Mr. Barnum's homestead, Lindencroft, is situated a short distance west of Bridgeport, in the town of Fairfield.

Chas. S. Stratton, better known as Gen. Tom Thumb, was born in Bridgeport Jan. 4, 1832. He weighed nine pounds at birth, and continued to grow until seven months old, when, from some unexplained cause, he ceased to increase in size and weight. His hight is 28 inches. In 1844 he visited Europe and has had the honor of appearing before nearly all the crowned heads of the old world. In 1863 he was married to Miss Lavinia Warren, a dwarf of about his own stature. The parents of the General have had two other children who have reached the usual hight.

The Naugatuck Railroad extending to Winsted, 62 miles, and the Housatonic, extending to Pittsfield, 110 miles, intersect the New York and New Haven Railroad, the former at this place, and the latter at Naugatuck Junction, east of Housatonic River. The trains on this road run into Bridgeport.

Stratford, about four miles from Bridgeport, is a pleasant, rural village. The principal street, about one mile in length, is ornamented with fine shade trees. Gen. Wooster, killed at Ridgefield in the Revolution, was a native of this town.

MILFORD.—SOLDIERS' MONUMENT.

Milford, 65 miles from New York and 8 from Bridgeport, is a quiet but beautiful town. It contains some elegant private residences, and the large elms which line the principal streets give the place a pleasant and ancient appearance. In Jan. 1777 two hundred American soldiers in a sick and dying condition, were brought from a British prison ship at New York, and suddenly cast on shore near this place. They were cared for by the inhabitants of the village, but in less than a month 46 of them died and were buried in one common grave. Near the railroad, in the old cemetery, east of the depot, a freestone monument, 30 feet high, has been erected to their memory. It can be seen from the cars, north of the track.

WEST ROCK.—THE JUDGES' CAVE.

As the traveler approaches New Haven from New York, he will notice West Rock, to the north, which is from three to four hundred feet high. The village of Westville is situated at its base and the church spires are seen from the cars. This is little more than two miles from the city of New Haven. On the summit of West Rock is the celebrated Judges' Cave, where the regicides, Goffe and Whalley, two of the judges who condemned King Charles I, concealed themselves when pursued by the King's officers. It is not a cave, strictly speaking, but an aperture in the rocks, which afforded shelter to the regicides. Upon the rocks are engraved these words, "Opposition to tyrants is obedience to God." Goffe and Whalley, previous to their concealment on West Rock, resided in New Haven, but their arrest being ordered, they were obliged to flee from the city.

EAST ROCK.

East Rock, two miles east of West Rock, and a mile north east of New Haven, is frequently visited. It is about the same hight as West Rock and the view of New Haven and the Sound from its summit is grand and beautiful. A better view of East Rock from the cars is had after the train leaves New Haven for Hartford and Springfield, a short distance out of the city.

NEW HAVEN.

Distance from New York, 74 miles; Montreal, 372; White Mountains, 258; Lake Memphremagog, 291; Quebec, 464.

On approaching New Haven the tourist will observe the church spires on the Public Square, the City Hall and other public buildings on the left. To the right is Long Wharf, and the Light House in the distance. Chapel Street, on which a larger part of the mercantile business is done, passes over the railroad at the north end of the depot. To reach the Public Square and the College buildings, take Chapel Street and a walk of five minutes, to the west, will bring you to them, located in the best part of the city. The magnificent elms, overarching the walks, and the general neatness of the city, at once attract the attention of the visitor, leaving an agreeable impression of the place upon his mind.

New Haven was settled in 1638, by a company of exiled Englishmen from London and vicinity, who had been merchants, and it is said that this was the most wealthy colony that had come to this country. The city was originally laid out in a plot half a mile square. It is beautifully situated on an extensive plain at the head of the bay which extends four miles in from the Sound. North of the city are high lands overlooking it and the Sound, the most prominent of which are East and West Rocks. Its public squares and ancient elms add greatly to the beauty of the city, giving it an appearance unlike any other place in this country, and as one walks underneath those living arches of green it is suggested that New Haven is truly entitled to the name of "Elm City," by which it is familiarly known.

The view in Temple Street, which extends through the Public Square, north and south, is particularly striking. For a long distance the broad elms form a magnificent arch, more perfect and beautiful than could be made by the hand of man. The view selected for illustration by the artist is from the center of the Green, looking north.

TEMPLE STREET, NEW HAVEN, CONN.

The Public Square, or Green, as it is frequently called, situated between Chapel and Elm Streets on the south and north, and College and Church Streets on the west and east, contains 16 acres. Temple Street extends through it from north to south, and the elms are so large that a complete arch is formed in the center. In this Square on the west side of Temple Street are Trinity, Center and North churches. Farther west is the State House, built in the Grecian Doric style. The basement is cased with Sing Sing marble and the walls above are stuccoed. The Legislature holds sessions here in the even years. Its other sessions are held at Hartford, where all of the State archives are kept.

Yale College, fronting this square on the west and occupying fourteen buildings, is one of the leading, if not the best, educational institutions in this country. It was founded in 1700, and in 1702 it held its first commencement at Saybrook. It was removed to New Haven in 1716, and received its name from Elihu Yale, one of its most liberal patrons, who was born in New Haven, and afterwards emigrating to the East Indies, became Governor of Fort George. Alumni Hall, built of Portland freestone, at a cost of $27,000, is a fine structure. The first floor is occupied by meetings of graduates and around this room are hung portraits of distinguished men, educated in the College, and others who have contributed to its endowment. The upper story is used by the two College societies. But the most magnificent building connected with the College is the one built by Mr. Augustus R. Street of New Haven, at a cost of not less than $150,000, which is to be used as a depository and school of fine arts. The historical paintings of the great battles in the Revolution, by Col. John Trumbull, son of the Governor of Connecticut during the war for Independence and an aid to Gen. Washington, which for many years have been kept in Trumbull Gallery, are to be removed to this building. These are the original paintings, and copies of them are now in the rotunda of the National Capitol. Trumbull Gallery was erected over the spot where Col. Trumbull was buried.

Of the public buildings of which New Haven may feel proud is the City Hall, situated on Church Street, fronting the Square on the east. It was completed in 1862, at a cost of $100,000. Henry Austin of New Haven was its architect, and the contractors for building it were Perkins & Chatfield of the same city. The building is of the Continental Gothic style, 91 feet front by 137 feet deep. It was built of Portland and Nova Scotia stone, laid alternately in courses. The tower is built of stone, 84 feet from the ground, surmounted by a spire 66 feet, making the whole hight 150 feet. The spire is slated and contains a fire alarm bell weighing 6,117 pounds, four illuminated clock dials, each seven feet in diameter, and an observatory or watch tower. The building is occupied by offices, city court, common council chamber, &c. Mr. Austin's plans were adopted after several others had been examined, and the building is creditable to his taste and skill as an architect.

There are nearly 40 churches in the city and the population is about 50,000. In 1800 the population was only a little over 5,000. A large variety of manufacturing is done in the city, but the most important is that of carriages. There are between 40 and 50 firms engaged in the business.

Here have lived and died some of our country's most eminent men. In the cemetery on Grove Street are the graves of Roger Sherman, one of the signers of the Declaration of Independence, Noah Webster, author of Webster's Dictionary and other books, Ezra Stiles and Timothy Dwight, Presidents of Yale College, Pierpont Edwards, Chief Justice of Connecticut, James Hillhouse, fifty years treasurer of Yale College and sixteen years United States Senator from Connecticut, Timothy Pitkin, the historian and United States Senator, Chauncey A. Goodrich—"Peter Parley," Margaret Arnold, wife of the traitor, Benedict Arnold, Eli Whitney, inventor of the cotton gin and many others more or less distinguished in various walks of life. Col. John Dixwell, one of the judges who condemned King Charles I, lived in New Haven, assuming the name of James Davids. He died at the age of 82 and was buried in the rear of Center church, on the Public Square, where a monument has recently been erected to his memory by his descendants.

James Hillhouse, who for so long a time was treasurer of Yale College and to whom New Haven is indebted for its noble elms, was very tall and striking in personal appearance. His complexion was so swarthy that some thought he had Indian blood in his veins. He frequently favored in a humorous way this idea. While a member of the United States Senate, a southern man challenged him for remarks made in debate. He accepted it, but said as the choice of weapons fell to him he should select *tomahawks!* The duel was not fought. One day while standing on the steps of the Capitol, a drove of donkeys were passing, on their way from Connecticut, where they were raised, to the South. Randolph, who was with him, said, "*there are some of your constituents.*" "Yes," replied Hillhouse, "they are going to be *schoolmasters* in Virginia."

New Haven formerly had considerable direct trade with foreign countries, and long wharf, commencing at the foot of Fleet Street and extending into the harbor to the channel, 3,943 feet, is the longest wharf in this country.

THE NEW HAVEN HOTEL, NEW HAVEN, CONN.

The New Haven Hotel, Mr S. W. Allis, Proprietor, is situated on the corner of Chapel and Church Streets, within five minutes walk of the depot. It fronts on the Public Square, and as it is provided with all the modern conveniences, bath rooms, &c., visitors find it a pleasant place of resort. During the summer, stages run from the Hotel to Double Beach and Branford Point, 7 miles distant, and to Savin Rock, 4 miles west of the city.

THE SHORE HOUSES.

Within a short distance of New Haven are several spacious and well kept Hotels, pleasantly situated along the beach, that have become favorite places of resort during the summer months with those who are fond of fishing, sailing and bathing.

The nearest one to New Haven is Savin Rock, four miles south west of the city, and a mile from West Haven depot, on the New York and New Haven Railroad. Omnibuses during the summer run hourly from New Haven to the Rock House. It is a delightful spot, affording a magnificent view of the Sound, and the beach is among the best bathing places found on the Connecticut shore. The Hotel will accommodate one hundred

THE NEW HAVEN HOTEL, NEW HAVEN, CONN.

and thirty guests, and communication can be had with all parts of the country by telegraph, the lines having been extended to it from New Haven. The proprietors are Burgess & Renshaw, well known in their profession.

The Branford Point House, kept by D. M. King, is seven miles from New Haven, east of the city, and is reached by cars on the New London and New Haven Railroad, which runs within a mile of the Hotel, or by stages from New Haven in the summer. It will accommodate two hundred guests and has long been a favorite resort with persons residing in all parts of the country, from the interior of New England to the far West.

The Double Beach House, and several others of less capacity, have their peculiar attractions and many friends, and nowhere can be found better facilities for recreation than along the shore of Long Island Sound.

GOING NORTH.

Leaving the "City of Elms," the train passes under Chapel Street, across the stone bridge over Mill River, past East Rock to the left and the broad salt meadows to the right, through the village of North Haven, immediately beyond which the scenery is of no particular interest, the surface of the country being level and the soil light and sandy.

WALLINGFORD.—THE WALLINGFORD COMMUNITY.

Twelve miles from New Haven, east of the railroad, will be noticed the village of Wallingford, situated on a commanding eminence. Express trains do not stop here. Quite an extensive business is done in manufacturing, and among some of the more important establishments are: Hall, Elton & Co., manufacturers of German Silver ware; Simpson & Co., German Silver spoons; Hall, Miller & Co., buttons; Albata Plate Co., &c.

Lyman Hall, one of the signers of the Declaration of Independence, was a native of Wallingford. After graduating at Yale he went to Georgia, where he established himself as a physician. Taking an active part in colonial affairs he was chosen to the General Congress in 1775, and afterwards Governor of Georgia. He died in 1790 and was buried in his adopted State. Just previous to the rebellion Georgia made Connecticut a present of his tombstones and they were taken to Wallingford and deposited in the cemetery south of the depot.

Situated on the slope of "Mount Tom," an eminence three-fourths of a mile west of Wallingford Station, is a branch of Oneida Community in Central New York, with which it holds a common interest. The Wallingford Society was organized in 1851 with a capital of $5,500. Its present capital is $30,625. The resident members average in number 45.

The primary object of the Community, it is claimed, is the religious culture of its members in accordance with what they conceive to be the spirit and doctrines of the New Testament. They believe in the power of Christianity to save individuals from all sin, from whence they are called Perfectionists. Their social system includes full Communion of property, or holding "all things in common," like that of the day of Pentecost.

The domain comprises 228 acres, of which 30 are in orchards, vineyards and small fruits. The strawberry crop of 1865, on five and two-fifths acres amounted to 850 bushels, worth $5,300. The income of this Community, like that at Oneida, was formerly chiefly derived from manufactures, but the last two years its mechanical industry has been limited to printing. A weekly paper called "*The Circular*," devoted to Christian Socialism and general intelligence, is published here, the type setting, folding, mailing, book-keeping, and in part the editing being done by women. Terms, free; or to those who choose to pay for it $1,00 per year.

A new building for publishing and educational purposes was erected in 1865, at a cost of $3,500. Three young men of the Community have been maintained as students in the legal and medical departments of Yale College.

This Community, being especially devoted to educational and publishing interests, is not at present self-supporting, but depends in part for its maintenance on a subsidy from Oneida Community, and on such contributions as are made by outside friends for the support of a free paper.

The cost of food and clothing during 1865, per individual, was $2.40 per week, or thirty-four cents per day, not including the ordinary household labor in preparing the articles consumed.

THE HANGING HILLS.

The tourist, while near Wallingford, will observe the Hanging Hills, or Sentinels of the Valley, west of Meriden. These peaks, which seem to rise abruptly to considerable hight, are the most elevated points of land in the State, and are the first objects seen by sailors coming in to Sandy Hook, below New York. A road has been constructed through a narrow glen in these hills, from Meriden to Berlin, known as Cat Hole Pass, which is much frequented by summer tourists and neighboring residents.

MERIDEN.

Distance from New York, 92 miles; Montreal, 354; White Mountains, 240; Lake Memphremagog, 262; Quebec, 446.

Meriden, where all express trains stop, is midway between New Haven and Hartford, it being just 18 miles to either place. It has a population of 10,000 and is one of the most active and prosperous towns in the State. From 1850 to 1860 it showed a greater proportionate increase in population than any other town in Connecticut. There is little or no inherited wealth in the town although the assessments now amount to between four and five millions. Twenty years ago there was no one residing in the town who was worth over $40,000. At the present time there are more than a dozen residents whose property is valued at from $100,000 to half a million each, while there are others who have accumulated large estates by their foresight and industry. Manufacturing is the principal business of the town, there being fifty different establishments, and a large variety of goods are made there and sent to all parts of the country. The most extensive concern is that of the Meriden Britannia Company, whose factory stands east of the railroad and near the depot. The building is 466 feet long, 40 feet wide and three stories high. In addition are three buildings in the rear, each one hundred feet long. The company employ 400 hands and include in their manufactures a large variety of plated table ware. A large business is done in the town in manufacturing ivory piano keys, ivory combs, cutlery, door knobs, lamp trimmings, balmoral skirts, hardware, castings, &c. The old town, where the first settlement was made, is delightfully situated on the hill, east of the depot and the large square brick building, standing at the head of the street is the Town Hall. That part of the village on the hill is known as Meriden and that at the depot and west of it, as West Meriden. Each village has a separate post office. There are nine churches in the town—three Congregational, two Baptist, an Episcopal, Methodist, Universalist, and Catholic. The State Reform School, a large brick building, will be noticed west of the railroad, and about a mile north of the depot.

MOUNT LAMENTATION.

East of Meriden is a range of mountains similar to the Hanging Hills on the west of the town, known as Mount Lamentation, a not very poetical name, but having its origin, it is said, in some sad local tradition. Continuing north the next stopping place for express trains is,

BERLIN JUNCTION.

The village of Berlin is situated on a hill east of the railroad, a little way south of the depot. From this place are two branch railroads, one extending north-west to New Britain two and a half miles distant, and the other south-east, ten miles, to Middletown on the Connecticut.

NEW BRITAIN.

The church spires of the town can be seen from Berlin Junction. This is a thriving and enterprising place, with a population of 6,000 and is pleasantly situated. The principal business is that of manufacturing, and among the most prominent are Russell & Erwin Manufacturing Company—locks and builders' hardware; Stanley Rule and Level Company—rules, levels, &c.; Stanley works—bolts, hinges, &c.; New Britain Knitting Company—shirts and drawers; P. & F. Corbin—cabinet hardware; North & Judd Manufacturing Company—harness and saddlery hardware; Landers, Frary & Clark—builders' hardware, &c.; New Britain Lock Company; North, Stanley & Co.—hooks and eyes; Churchill, Dana & Co.—jewelry; Butler & Gross—saddlery hardware; Judd & Blakeslee—sash fastener and curtain fixtures; Malleable Iron Works, &c. The manufacturing is all done by steam power and has been thus far successfully conducted.

The village is supplied with water brought two and a half miles, from Shuttle Meadow Lake. The fountain on the Green is said to be the largest in the country and will throw a stream to the hight of 140 feet.

The State Normal School is located in New Britain and has from eighty to a hundred pupils.

MIDDLETOWN.

Middletown, although ten miles from the main line of travel, is one of the most desirable places for a summer residence in Connecticut. The streets are broad, and the private residences are large and elegant. The city is situated on a considerable eminence, sloping eastward to the river, and from High Street which extends north and south, a fine view is had of the river and the region lying beyond. On this street is located Wesleyan University, a Methodist institution, founded in 1831. The buildings are finely situated on the west side of the street, in front of which is a large shaded lawn. The eminence on which the University stands is 160 feet above the river. The College buildings were originally built for and occupied by a military school, under Capt. Alden Partridge, who afterwards established a similar institution at Norwich, Vt.

Main Street lies below High Street, running parallel with it, and is a short distance from the river. The street is broad and has quite an ancient appearance. The Berkley Divinity School, an Episcopal institution, is located on the corner of Main and Washington Streets. Middletown is 34 miles from the Sound, at the head of ship navigation, and 15 miles from Hartford. During the summer many New York people have resided in the town, and as the drives and scenery are good, and the place easy of access, either by steamboat or railroad, it will continue to have many admirers. The population is about 10,000.

There are also several large manufacturing establishments in the town and among them are: The Russell Manufacturing Company—rubber goods, webbings, &c.; The Hubbard Hardware Company; Savage Fire Arms Manufacturing Company; two sewing machine manufactories, &c. Britannia ware, Douglas pumps, files, &c., are also extensively made.

THE MC DONOUGH HOUSE.

This house, kept by Dickinson & Craig, is four stories high and will accommodate 150 guests. It is situated at the corner of Main and Court Streets. The rooms are large and pleasant and it is a favorite place with summer tourists.

THE PORTLAND QUARRIES.

Opposite Middletown are the famous Portland freestone quarries—the most extensive in the world. They are operated by the Middlesex Company, Brainard & Co., and Shaler & Hall. They employ from 600 to 800 hands, 100 horses and 200 oxen, in getting out the stone, and 40 schooners in freighting it to various coast cities from Eastport to New Orleans. In addition large quantities are sent to the interior by railroad. The quality of this stone is much superior to that found at any other quarry. It covers a circuit of half a mile and is supposed to be 500 feet in thickness. It is claimed by geologists that underneath the stone is a strata of coal, but this statement has not yet been verified, although excavations have been made 150 feet below the bed of the river where some of the best stone for building material is found.

HARTFORD.

Distance from New York, 110 miles; Montreal, 336; White Mountains, 222; Lake Memphremagog, 255; Quebec, 428.

A ride of a few miles from Berlin Junction brings you within sight of the tall spires of Hartford. East of the railroad, in the suburbs of the city, will be noticed the Sharps Rifle Factory, where are employed from 600 to 700 hands. Still further north and on the same side of the railroad is Trinity College, standing on an eminence and fronting the east. Adjoining the College grounds on the north, and south of the depot and Asylum Street, is the Park, which was purchased and laid out by the city a few years since at a cost of over $270,000. It contains 30 acres and in addition to this are 15 acres on the south belonging to the College, which are open in connection with the Park, to the public. Park River forms the northern boundary of the Park and is crossed by several stone bridges, and that at the junction of Ford and Pearl Streets, in sight of the depot, built of Portland freestone, is a beautiful structure. The River affords an excellent place for skating in winter. A speaker's stand, built of stone, will be seen to the right and south of the bridge, from which public addresses are sometimes delivered. Out-door concerts are also given here at stated periods in summer. The grounds are neatly and tastefully laid out, and the whole is alike creditable to the wisdom and liberality of the people of the city.

Hartford has a population of 40,000. In 1800 it was only a little more than 5,000 and up to 1840 it had reached only a little over 12,000. Within the last ten or fifteen years new enterprises have sprung up and its growth has been quite rapid, and at the present time there are few places of its size that have so much real and lasting prosperity. Statistics show that it has more wealth in proportion to its inhabitants than any other city in this country. It has a large mercantile and manufacturing business, but it is chiefly known abroad on account of its numerous insurance companies. In this respect it is the leading city in the country. There are no less than eighteen insurance companies in operation, with a capital of $18,000,000, and all of them are doing a large and successful business. Of this number eleven are devoted to fire, six to life and one to accident insurance. The latter is the first of its kind in the country. Its moneyed institutions stand equally high in public estimation although confined to a more limited sphere of action. There are twelve banks of issue with a capital of $8,000,000, and four savings institutions.

In Colonial times, Hartford took a leading position, and then as well as now was a place of no small consequence. There are still many things in existence in the city that are of historical interest, especially to those having a taste for the rare and curious belonging to other days. No one passing through the city, with time at his command, should fail of spending a few days in visiting its many interesting localities. He could not go away without feeling doubly paid for his time and trouble.

Although a severe gale in 1856 blew down the famous Charter Oak, pieces of it are preserved, and at the State House in the office of the Secretary of State, is the identical charter, framed in the wood of the tree that once concealed it from Sir Edmund Andros, the first Governor-general of New England, who in 1686 attempted to wrest it from the people of Connecticut. The demand for building lots has greatly changed the old Wyllys place, where the Charter Oak stood, situated east of Main Street, in the southern part of the city, but a marble slab at the side of the walk in Charter Oak Place, has been placed over the spot where the old tree took root and spread its noble branches.

The State House, which in point of beauty is hardly worthy of Connecticut, was built in 1794. A new one would have taken its place some years since if the Legislature held all its sessions here. In the State Library are preserved many letters from the kings of England during Colonial times to the Governors in Connecticut. The oldest one was written in 1666 and bears upon it the autograph of Charles II. In the Senate Chamber is the Governor's chair that was made of wood from the Charter Oak. It is handsomely carved and inlaid, and upon it is the State Coat of Arms. Here is a full length, original painting of Washington by Stewart. Here also hang the portraits of twenty-four governors, from the John Winthrop of Colonial days to Gen. Hawley. Oliver Wolcott, Sr., whose portrait is among the number, was one of the signers of the Declaration of Independence, and afterwards Secretary of the Treasury during Washington's and John Adams' administrations. In this chamber was held the famous Hartford Convention.

In the Historical Rooms in Wadsworth Athenæum, will be found some rare relics of olden times. Among them, Elder Wm. Brewster's chest, that came over with him in the Mayflower; Miles Standish's dinner pot; Benedict Arnold's watch; Gen. Israel Putnam's tavern sign and the sword carried by him at Bunker Hill; a link of the chain stretched across the Hudson at West Point, in the Revolution; bomb-shells that were thrown into Stonington during the last war; an arm chair made in the 13th century; the vest and shirt of Col. Ledyard, commander of Fort Griswold when surrendered to the British Sept. 6, 1781, and who was massacred after the surrender; Nathan Hale's powder horn, made by him during his college vacations; a mortar captured at the city of Mexico; the first telegraph message sent in this country, between Washington and Baltimore; an old drum used at Farmington to call the people to church; Dr. Robbins' collection of bibles, one of them printed in 1478.

But of all the rare and curious things found here none are of more interest by way of showing the rapid development of the country, than the little six by nine mail bag used in 1775, to carry the mail between Hartford, Middletown and New Haven.

The first settlement made in Hartford was by the Dutch in 1633, who landed on the point of land at the junction of Park River with the Connecticut, where they built a Fort. One of the bricks used in its construction is now in the Historical Rooms. This place is still known as Dutch Point. The first English settlement was made in 1635, the settlers coming from Cambridge, Mass. The first meeting house in Connecticut was built at Hartford in 1638, and some of its timbers are said to have been used in the construction of the present Center Congregational Church. Thomas Green established the Connecticut *Courant* in October, 1764, the first paper and printing office in Hartford, and John I. Wells received in 1819 a patent for the first lever printing press. Dr. A. Kinsley, invented the first steam-engine ever made, in 1797–9, and set it running in Main Street. He also invented the first brick pressing machine. The "Mansion House" on Kinsley Street, built in 1796 is probably the oldest house in this country, built of pressed bricks that were made here.

Main Street, one of the finest in any New England city extending from north to south, is two miles in length. The retail trade is principally done here. State Street, extending east from Main Street to the River is occupied by those doing a wholesale business in groceries, dye stuffs, wool, tobacco, leather and iron. Hartford is one of the largest markets for wool and tobacco of any city in New England. An extensive wholesale trade is done on Asylum Street in dry goods.

The factory built by Col. Samuel Colt, for the manufacture of his celebrated revolvers was one of the largest enterprises ever undertaken. Since Colonel Colt's death it has been conducted by a company, of which Brig. Gen. Franklin is now President. Employment is given to eight hundred hands. The front building was burnt in 1864, but it was rebuilt in 1866. The establishment is situated in the south-east part of the city, near the Connecticut, and is inclosed by a dyke, fifty feet broad at the top and 8,698 feet in length. It incloses 23 acres of land, and cost over $80,000. Col. Colt assumed the responsibility and built the dyke at his own expense, but the city afterward paid part of the cost.

Few men had so determined a purpose, and were so hard to be swerved from their line of policy as Col. Colt. Starting as a poor boy, he worked his way to fame and wealth, and when he died he left an immense fortune to his wife and young son. His dwelling, grounds and extensive green house on Wethersfield Avenue, which overlook the Armory, built by himself, surpass anything in the city. Within the dyke enclosure is a colony of Swiss, brought to this country by Col. Colt to manufacture willow ware, the material for which is grown along the dyke.

Of the public institutions may be mentioned the Wadsworth Athenæum, Trinity College, The Connecticut Theological Institute, Deaf and Dumb Asylum, Retreat for the Insane and Hartford Hospital. The Athenæum, was erected by contributions from citizens of Hartford, at a cost of $52,000. It was constructed of granite and is 80 by 100 feet. In this building are the Connecticut Historical Rooms, Young Men's Institute, and the Watkinson Library. Also rooms devoted to paintings and statuary. The Watkinson Library is one of reference and no book can be taken from it except on the written consent of the trustees. It was founded by David Watkinson, who died Dec. 13, 1857, aged 80 years, leaving $100,000 for the purpose of establishing the library. Rare works were purchased in Europe, and the library was first opened to the public in the early part of 1866. The Young Men's Institute contains 13,000 volumes which can be taken from the rooms. The Statuary Room on the first floor contains the marbles and casts made by Edward S. Bartholomew, a native of Hartford, who died abroad in 1858, aged 36 years, after having gained an enviable reputation as a sculptor. The Picture Gallery contains about 150 elegant paintings, including Trumbull's famous battle pieces, illustrating scenes in the Revolution. An admission fee is charged to the Statuary Room and Picture Gallery. The Historical Rooms are open each day, free to the public and the janitor in attendance will point out to the visitor the more rare and curious specimens of antiquity. The Deaf and Dumb Asylum, located on Asylum Street, west of the depot is the oldest institution of its kind in this country, having been incorporated in 1816. The late Rev. T. H. Gallaudet, LL.D. visited Europe for the purpose of ascertaining the best method of imparting instruction to the deaf and dumb, and brought with him on his return M. Laurent Clerc, a deaf mute who had been a successful teacher in Paris, and who acted as an assistant to Mr. Gallaudet. It was opened with seven deaf mutes as pupils, and the number has since been increased to 275. The main building was erected in 1820 and is 130 by 50 feet, four stories high. The Retreat for the Insane was opened in 1824. It is situated in the southern part of the city, on Washington Street, on a gentle elevation commanding an extensive view of the city, the river and the valley beyond. The grounds contain 17 acres and are tastefully ornamented with walks and shade trees. During the 40 years of its existence there have been admitted to it some 4,000 patients, more than half of whom were discharged as cured. The average number of patients is about 150. The Hartford Hospital was dedicated in 1859. The main building is 72 by 48 feet, three stories high, with a wing 113 by 30 feet. It is built of Portland stone, and cost, including grounds, over $48,000. Any person paying $1,000 at one time will be entitled to a free bed.

There are 24 churches in the city—seven Congregational, four Episcopal, three Methodist, two Presbyterian, two Baptist, two Catholics, and one each of Unitarian and Universalist, Second Advents and Israelite.

The Hartford and Wethersfield Horse Railroad Company's tracks extend from Spring Grove Cemetery through Main Street, to Wethersfield, a distance of seven miles, and from the Connecticut River west two miles, through State and Asylum Streets.

Hartford has a paid fire department with four steam fire engines. It is a significant fact that since the paid system went into operation there has not been as many fires as formerly. The city is supplied with water from the Connecticut River, the reservoir being located on Garden Street, west of the depot. Within ten years the daily consumption of water has increased from less than half a million gallons to about two millions. Owing to the great increased demand the commissioners are procuring a supply from Trout Brook, five miles west of the city. The fall from Trout Brook to foot of State Street is 210 feet.

Of the persons who have gained distinction in various pursuits, who reside in Hartford, may be mentioned Mrs. Harriet Beecher Stowe, Prof. Stowe, Rev. Dr. Bushnell, Rev. Dr. Hawes, Rev. Dr. Burton, Hon. Gideon Welles, U. S. Senator James Dixon, Hon. Isaac Toucey, Ex-Gov. Thos. H. Seymour, Hon. Henry C. Demming, Brevet Major Gen. Joseph R.

Hawley, now Governor of the State, and Rose Terry, contributor to the periodical literature of the country. Gail Hamilton was formerly a teacher in the public schools in this city.

Mrs. Sigourney, whose death occurred in 1865, resided for many years in the dwelling on the south side of Asylum Street, and next to the railroad. It will be observed a few rods south of the depot. It is now owned by Hon. Julius Catlin. She resided several years before her death in a cottage on High Street. Mrs. Harriet Beecher Stowe resides on Sigourney Street in the west part of the city.

The repair shops of the New Haven, Hartford and Springfield Railroad, are located at this place, a short distance south of the depot. The passenger depot, occupied jointly by the New Haven, Hartford and Springfield and the Providence, Hartford and Fishkill Railroads at this place is one of the finest in the country. It was built of Portland freestone, and is a large and substantial building.

THE ALLYN HOUSE.

Hartford has several hotels, the largest and most elegant of which is the Allyn House, situated at the corner of Asylum and

Trumbull Streets. It was erected in 1857 at a cost of $125,-000. It is four stories high, with a front of 155 feet on Asylum Street, and 105 on Trumbull. The front is built of Portland stone and altogether is not surpassed by any hotel in New England. The first floor of the building is occupied by stores, and the remainder is used for hotel purposes. There are accommodations for nearly 300 guests. Everything connected with it is neatly and conveniently arranged, and no pains have been spared to make this a first class hotel in every respect. The proprietor, Mr. R. J. Allyn, is courteous and obliging, and makes the stranger at once feel at home.

Adjoining the Allyn House, on the west, and connected with it by a private entrance, is Allyn Hall, one of the largest and finest in Connecticut. It will seat 1,500 people.

The streets of the city are McAdamized, and the drives through and about it are unsurpassed. Among them may be mentioned,—to Tumble Down Brook, eight miles west by Albany road; to Talcott Mountain, nine miles west; to West Hartford, three and a half miles; to Wethersfield, four miles; to Glastenbury, four miles; over Newington Mountain, three and one half miles; to Prospect Hill; to Bloomfield, and last to Shipman's at Rocky Hill, some seven miles, which by city people is considered an "institution."

WINDSOR.

The first English settlement in Connecticut was made at Windsor in 1633. William Holmes and others erected a house on the Farmington River near its mouth, and the land in its vicinity is still known as Plymouth Meadow. The Dutch Governor at New York sent a force to assault the house erected by Holmes and drive the English away, but it was so well fortified that the expedition returned without doing it, after making friends with the English. Roger Wolcott, Governor of Connecticut from 1751 to 1754, and Oliver Ellsworth, Senator and Chief Justice of the United States, were born in this town. Windsor is a pleasant country village, but is not a place of much business.

SOUTH WINDSOR.

South Windsor, situated on the east side of the Connecticut, and six miles north of Hartford, is distinguished as being the birthplace of Jonathan Edwards, the great American divine, John Fitch, the inventor of the steamboat, and Oliver Wolcott, one of the signers of the Declaration of Independence, and Governor of Connecticut in 1796. During the Revolutionary war many prisoners were sent here for safe keeping, and among them were William Franklin, the royal governor of New Jersey, and son of Dr Franklin, Gen. Hamilton and Gen. Prescott. Gov Franklin was quartered at the house of Lieut. Diggin, about a mile south of the Congregational church, where with his servants, he lived in princely style. He was extremely fond of *sour* punch, and in a bower situated in a retired spot, back of the street near Podunk Brook, he prepared and served his favorite beverage to the French visitors, who styled it "*one grand contradiction.*" South Windsor was the headquarters of Gen. LaFayette, in 1788, after the project of invading Canada had been abandoned, and he remained at the house of Mr. Porter during his stay in town, about three-quarters of a mile south of the Congregational church, which was provided for defense by port-holes for muskets. Many of the elm trees now standing were set out by the British and Hessian prisoners at the suggestion of Gen. LaFayette, who held one end of the line while Mr. Porter held the other. The trees were planted in rows parallel with the street. While LaFayette resided here he was visited by Washington and in order to do honor to the occasion he requested Lieut. King to appear with a company of mounted men. Forty-two men were mustered, equipped somewhat ludicrously with sheep skins for saddles and canes for swords, and LaFayette introduced them as follows: "Gen. Washington, I presume you are acquainted with this troop." The General replied, "I do not remember that I ever before had the honor of seeing them." Much to Washington's amusement, LaFayette expressed his surprise, remarking, that they had seen much service and were known as the "Old Testament Guard."

THE STONE BRIDGE, NEAR WINDSOR.

North of Windsor station the railroad company are building across Farmington River a substantial stone bridge, 450 feet in length, with seven arches, at a cost of $40,000.

WINDSOR LOCKS.

A few miles further north, on the banks of the Connecticut is the manufacturing village of Windsor Locks. The water power is furnished from a canal on the west side of the river, five miles in length, that was built many years ago around Enfield Falls, for the purpose of improving the navigation of the Connecticut. Sloops and small steamboats laden with merchandise going to towns higher up the Connecticut, used to pass through the canal and thence around the rapids in the river. Since the construction of the railroad this canal has become of no use so far as its original purpose is concerned, but the ingenuity of man has seized upon it and compelled it to contribute to his material wants.

Here are located the Seymour Paper Company, manufacturers of Printing and Envelope paper; J. Francis & Co.'s Rolling Mills; the Foundry of H. A. Converse, the Spool Cotton manufactory of L. M. Pinkham, the Chuck mills of Horton & Son and the Manilla paper mill of C. H. Dexter.

THE IRON BRIDGE OVER THE CONNECTICUT.

THE GREAT IRON BRIDGE ACROSS THE CONNECTICUT AT WAREHOUSE POINT.

Passing Windsor Locks you come to one of the finest bridges in this country—the great Iron Truss Bridge across the Connecticut at Warehouse Point, midway between Hartford and Springfield. It is 1,525 feet long, weighs including track and floor beams upon which the track rests, about 800 tons, and cost $265,000. The chief engineer of this noble structure was Mr. James Laurie, a Scotchman by birth, who, for several years was President of the board of Civil Engineers in this country, and for a time at the head of the Government engineers in Nova Scotia. He was assisted by Theo. G. Ellis, Engineer of the Hartford Dyke. The plans were made in 1862 and submitted to a Philadelphia firm, but owing to the great demands upon American iron workers, for Government work, for war purposes, it could not be built in this country as soon as required. After some delay it was decided to have the bridge built in England, and in January, 1864, Mr. Laurie sailed for Europe to give out the contracts. On arriving in England he proceeded to Manchester where he contracted with William Fairbairn & Sons, they agreeing to make the iron for the bridge by the first of December. Subsequently it appearing that they would not be able to finish the work as soon as specified, part of it was given to the London Engineering and Iron Ship Building Company. In about a year the bridge was shipped from Liverpool and London, and in June, 1865, work upon its erection was begun. About one hundred workmen, many of whom came specially from England, were employed and in Feb. 1866 it was completed.

There are seventeen spans in the bridge, the longest of which, the channel span, in the center of the river, is 177⅓ feet. Eight of the other spans are 88½ feet each, another is 140 feet, another 76¾ feet, another 43 feet and another 25½ feet, making the exact total length of the bridge 1,524½ feet.

Each span consists of a wrought iron truss, composed of horizontal plates, angle and T iron. The width of the deck of the bridge upon which the track rests is 17¾ feet. Of the iron truss, canal span, 16 feet, of the channel span 12⅝ feet, and of the others, 10⅓ feet. The hight of the truss—channel span, 16⅝ feet, canal span 12⅓ feet, and of the others 11 feet.

The horizontal plates in the four chords are from 15 to 25 feet in length, from one-fourth to three-fourths of an inch in thickness, and about eight inches in width. At the joints a short plate is riveted to each side of the main plate, and is so arranged that no two joints meet in the same place. The plates and angle iron, which are riveted together, give each chord a trough like shape. From the upper to the lower chord on each side of the bridge, are iron posts, made of plate, angle and T iron. Across the posts on an angle of 45 degrees, extending from the bottom to the top chord on each side of the bridge, are bars of a few inches in width. In the short span these bars cross but one post to which it is firmly riveted, in the next longer two posts, and in the channel span three. The posts being several feet apart, from five to five and three-fourths feet, they give a lattice like appearance to the bridge. Extending through the truss are lateral and vertical tie bars which help support it.

The spans are securely fastened to the piers below. One end of each span rests upon four iron rollers which turn upon an iron bed-plate, and between the ends of the spans is a space of an inch and a half, allowed for expansion. These rollers are upon every other pier—the ends of the spans upon the intervening ones are firmly secured to the masonry, so there can be no possibility of the bridge getting out of place.

The frame of the bridge was all put together in England before shipping and then part of it taken down. This was done to detect any mistake that might have occurred.

There are 175,000 rivets, from three-fourths to one and one-eighth inches in diameter, in the bridge. Part of them were put in by machinery in England and the remainder by hand while the bridge was being erected.

The piers of the old bridge, which are of Monson granite, were used, after raising them to a greater hight, and new ones were built between the old, doubling the number. To build the bridge and maintain the old one so as not to delay the trains, while the work was in progress was an undertaking of no small magnitude. It was however accomplished and of the 22 to 28 trains that crossed the bridge daily not a detention of a single minute was caused to them. The lower chords of the iron bridge were placed upon blocking two feet in thickness, which rested upon the piers, and during Sunday when there was no train to pass the completed span was lowered to its place by means of hydraulic jacks.

The weight of the bridge, not including track and floor beams, is 624 tons and its cost in England in gold was $85.58 per ton. In New York in currency, its cost was $241.54 per ton. The freight from London and Liverpool to New York was $3.75 per ton. Some of the other items of cost are as follows: Freight from London and Liverpool to New York, $2,342.10; duty, $30.12 per ton; making a total of $18,796.40; paid premium on gold, $73,120.68; cost of bridge in England, $53,400.22; cost of iron work, erected, $173,109.62; cost of labor for erection, including tools, $16,985.34; cost of masonry, $15,744.07. It will be seen by this that the premium on gold which was then in the vicinity of 100, amounted to $19,720.46 more than the cost of the bridge in England, when ready for shipment.

The track passes over the top of the bridge, excepting the span over the canal, and the view up and down the river is very fine. The distance from the top of the rails to low water mark below is 47 feet.

This is the most extensive iron bridge in the United States, but for several years, the New York Central, Baltimore and Ohio, and Pennsylvania Central Railroads have tested them on a smaller scale and have become satisfied of their durability. It is thought that this bridge will last a century. The strength of the bridge must be very great, and it is estimated that a continuous line of locomotives, from one shore to the other, would not exceed more than one-seventh of the weight that it is capable of sustaining.

Two wooden bridges have been built in this place—the first one in 1844, when the road was opened. It was blown down in October, 1846, and rebuilt in forty-five days.

The iron has all been painted red and the appearance of the bridge in the distance is very fine. A good view of it can be had soon after the train passes Windsor Locks, going north, or before it reaches Warehouse Point going south. To get a correct estimate of its great magnitude one wants to leave the train and pass through its entire length, underneath the railroad track. There is a narrow plank on either side, extending through the bridge, but unless one has good nerves the rushing waters below might disturb his equilibrium.

During the construction of the bridge no serious accident occurred. One workman fell through a thirteen inch hole into the river, a distance of forty feet and struck in water that was only nine inches deep. He was disabled only for a few days and then continued work until the bridge was completed.

WAREHOUSE POINT.

Crossing the Connecticut on the iron bridge you come to Warehouse Point, a way station at the east end of the bridge on the bank of the river. Formerly this was a place of some note, it being the head of sloop navigation. The place received its name from the fact that warehouses for the storage of merchandise were located here. The boats unloaded at this place and their cargoes were transferred to wagons and carried to the several towns farther up the Connecticut.

ENFIELD.—COL. HAZARD'S POWDER WORKS.—THE SHAKERS.

Passing Warehouse Point, the village of Enfield will be noticed on the hill to the east. This is a quiet, rural town, overlooking the Connecticut and the valley for many miles. The northern limits of the town extend to the boundary line between Connecticut and Massachusetts. Four miles east of the river is Hazardville where are located part of the powder mills of Col. A. G. Hazard. He also owns mills at Scitico, (in Enfield,) at East Hartford, and Canton. During the Rebellion he furnished a large quantity of powder for the Government, and England, during the Crimean war, purchased a million and a quarter dollars worth of him. There are no powder works in England so large as those owned by the Colonel, and himself and Dupont make one-half of the powder that is manufactured in this country. The powder is taken to the magazine, near Enfield station and from there sent down the river in small boats. He has been thirty years in the business and has acquired a large property. His acquaintance with the public men of the country is extensive, and when Webster was at the zenith of his fame he was among his personal friends. Gov. A. H. Bullock of Massachusetts married one of his daughters.

The Shakers have one of their largest communities in this town, six miles east of the river. They number several hundred members, and are a very industrious and thriving people.

THOMPSONVILLE—THE HARTFORD CARPET WORKS.

Two miles north of Enfield bridge, and in the town of Enfield, is the manufacturing village of Thompsonville, named in honor of Col. Orrin Thompson, the founder of the Hartford Carpet Works located at this place. The manufacture of carpets was begun here in 1828 and this establishment is now one of the largest of its kind in the country. The varieties made are Ingrain and Venetian, and the quality is said to be superior to anything found in the American market, so much so that foreign Ingrain carpets have been superseded by them. The machinery at these mills is driven entirely by steam, three engines, one of them 500 horse power, being used for that purpose. The consumption of coal in a single year amounts to 3000 tons. There are in the mills 127 Ingrain and 14 Venetian power looms, and there are manufactured daily 6000 yards of Ingrain carpeting. The wool consumed is all imported, as there are no breeds of sheep in this country producing a quality sufficiently coarse to be used in manufacturing carpets. It requires 6000 pounds of wool per day to keep the mills in full operation. The capital of the Company is $1,500,000; President and Treasurer, Geo. Roberts, Hartford; Superintendent at Thompsonville, J. L. Houston. The Company also have mills at Tariffville, where they manufacture Brussels carpeting.

The Enfield Manufacturing Company, with a capital of $250,000 employ 300 hands, and manufacture shirts, hosiery, &c.

LONGMEADOW.

Within four miles of Springfield, on the plateau, east of the railroad, will be noticed the village of Longmeadow. The boundary line between Massachusetts crosses the Connecticut between this place and Thompsonville. Longmeadow was settled in 1644, eight years after the settlement of Springfield.

SPRINGFIELD.

Distance from New York, 134 miles; Montreal, 310; White Mountains, 184; Lake Memphremagog, 229; Quebec, 402.

In approaching Springfield from the south, as the train passes around the bend in the river, the city will be noticed on the left, and then again on the right, spread out over the hillside, more than a mile distant. The most prominent buildings to be seen are the United States Arsenal on Armory Square, and St. Michael's (Catholic) Church, west and below it. The city contains 25,000 inhabitants and is rapidly increasing in wealth and importance. It is compactly built for a provincial city and numbers among its inhabitants some of the most enterprising people in New England.

In a comparative sense Springfield has not been so much distinguished for its manufactories as for being a great natural commercial center. A few years ago, with few exceptions, very little manufacturing was done within what are now the limits of the city; but more recently the manufacturing interests have been greatly increased. Here center long lines of railways, from north, south, east and west, with direct communication with all the large cities of the country, while for nearly fifty miles on either line, out of Springfield, and contributory to its trade and business, are large and thriving towns.

The United States Armory, which was established here in 1795, has probably been the chief source of prosperity to the town, although the number of hands employed previous to the Rebellion seldom exceeded 400. After the destruction of the Harper's Ferry Armory, early in the war, a large force, at one time 3,200 men, were kept at work divided into two sets—one party working at night, and another during the day. There were manufactured during the four years of the Rebellion, from April, 1861, to June 30, 1865, 791,134 guns of various patterns, nearly all of which were borne over many a bloody battle field in defense of free institutions. This is a larger number of muskets than was manufactured during the first 65 years of the existence of the Armory, up to the commencement of the Rebellion. The amount of disbursements in 1865 that passed through the paymaster's hands, Mr. Edward Ingersoll, including money and material used at the Armory, was $4,677,422, and for the whole time during the war it was over $12,000,000. The two squares on the hill, owned by the Government comprise more than 72 acres. The Arsenal and the shops in which the muskets are made, excepting the welding of the barrels, are located on the western square overlooking the city and the valley beyond. It is inclosed by an iron fence nearly nine feet high, and the grounds are neatly and tastefully laid out. The view from the top of the Arsenal is particularly fine, exceeding in some respects that obtained from any other point in the city. The Arsenal, which is three stories high, will hold three hundred thousand muskets, and they are so regularly and neatly arranged in columns that they make a striking display. Some years ago Longfellow, after visiting the place previous to the Rebellion, and when such a thing seemed impossible, wrote the following lines, which were so prophetic and so expressive in the portrayal of the evils of war and bloodshed that they will be read with renewed interest by every one who has been at the Arsenal:

THE ARSENAL AT SPRINGFIELD.

This is the Arsenal. From floor to ceiling,
  Like a huge organ, rise the burnished arms;
But from their silent pipes no anthem pealing
  Startles the villages with strange alarms.

Ah! what a sound will rise—how wild and dreary—
  When the death-angel touches those swift keys!
What loud lament and dismal Miserere
  Will mingle with their awful symphonies!

I hear even now the infinite, fierce chorus—
  The cries of agony, the endless groan,
Which, through the ages that have gone before us,
  In long reverberations reach our own.

On helm and harness rings the Saxon hammer,
  Through Cimbric forest roars the Norseman's song;
And loud, amid the universal clamor,
  O'er distant deserts sounds the Tartar gong.

I hear the Florentine, who from his palace
  Wheels out his battle-bell with dreadful din,
And Aztec priests upon their teocallis
  Beat the wild war-drums made of serpent's skin,

The tumult of each sacked and burning village;
The shout that every prayer for mercy drowns;
The soldiers' revels in the midst of pillage,
The wail of famine in beleaguered towns;

The bursting shell, the gateway wrenched asunder,
The rattling musketry, the clashing blade—
And ever and anon, in tones of thunder,
The diapason of the cannonade.

Is it, O man, with such discordant noises,
With such accursed instruments as these,
Thou drownest Nature's sweet and kindly voices,
And jarrest the celestial harmonies?

Were half the power that fills the world with terror,
Were half the wealth bestowed on camps and courts
Given to redeem the human mind from error,
There were no need of arsenals nor forts;

The warrior's name would be a name abhorred;
And every nation that should lift again
Its hand against a brother, on its forehead
Would wear forevermore the curse of Cain!

Down the dark future, through long generations,
The echoing sounds grow fainter and then cease;
And like a bell, with solemn, sweet vibrations,
I hear once more the voice of Christ say, "Peace!"

Peace!—and no longer from its brazen portals,
The blast of war's great organ shakes the skies;
But beautiful as songs of the immortals,
The holy melodies of love arise.

The Water-Shops, located about a mile south east of the Arsenal, are particularly well adapted to the purposes for which they were constructed. Here all the barrels are made and tested.

Springfield cannot boast of so many pleasant drives as some of the other towns in its vicinity, but it has a few charming views. That from Long Hill, in the south part of the city is as grand as it is extensive. The city on the right, the winding river on the left, the broad valley, checkered with a thousand fields, and the towering mountain peaks skirting the western horizon, present a beautiful and picturesque scene.

The cemetery, the principal entrance to which is from Maple Street, has few equals in natural beauty, or artificial adornment, when Mount Auburn and Greenwood are excepted. Inroads have been made upon Puritanical ideas even here in the heart of New England, and the last resting places of the dead are now adorned by loving hands, stripping them of the more forbidding aspects that once distinguished them. No one should fail of spending a few hours in this secluded and beautiful spot.

Hampden Park, in the north part of the city, lying between the Connecticut River Railroad and the river, is conveniently situated and comprises a large number of acres. Here have been held several National Horse Shows and the County Agricultural Fairs. There are no better show grounds in New England.

Springfield is the oldest town in Massachusetts on the Connecticut River, having been settled in 1636 by a colony from Roxbury, and many of the descendants still live in the vicinity.

The two principal business streets are Main and State—the former running parallel with the river, and the latter crossing it at right angles, extending from the Connecticut eastward past the United States Armory. Many large and magnificent brick blocks have been erected on Main Street within the last few years. During the war, owing to the large number of workmen employed at the armory, few towns were so prosperous.

The railroads terminating here are the New Haven, Hartford and Springfield, and the Connecticut River—the former 62 miles in length, extending from New Haven to Springfield, and the other north from Springfield to South Vernon, at the State line, between Massachusetts and Vermont, a distance of 50 miles. The Western Railroad, connecting at Worcester with the Boston and Worcester, passes through Springfield and terminates at Albany. The distance to Boston and Albany from Springfield is about the same, it being about 100 miles to either place. Here are located the repair shops of the Western and Connecticut River Railroads, giving employment to a large number of hands.

Of the several manufacturing establishments, the largest and most important are the Wason Manufacturing Company, and the Smith & Wesson. The former manufacture railroad cars of all descriptions, including passenger, sleeping, freight, coal and horse railway cars. They employ 350 hands, and in 1865 their business amounted to $700,000,—$300,000 of which was for cars furnished to the New Jersey Central.

The cars used by the Western, Central and Union Pacific Railroads, divisions of the great line across the continent, were made by them. The royal car, made several years since for the Pasha of Egypt, one of the most elegant ever made in this country, was turned out at their establishment. The principal officers of the Company are, T. W. Wason, President; G. C. Fisk, Treasurer and General Agent; H. S. Hyde, Secretary.

Smith & Wesson manufacture five, six and seven shot revolvers, employing 350 hands. They turn out 350 revolvers a day, amounting to a million of dollars per year. Their revolver is so well known and so much of a favorite that up to 1866 they were two years behind their orders, and now they are more than a year behind.

The manufacture and sale, at wholesale and retail, of harnesses, saddles, trunks, &c., has become a large business in Springfield within the last few years, and one of the most extensive concerns is that of W. H. Wilkinson, who, during the Rebellion was largely engaged upon government work. He employed at one time as many as 400 hands, and made for the Government during the war $1,500,000 worth of harnesses and saddles. He delivered to the Government, $75,000 worth of work after the fall of Richmond. The teams of the first ten regiments that left Connecticut were equipped by him, and he also made the model Artillery harnesses for the Government, a complete set of which were presented to each of the Governments of Switzerland and Italy. Mr. Wilkinson employs one hundred hands at the present time, and his work is sold in New England, in the West and South. Commencing at twenty-one without any capital, he has by perseverance accumulated a handsome property.

Josiah Cummings, formerly a partner with Mr. Wilkinson, was also largely engaged upon Government contracts during the Rebellion, employing 300 to 400 hands and making a million of dollars worth of work. He now employs about a hundred hands, and manufactures harnesses, saddles and trunks. His trade extends all through the United States, and his harnesses are bought by the most wealthy gentlemen in the large cities. He is now manufacturing as elegant and durable work in either branch of his business, as can be purchased in New York or Boston.

The manufacture of paper collars, envelopes and paper boxes, has become an important business, and at the present time a large number of hands are employed upon this kind of work in Springfield.

THE MASSASOIT HOUSE, SPRINGFIELD, MASS.

No hotel in New England has acquired so extensive and deservedly good reputation as the Massasoit House, and very few in the country are better known, and none are better kept. It is the pride of its proprietors, the boast of every Massachusetts man abroad, and the haven of rest to the weary and dusty traveler. The experience of hotel life is incomplete to all who have not past its portals. It is located close to the depot, and ample time is given the tourist for meals. The proprietors, M. & E. S. Chapin, have long been engaged in the hotel business,—landlords of the Massasoit.

THE WEST SPRINGFIELD CHURCH—ANECDOTE OF DR. LATHROP—A REMARKABLE WAGER.

Leaving Springfield for the north, the West Springfield Church, standing on a high bluff, on the west bank of the river, will be noticed. This church is seen for many miles up and down the valley. Here have preached more Doctors of Divinity than at any other country church in New England, and some of them have been quite distinguished. Among them were Rev. Dr. Joseph Lathrop, Rev. Dr. Wm. B. Sprague, of Albany, and Rev. Dr. Thomas E. Vermilye, of New York. Rev. Henry M. Field, of New York, editor of the Evangelist, son of Rev. Dr. Field of Stockbridge, preached here several years. Dr. Lathrop, it is said, was one of the most remarkable divines that ever lived in the Connecticut Valley, and during his ministry of 65 years he wrote five thousand sermons, seven octavo volumes of which have been published. An anecdote is related of him which is said to be a good illustration of his character. A parishioner, for some trivial reason had become very angry with him. Meeting him one day, he said, "Doctor, have you any religion?" "*None to boast of,*" was the laconic reply.

Another anecdote, concerning the erection of the church is told by some of the old residents, which illustrates some of the habits incident to earlier days: Many years ago, when

BRIGHTWOOD, THE RESIDENCE OF DR. HOLLAND.

the church was built, the whole town turned out on "raising" day to put up the frame. That being accomplished the "boys" resolved upon having some fun. Going to the village tavern where liquor was sold, one of the party informed the landlord that he had just "bet the drinks" for all with another of their number and as soon as a decision could be made the losing side would pay for what was drank. The liquor was brought out and many a glass was emptied. Then the landlord inquired the nature of the wager, and received the following explanation: "Why," says the leader of the party, "I have just bet Jones that when that steeple falls it will go to the south, and he bets that it will fall to the north. When it goes over let me know and you shall have your pay." As the steeple still stands, it is presumed the bet of fifty years ago is yet unpaid.

THE RESIDENCE OF DR. HOLLAND.

Passing Hampden Park on the left, and Round Hill on the right, in leaving Springfield, Brightwood, the home of Dr. J. G. Holland, known in literature as Timothy Titcomb, can be seen some distance east of the railroad upon an eminence, half hidden among stately trees. The Doctor is a genial, warm hearted gentleman, now, after years of toil in full fruition of his fondest hopes, dwelling beneath his own vine and fig tree, and yet on the sunny side of life, not having past into the fifties. He was born in Belchertown, Mass., and was the son of a mechanic who was more noted for piety than riches. Moving from town to town as demand for his labor made it necessary, his father resided in Belchertown, Heath, Granby, South Hadley and Northampton, before the Doctor reached manhood. In the High School at Northampton he received the greater part of his scholastic acquirements, and after trying his hand at various employments, working in a silk factory, teaching penmanship and the English branches, taking daguerreotypes, &c., he finally settled down upon the conviction that *his* sphere was to be that of a country doctor—a vender of pills and powders. Studying medicine at Northampton and attending medical lectures in Pittsfield, he took his "sheep-skin" and went out into the world with the vague impression that fame and fortune were at the top of a not very long ladder. Ah, well it is, that in the conflict of life the future is hidden from human eyes. He settled finally in Springfield, where the stern realities of every day life widened his knowledge of human nature and modified some of his enthusiasm. Meeting with little encouragement in the practice of his profession, or in the publication of a weekly paper, he turned his steps southward, somewhat discouraged. He went to Richmond, Va., where he taught school and afterward to Vicksburg, Miss. In the latter place he received a salary of $1000 per annum, as Superintendent of public schools. While here the sickness of a near relative called his wife north. After her departure he became disheartened, and giving up his place left for Springfield. On the day of his arrival in that city, less than twenty years ago, the associate editor of the Springfield Republican, a son of Rev. Dr. Davis of Westfield, was buried. On the way from the depot to the home of a friend the argus eyes of the editor-in-chief, who scenteth smartness afar off, fell upon him and then came the thought "Here's my man." A proposition was made and accepted, the Doctor commencing on a salary of *five hundred dollars*—half the amount he had received in Mississippi. "There is a tide in the affairs of men," says Shakespeare, "which taken at the flood leads on to fortune." This was true of the Doctor. In earlier years he had shown fondness for rhyming, and here in his new field he found ample scope for his brilliant imagination. He soon won success as a writer and author, and the dark halo that had dimmed his horizon gave place to the broad, glorious sun-light. His first book was a history of Western Massachusetts, written for the columns of the Springfield Republican, as have been a larger part of his publications.

Following this, appeared from his pen, Bay Path, Letters to the Young, Bitter Sweet, Gold Foil, Miss Gilbert's Career, Lessons in Life, Letters to the Joneses, Plain Talk on Familiar Subjects, and Life of Abraham Lincoln. His reputation as an author was established on Letters to the Young, which has had a very extensive circulation, although not as great as his Life of Lincoln, which has gone above one hundred thousand copies. This is an octavo volume of some 700 pages, and every line of it, and in fact all the labor bestowed upon it, commencing with the first collection of material, was done inside of four months. When his publisher made application to have the work written a difference of opinion rose in regard to compensation. The Doctor demanded $5000 and the publisher would give only $3000. A compromise was finally made by fixing the price at 20 cents per copy. As over a hundred thousand copies have been sold it will be seen that this was a compromise productive of good to the deserving party, unlike most of those made in higher places. In the early part of 1866 he sold his interest in the Springfield Republican—twenty-six shares, a little over a quarter of the whole concern—for $26,000, and he now retires to green fields, poetry and books, with a fortune sufficiently ample to supply the wants of station and reasonable desire, and all made, too, since his connection with the Springfield Republican.

CHICOPEE.

Nearly four miles north of Springfield is the manufacturing town of Chicopee, situated on the south bank of Chicopee River. The Dwight Manufacturing Company's mills, seven in number, will be seen on the Chicopee River, nearest the railroad. This corporation has a capital of $1,700,000, employs, when in full operation, 2,000 hands and manufactures $20,000,000 worth of goods annually. There are 70,000 spindles in the mills and the goods manufactured consist of sheetings, shirtings, drills and print cloths. Sylvanus Adams is Agent and S. H. Brigham, Superintendent.

The Ames Manufacturing Company, whose buildings can be seen east of the tall chimney, employs 400 hands in manufacturing gun-stocking machinery, water wheels, bronze cannon, swords, bronze statuary, silver and plated ware, &c. They are the largest manufacturers of bronze cannon in the country and during the war they made over a thousand cannon for the Government, besides a large quantity of shot and shell, running their works night and day, for three years and employing 600 to 700 hands. In every gunboat and on every battlefield their cannon played a prominent part in overcoming treason. The capital of this corporation is $250,000. James T. Ames is Agent and Geo. Arms, Superintendent.

The Gaylord Manufacturing Company employ about 100 hands in making mail-bags, military accoutrements, locks, steel pens, &c.

At Chicopee Falls, two miles east of Chicopee, are several large manufacturing establishments. The Chicopee Manufacturing Company employ 1,000 hands and manufacture sheetings, shirtings, print flannels, drills and counterpanes. Their capital is $420,000. E. Blake, Agent; Charles Green, Superintendent.

The Belcher & Taylor Manufacturing Company employ about 50 hands in manufacturing agricultural implements. Capital, $50,000; B. B. Belcher, Agent.

Whittemore & Belcher also manufacture a large variety of agricultural implements. This is one of the oldest and largest concerns of its kind in this country.

WILLIMANSETT.

This station is four miles from Chicopee. Passengers for South Hadley Falls, opposite Holyoke, leave the railroad at this place. A few rods north of the station the Connecticut River is crossed on a bridge 700 feet in length.

DAM ACROSS THE CONNECTICUT AT HOLYOKE, MASS.

HOLYOKE.

Distance from New York, 144 miles; Montreal, 302: White Mountains, 176; Lake Memphremagog, 228; Quebec, 374.

Shortly before reaching Willimansett the factories, public and private buildings of Holyoke are seen in the north-west. Here, eight miles from Springfield, is the greatest water power in New England, and here at some future day will be one of the largest manufacturing cities in America. Just north of the town, a dam, 30 feet high and 1,017 feet in length, is built across the Connecticut. The river at this point falls 60 feet in a mile and a half, and furnishes power sufficient to drive more than a million of cotton spindles, three times greater than there are at Lowell. There are three canals, (along which are situated the factories,) so arranged that the water is used three times over, the mills on the upper canal discharging the water from their wheels into the canal of the second level, from the second into the third, and from the third into the river below the rapids. The upper canal is 140 feet wide, 20 feet deep and lined on both sides by heavy stone walls. The upper canal is now 3,000 feet in length, the middle 7,000 feet, and the lower 3,600 feet. They are to be extended when there is demand for more power and their united length, when completed will be nearly six miles. The dam, canals, and some 1,100 acres of land are owned by the Holyoke Water Power Company, who lease the power for a term of years, or in perpetuity to parties wishing to erect manufacturing establishments. There is never a deficiency of water, even in the driest seasons, nor can the mills on the two upper canals be obstructed by back water, as in some localities.

The project of a dam across the Connecticut at this place was first suggested in 1847, and in the following year it was completed, but was so poorly built that it was carried away a few hours after the gates were closed—just before the water had reached the top of the dam. In 1849 another one was built which has withstood the greatest freshets ever known in the Connecticut. It is built of wood and contains more than four millions feet of lumber, all of which being under water is protected from decay. The top of the dam is covered with sheets of boiler plate iron, from one shore to the other. The dam is spiked to the solid rock in the bottom of the river by three thousand one and one-quarter inch iron bolts, thus preventing any possibility of its ever giving way. During the construction of the dam the water passed through 46 gates, 16 by 18 feet each, and when completed at twenty-two minutes before one, in the afternoon of Oct. 22, 1849, the engineer gave the signal, and half of them (alternate ones) were closed. Another signal was given and the remaining gates were shut. The river ceased its flow until its waters gradually collecting, rose upon the face of the dam and finally fell in an unbroken sheet over its crest. This water fall, considering its length, is the most beautiful in New England, and the traveler can obtain a good view of it soon after leaving the depot, by taking a seat on the east side of the car.

The village is pleasantly situated on a hill-side facing the east, which affords delightful sites for elegant residences. At the present time there are some 6,000 inhabitants in the town, and as manufacturing interests are improving it will be largely increased. The Water Power Company supply the town with gas and water. The reservoir, which will hold 2,000,000 gallons, is filled from the Connecticut by force pumps, and as it is 72 feet above the dam there is sufficient head to throw the water over the highest mill in the town.

Among the corporations and manufacturing companies doing business in the town are the following:

Holyoke Water Power Company owns dam, canals, and 1,100 acres of land. Leases power for manufacturing purposes. Capital, $350,000. George M. Bartholomew of Hartford, President; S. Stewart Chase, Agent and Engineer.

The Lyman Mills employ 1,200 hands in manufacturing sheetings, shirtings, lawns and print cloths. The capital of this corporation is $1,500,000, and the capacity of the mills is 50,-000 spindles. The aggregate yearly product amounts to three and a half millions yards, which is all sold in Boston and New York. The Agent is J. S. Davis.

The Parsons Paper Company manufacture writing papers of every description. They have nineteen engines for grinding rags, and turn out 800 tons of paper yearly, valued at $500,000. Their capital (nominal) is $60,000. The number of hands employed is 150. Aaron Bagg is President, J. C. Parsons, Agent and Treasurer.

The Holyoke Paper Company manufacture writing papers. When their additions are completed they will employ 300 hands and turn out four tons of paper daily. President, Daniel Ashley; Agent, O. H. Greenleaf; Treasurer, C. H. Haywood.

The Whiting Paper Company manufacture collar paper, turning out three and a half tons daily. They have a capital of $100,000 and employ 100 hands. President, L. L. Brown; Agent, Wm. Whiting.

The Hampden Paper Company employ 75 hands and manufacture one and a half tons of collar paper daily. Their capital is $60,000.

The Franklin Paper Company have a capital of $60,000, employ 75 hands and turn out one and a half tons of collar paper. The Agent is J. H. Newton.

The Bemis Paper Company manufacture Manilla paper. Their capital is $50,000. President, Stephen C. Bemis; Agent, R. P. Crafts.

The Holyoke Manilla Paper Company have a capital of $30,-000, employ 15 hands and manufacture one and a half tons of paper daily, amounting in value per year, to $125,000. President, J. C. Parsons; Agent and Treasurer, Henry S. Adams; Clerk, James G. Smith.

C. L. Frink employs 14 hands in manufacturing envelopes, paper shirt bosoms, collars, &c.

The Holyoke Machine Company manufacture castings, all

kinds of machinery, water wheels, &c. Number of hands employed, 80; capital $40,000. T. B. Flanders, Agent.

The Hampden Mills, with a capital of $270,000, employ 700 hands in manufacturing ginghams, cottonades and tickings. The capacity of the mills is 10,000 spindles and the yearly product is two millions yards, valued at $400,000. The goods are sold in Boston and New York. The Agent is John E. Chase.

The Hadley Company manufacture a superior article of fine yarns and threads. They have a capital of $800,000, employ 450 hands, and turn out one thousand pounds of yarns and threads daily. Number of spindles in this establishment, 16,000. J. S. Davis is the Agent.

The Merrick Thread Company, successors of Merrick Brothers & Co., whose goods have been favorably known for quite a number of years, employ 300 hands in manufacturing spool cotton and fine yarn. They have a capital of $200,000. The company have an office at 28 Warren Street, New York.

The Holyoke Warp Mills employ 50 hands, have a capital of $75,000, and manufacture cotton warps and balmoral skirts. H. M. Tinkham, Treasurer; A. L. Maxfield, Agent.

Geo. W. Prentiss manufactures piano, broom and other wires.

The Germania Mills, with a capital of $250,000, employ 150 hands and manufacture about 200,000 yards of fine beevers.

The J. Beebe Woolen Mill employs 150 hands and manufactures 500,000 yards of doeskins per annum.

The New York Woolen Mill employs 125 hands and manufactures from 300.000 to 400,000 yards of fancy cassimeres per annum.

E. Chase & Sons are extensively engaged in the lumber business, and probably have a larger trade than any other lumber firm in the valley.

SOUTH HADLEY FALLS.

Opposite Holyoke is the village of South Hadley Falls. The large brick factory on the bank of the river is the Glasgow

Gingham Works, and north of it a paper mill owned by the same corporation, and the Carew Paper Company.

Leaving Holyoke the tourist passes the dam and around the great bend in the Connecticut, continuing along the bank of the river. The scenery for several miles is particularly fine.

SMITH'S FERRY.—MT. HOLYOKE FEMALE SEMINARY IN THE DISTANCE.

This station is nearly five miles from Holyoke and four from Northampton. Here passengers for South Hadley cross the Connecticut. The village is in full view, situated on a commanding elevation, about a mile from the river. In South Hadley is located the celebrated Mt. Holyoke Female Seminary, established through the untiring efforts of Mary Lyon, in 1837, who became its first preceptress. The main building is 50 by 94 feet, five stories high, including basement, and has two wings, one at each end. This is strictly a family school on a large scale, to which no day pupils are admitted and no domestics are employed. The labor is divided among the whole number, each young lady having a particular portion of work assigned her for a given time. The principal object of the institution is to furnish a supply of well qualified female teachers. Soon after leaving Smith's Ferry going north, a good view of the Seminary is had, which is situated a short distance south of the village church.

SCENERY OF UNUSUAL INTEREST.

From Smith's Ferry to Northampton, a distance of four miles, the varied objects which can be seen are of more than usual interest. Nowhere along the whole route, crowded into so small a space is there so much to attract the attention of the tourist. North and on the right, rises Mount Holyoke, on the summit of which is seen the Prospect House. The train is soon passing between Mounts Tom and Holyoke, both of which approach close to the river. Here the Connecticut, or the vast body of water that once made this region a great lake, gradually wore through the barrier of rock, leaving a magnificent valley, one of the most fertile upon the face of the globe. On the east side of the river, at the western end of Mount Holyoke, are columnar rocks, rising perpendicularly from the water to the hight of near a hundred feet, which resemble those on the coast of Ireland, forming Fingal's Cave and the Giant's Causeway. President Hitchcock, in his Geology of Massachusetts has given them the name of Titan's Pier.

Looking up the Connecticut, on the right, will be noticed Amherst College, eight miles distant. A little to the left and farther north is Mount Toby, apparently extending towards the east. A little to the left and still farther north is Sugar Loaf Mountain, on the west bank of the Connecticut, and twelve miles from Northampton. After passing over the railroad bridge to what is known as Ox-Bow Island, the former course of the Connecticut will be seen. Here the river, which formerly made a circuit of three and a half miles to gain a distance of thirty rods, received the name of Ox-Bow. It curved to the west and thence to the east, coming back to what is now the main channel, east of the bridge. In 1840 a freshet washed through the "neck" east of the railroad, making an island of the land lying in the Bow. While crossing the island, which contains 400 acres, and now connected to the main land on the north by the railroad embankment, can be seen in the west the factories and church spires of Easthampton. South of the Ox-Bow and under Mount Tom is Pascommuck, where in 1704 nineteen or twenty persons were slain by Indians, and the village burnt. The highest elevation seen west of Easthampton is Pomeroy's Mountain, and at its eastern base are several lead mines that were opened during the Revolution, but owing to the great depth of the ore in the rock, they were abandoned. They have recently been re-opened and worked. The meadows north of the Island are very broad, and including those extending to the right, they contain 8000 acres, valued at $150 to $250 per acre. On approaching Northampton a good view of the State Lunatic Hospital is had, which is located a mile west of the town. In the center will be noticed the High School building, the Town Hall, the First Church, and also Round Hill beyond with its Water-Cure buildings.

MOUNT HOLYOKE—THE PROSPECT HOUSE.

In going north, the first distinct view of Mount Holyoke, which is situated on the east side of the Connecticut, within two miles of Northampton, is had soon after leaving Holyoke. On the summit will be noticed the Prospect House, one thousand feet above the Connecticut. Coming from the north, the mountain is seen at South Deerfield, and most of the way to Northampton the Prospect House is prominently outlined on the sky beyond. Here in 1821 was built the first house erected on any mountain in New England. It is a favorite place of resort and during a single season from fifteen to twenty thousand people visit its summit, coming from nearly every northern and western State in the Union. The view is beautiful and picturesque, and is pronounced by distinguished travelers to be the *finest in America.* N. P. Willis, and President Hitchcock, the latter distinguished as a geologist, have written glowing descriptions of its unrivaled beauty, while Jenny Lind, during a visit to it when on her concert tour through this country, spoke of it in terms of unqualified praise. So great a diversity of scenery is rarely met with. Mountain, meadow, river and valley are harmoniously blended, while here and there the tall spires of hundreds of churches are seen pointing heavenward. The view is much more extensive than one would suppose, reaching from the Green Mountains in Vermont and Monadnock in New Hampshire on the north, to East and West Rocks on the Sound in the south, a distance of more than a hundred miles. On the west, Greylock rears its stately peak, while in the east the rounded form of Wachusetts meets the eye. The view embraces no less than ten mountains in four States, and about forty villages. But on the whole, the most pleasing scene is that of the river and meadow beneath. The latter diversified by the different crops under cultivation, resembles a magnificent carpet, the beauty and richness of coloring transcending anything produced in art. In looking at this scene, one is reminded more of a great painting than an actual landscape. The proprietor of the Prospect House, J. W. French, has resided on the mountain nearly twenty years, and half of that time both summer and winter. The present house is 55 by 70 feet, two stories high. Visitors are taken to the summit by steam power, an inclined railway having been constructed in 1854, extending 600 feet down the mountain to the carriage road, where it is to connect with a horse railway to the Connecticut River. A steamboat was built in the spring of 1866, by Mr. French, of the Prospect House, and makes trips on the Connecticut, carrying passengers to and from the terminus of the mountain railway.

The summit is less than three miles from Northampton, from which place it is easily reached by carriages or otherwise.

MOUNT TOM.

Mount Tom, on the west side of the Connecticut, will be noticed first, soon after leaving Springfield, in the north-west. The point seen, which is the southern end, is 1,200 feet high, the greatest elevation of any part of the mountain range. The south-eastern face is comparatively gradual in ascent, and reaches nearly down to the Connecticut. The north-western side is more precipitous, and in some places is nearly perpendicular. It is some three or four miles in length, and its northern end terminates within a few rods of the Connecticut, opposite Mount Holyoke.

NORTHAMPTON.

Distance from New York, 153 miles; from Montreal, 293; White Mountains, 167; Lake Memphremagog, 212; Quebec, 385.

Northampton, which is 17 miles from Springfield, is among the oldest towns in the Connecticut Valley, having been settled in 1654 by 21 planters from Hartford and Windsor, who purchased it of the Indians for "one hundred fathoms of wampum, ten coats and some small gifts." The Indian name of the town is Nonotuck. The whites gave it the name of Northampton after a town of the same name in England. There are few villages in New England which present so many attractions to the summer tourist, and few are so widely and favorably known. A traveler writing of it, very appropriately remarks: "We must peep at Northampton with loving leisure. It is the frontispiece of the book of beauty, which nature opens wide in the valley of the Connecticut, and one of the most winsome pictures in the volume."

Its broad and extensive meadows, its river and mountain scenery, its ancient elms and shaded streets, distinguish it from all the other towns on the banks of the noble Connecticut. It has always been noted for its culture and refinement, as well as for its great natural beauty, and many distinguished men have been among its residents, including Maj. Joseph Hawley, a distinguished lawyer and statesman, who died in 1788; Rev. Jonathan Edwards, the third minister of the town, who preached here 23 years, from 1727 to 1753; Gov. Caleb Strong, who was a member of the provincial Congress in 1774, of the Convention for drafting the Constitution of the United States, and one of the committee to draft a Constitution to be submitted to the people; a member of the United States Senate in the first Congress, and for eleven years Governor of Massachusetts, commencing in 1800.

In the cemetery are buried four persons who were once United States Senators from Massachusetts, Gov. Caleb Strong, Eli P. Ashmun, Elijah H. Mills and Isaac C. Bates. David Brainard, the missionary to the Stockbridge Indians, and Dr. Sylvester Graham, one of the first lecturers on health in this country, are also buried in the same cemetery.

The Edwards Elm on King Street, the top of which can be seen west of the railroad, shortly after crossing Main Street, is among the oldest and most beautiful trees in Northampton. It was set out by President Edwards, in front of his dwelling, during his ministry in the town.

DR. DENNISTON'S HOME FOR INVALIDS.

Dr. Denniston's Water Cure and Home for Invalids, is at Spring Dale, just west of the village. It is pleasantly situated, and will accommodate fifty patients. The Doctor, who devotes his time to the interest of his patients, has been quite successful in the treatment of disease.

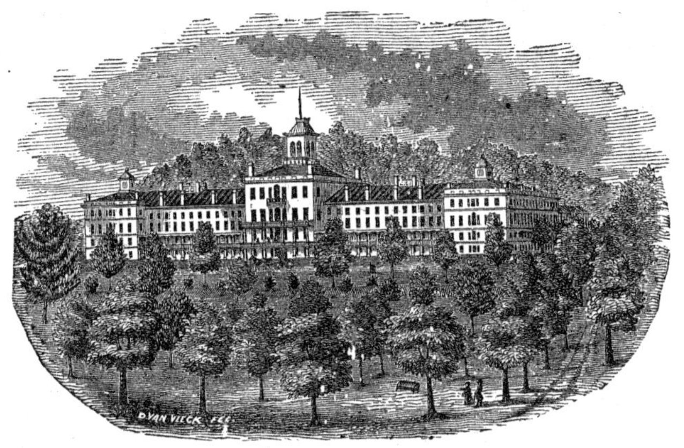

ROUND HILL WATER CURE AND HOTEL.

Round Hill, a beautiful eminence overlooking the town, with its water-cure buildings, and its grove of native forest trees, will be noticed in the north-west, and about a quarter of a mile west of the railroad.

Here George Bancroft, the historian, and J. G. Coggswell, for some years Librarian of the Astor Library, had a famous classical school—one of the most noted in this country. Dr. H. Halsted now occupies the buildings for a water-cure. Jenny Lind spent several months there just after her marriage, previous to returning to Europe. The view from the piazza of the water-cure is extensive and beautiful, and is nowhere surpassed.

The State Lunatic Hospital, located one mile west of the village, is a large and elegant structure. The erection of the building was commenced in 1856, and completed in 1858. The length of the two wings and main building is 512 feet. The wings are three stories high, and the main building four. The floors cover an area of four acres. The first Superintendent was Dr. William Henry Prince, of Salem, now residing in Cleveland, Ohio. Resigning in 1864, Dr. Pliny Earle, formerly

Superintendent of the Bloomingdale Hospital, was appointed Superintendent, which position he now holds. Its average number of patients is about 350.

Northampton has always been celebrated for its beautiful drives, which, with the many other pleasing features of the town, attract hundreds from the cities to spend the summer months. It has also taken great interest in educational matters, and within the last few years there has been erected a High School building, at a cost of about $40,000.

Florence, a village within the limits of the town, and about two miles and a half west of the center, in point of business has perhaps shown the greatest enterprise. Here are located the shops of the Florence Sewing Machine Company, the Nonotuck Silk Company, a Button and Daguerreotype Case factory, Cotton factory, &c. Dr. Charles Munde, a participator in the German revolutions, and a refugee, for many years had a water-cure establishment there, but it was burnt in 1865, and he has since returned to Europe to educate his children, having received a pardon from the King, and an appointment under our government.

Some years ago there was an industrial association in Florence, called the Community, similar to those advocated by Fourier, the distinguished French philanthropist. Considerable land was purchased and held by the association. Here were gathered some of the brightest intellects of the country, who joined the association to achieve an ideal life. Failing to make it pecuniarily self-sustaining, the project was abandoned, but some of its members still reside in the town, and are among its best and most worthy citizens. There has recently been erected in Florence a school house, costing about $30,000; nearly all of it a free gift from one of its most esteemed residents, Mr. S. L. Hill.

Of the other manufacturing establishments in the town, the most important are the Bay State Works, where hoes, rakes,

&c., are made; the Paper Mill of Wm. Clark & Co., L. B. Williams & Co's Basket Factory, and Arms, Bardwell & Co's Skirt Factory. The International Screw Company are about to erect shops in the town, and will give employment to a large number of hands.

The construction of a Horse Railway through the streets of Northampton to the village of Florence, was commenced in the spring of 1866. This, now completed, is the only street railway in Massachusetts west of Worcester.

The Northampton Indelible Pencil Company are doing considerable business in the manufacture of Indelible Pencils for marking fine linen. This is an article designed to take the place of indelible ink.

THE MANSION HOUSE AT NORTHAMPTON.

This popular and well known hotel, kept by William Hill, is centrally located, within five minutes walk of the depot. Under

Mr. Hill's management it has come to be regarded by summer tourists with great favor. A good livery stable is connected with the house, and carriages are furnished to parties wishing to visit Mt. Holyoke and the neighboring villages.

THE WARNER HOUSE,

On Main Street, Northampton, kept by Roswell Hunt, is one of the oldest hotels in the valley. For many years it was kept by the late Hon. Oliver Warner, and under his management it became widely known. It has been for many years a favorite stopping place with business men, and has always received a large patronage.

THE FLORENCE SEWING MACHINE.

The manufactory of the Florence Sewing Machine at Florence, in the town of Northampton, is quite extensive, as will be seen by the birds-eye view given of it by the artist. Here are employed a large number of hands in manufacturing what is acknowledged to be the best Sewing Machine now in use in this country. This machine makes *four* distinct stitches, lock, knot, double lock and double knot; either of which is stronger and more elastic than that made by many other machines, and it has become so popular that it has been almost impossible, much of the time, to fill the orders for it. Some of the more important features of this machine were invented by L. W. Langdon, then of Rochester, N. Y. Placing his invention on exhibition at Crystal Palace, New York city, it came under the observation of Mr. S. L. Hill, of Florence, who made arrangements to have its manufacture begun in the place of his residence. A company was formed, and after experimenting four years, they commenced to build some of the machines. In a year and a half, after surmounting many obstacles, they completed ten machines, at a cost of $10,000. Since that time there has been no difficulty, and the machine has risen rapidly into popular favor.

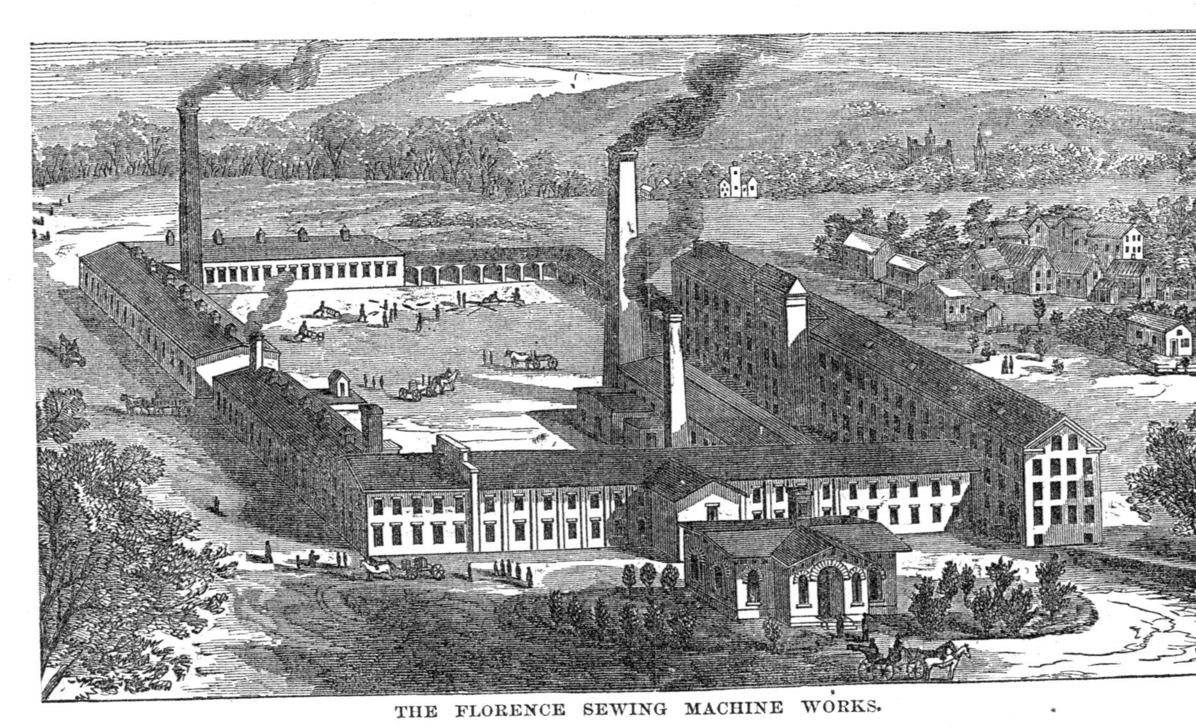

THE FLORENCE SEWING MACHINE WORKS.

The usual number of machines manufactured is from 1,000 to 1,200 monthly.

The advantages of this machine over all others is stated as follows:

"*It makes four different stitches*, the *lock*, *knot*, *double lock*, and *double knot*, on one and the same machine. Each stitch being *alike on both sides* of the fabric.

Every Machine has the *reversible feed motion*, which enables tbe operator, by simply turning a thumb screw, to have the work run either to the right or left, to stay any part of the seam, or fasten the ends of seams, without turning the fabric.

The only machine having a self-adjusting shuttle tension—the amount of tension always being in exact proportion to the size of the bobbin.

Changing the length of stitch, and from one kind of stitch to another, can readily be done while the machine is in motion.

The needle is easily adjusted.

It is almost *noiseless* and can be used where quiet is necessary.

Its motions are all *positive*; there are no springs to get out of order, and its simplicity enables the most inexperienced to operate it.

It does not require finer thread on the under than for the upper side, and will sew across the heaviest seams, or from one to more thicknesses of cloth, without change of needle, tension, or breaking thread.

The Hemmer is easily adjusted, and will turn any width of hem desired.

No other machine will do so great a range of work as the Florence.

It will hem, fell, bind, gather, braid, quilt, and gather and sew on a ruffle at the same time."

To use a poor and worthless tool of any kind is poor economy, and to nothing is this rule more applicable than to a second rate sewing machine.

The Company have offices in New York, Boston, Philadelphia, Cincinnati, Chicago, St. Louis, San Francisco, and in all the important places in the country, while a considerable number of machines have been sold in Europe.

The manufactory is only about two and a half miles from Northampton, and is worthy a visit.

THE SMITH CHARITIES.

Oliver Smith, of Hatfield, a bachelor, died in 1845 worth $370,000, which he left by will to be devoted principally to charitable objects. Among the provisions of the will was the establishment of Smith's Agricultural School at Northampton, 60 years after his decease, and to assist poor and worthy young men and women and widow ladies. The will provides that young men and women, taken from families residing in Northampton, Williamsburg, Hatfield, Hadley and Amherst, in Hampshire County, and in Whately, Deerfield and Greenfield, in Franklin County, and bound out to persons residing in those towns, shall receive: girls, when married, as a marriage portion, the sum of $300; boys, when of age, a loan of $500 for five years—interest to be paid annually. At the end of the five years, if they prove themselves worthy, then they shall have the $500 outright, as a present, to assist them in commencing business. Under certain conditions, the will also provides that indigent young women, about to be married, can have $50 as a marriage portion, and that indigent widows, who have children dependent upon them, can receive $50 annually, to assist them in supporting their families.

When the Annual Report was made in May, 1867, the aggregate amount of the several funds was $853,776, divided as follows: Joint and Miscellaneous Fund, $451,168; Contingent Fund, $341,627; Agricultural Fund, $54,997.

These funds are managed by a Board of three Trustees, all of whom are chosen annually by electors—one from each of the eight towns receiving benefits of the will. The electors are chosen at the annual town meetings. The President of the

Board is Hon. Osmyn Baker, of Northampton. In 1866 the Trustees completed the erection of an office and banking building, at Northampton, of Portland freestone, at a cost of about $30,000.

THE SILK FEVER—REMARKABLE PERSEVERANCE OF ITS ORIGINATOR.

The speculative mania which swept over this country some 30 or 40 years ago, concerning the production of raw silk, had its origin in Northampton. The motive however of the one who suggested it, was not of a speculative nature, but had its foundation in a desire to do a great public good. The originator of it has had remarkable experience, and his history is of more than ordinary interest. Few men have ever labored so perseveringly against so many discouragements, without being disheartened and turned from their purpose. From the attempt to introduce the production of raw silk into this country he turned his attention to invention, but from a variety of causes, when, seemingly on the point of realizing an immense fortune, his expectations and years of anxious labor have come to naught. Few have had the capacity to bring their inventions so successfully before the public, or have secured so large sums to have them tested. In several instances large companies have been formed, and altogether, himself and those concerned with him have expended not less than half a million of dollars in his various enterprises. Yet, nearly every one of his inventions have failed in securing to him, or those interested, a remuneration. Not, it is claimed, because they possessed no real worth, but from other causes over which he had no control. He has at last, however, perfected an invention, after six years of most constant labor, that promises to be one of great usefulness. It is an indelible pencil for writing on paper—a substitution in many cases for ink.

Mr. Samuel Whitmarsh, the gentleman referred to, was formerly a dry goods merchant in New York. In 1830 he went to Northampton to reside. It occurring to him that the production of raw silk might be successfully done in this country, he traveled through the silk regions of the Old World to make investigations. He returned home with full belief in its practicability and at once made arrangements to commence the business in Northampton. Mulberry trees were planted and cocooneries established. The subject was then discussed in the public prints and thousands rushed into the business without any knowledge of it. Speculators seized upon it and fanned the flame, and it soon become a mania, running through the country like wild-fire. As a natural result the whole thing proved a failure.

A company was formed in Northampton and a factory was established in the village of Florence for the manufacture of silk. In that factory was woven cloth for a silk vest which Mr. Whitmarsh presented to Henry Clay. In Northampton a smaller factory was also built and in it ribbons of various qualities were woven.

After making a series of experiments, Mr. Whitmarsh became satisfied that a warmer climate would be more favorable to the production of raw silk. He went to the island of Jamaica to make investigations, and was convinced that the business could be successfully carried on there. He formed a company with a capital of $200,000, and in 1848 erected extensive buildings.

Through the various discouragements that have been passed, Mr. Whitmarsh has been unwavering. He visited England to interest the people in the enterprise, and while at London sold $50,000 worth of stock in the Company. The samples of silk he had with him were pronounced to be the best in the London market. Lord Metcalf, just appointed Governor of Jamaica, took great interest in the enterprise, and declared to Mr. Whitmarsh that he was deserving of the highest monument that could be erected, for what he had already accomplished. Returning to Jamaica, to his great chagrin and disappointment, he found that one of the directors in the Company, a lawyer by profession, had had some difficulty with the owners of an ice-house in which the worms had been placed, and had removed them to a cellar, the dampness of which killed them. As they had long been undergoing the process of acclimation, this put the enterprise back five years. Following this began a long and unprofitable litigation, and finally the project was abandoned altogether. In 1846 he loaded a small vessel with tropical plants, orange trees, century plants, &c., and accompanied with his family and some 30 American workmen, sailed for Boston, with a view of opening a botanical garden, under the patronage of the city, the ship and cargo being all that was left of a large property, and what at one time promised a great enterprise. In Boston the proposition to establish a conservatory and garden did not meet with success, and it was abandoned. Before leaving Jamaica he took up a century plant and sailed for London, where he sold it for a hundred guineas, and returned home by the same steamer.

Since the silk enterprise he has devoted himself to developing several inventions. Among them, after spending some six or eight years in experimenting, was a steam furnace for warming buildings. A company was formed of New York capitalists, and their manufacture commenced at Northampton. Some difficulty arose in the company and this was abandoned, Mr. Whitmarsh alone losing $30,000.

He next invented a kind of belting, and some New York men began its manufacture at Northampton. This company too got into difficulty, and after losing from $60,000 to $80,000 gave up the business.

In December, 1859, Mr. Whitmarsh commenced experimenting with a view of inventing an Indelible Pencil for writing on paper, and after six years of the most patient labor, he has at last succeeded. The patent is in the hands of Mr. A. G. Day, of Seymour, Conn., and Mr. Whitmarsh, and it will soon be brougnt before the public.

EASTHAMPTON.

Four miles south-west of Northampton, is the town of Easthampton, noted for its schools and factories. It presents a very neat appearance, much more so than is usual in a manufacturing village, and its rapid growth is due to the enterprise of Hon. Samuel Williston, son of Rev. Payson Williston, the first minister of the town, who was settled in 1789. Williston Seminary, which, as a classical school, to prepare young men for college, has few equals, was established by Mr. Williston, who has given $225,000 for that purpose.

He first commenced the manufacture of buttons in a small way by hand, his wife assisting him. Meeting with great success, he enlarged his business, and finally, in 1847, began the erection of a factory at Easthampton. Previously he had manufactured suspenders as well as buttons, and when his factory was completed his business was transferred to it and greatly enlarged. In later years other kinds of manufacturing have been entered upon, and all of his enterprises have proved immensely profitable. He is probably the richest manufacturer in the western part of the State, and in 1864 he returned an income of over $200,000. His gifts for religious and educational purposes in this vicinity amount to $318,000. Of this amount he has given $225,000 to Williston Seminary, $50,000 to Amherst College, and $43,000 to Payson church in Easthampton. When the Canal Railroad was built, he subscribed $35,000 to its capital stock, and as that enterprise, owing to bad management, did not pay as an investment, that sum can be regarded as a gift, which will make the aggregate of his public donations $353,000.

There are now in the town some half a dozen factories, with a total capital of $1,600,000. The different corporations are:

Nashawannuck Manufacturing Company, capital $300,000, employs 300 hands in manufacturing suspenders and frills.

Glendale Vulcanized Rubber Company, capital $250,000, employs 300 hands, and manufactures elastic shoe webbing.

National Button Company, capital $150,000, employs 125 hands, and manufactures 1200 gross of buttons per day.

Easthampton Rubber Thread Company, capital $100,000, manufactures rubber thread used in webbing.

Williston Mills, capital $800,000, has two mills, and manufacture cotton yarn for warps.

HADLEY.

Both above and below Northampton the church spires of Old Hadley can be seen, about three miles east of the railroad, the streets of which extend from the Connecticut on the north, to the same river on the south, a distance of about a mile, the town lying in the neck or base of the peninsula. The Connecticut here makes a curve to the west, and thence to the east in its southerly course of seven miles. The town was settled in 1650, by a colony from Hartford, Windsor and Wethersfield, Conn. There are three streets running north and south, parallel with each other. West street was laid out before the colony came to the town, with "home lots" of several acres each on either side of the street, which was originally twenty rods wide and one mile in length. In 1773 the original width was reduced to eighteen rods. Since that time still further reductions have been made which have cut it down to seventeen and one-half rods at the South, and fifteen and one-half rods at the North. Various causes, including the encroachments of the river at the north end, have reduced its length to 300 rods, consequently it contains not far from twenty-one acres. On each side of the street are two rows of ancient elms, nearly 1,000 in number;

and the quiet, rural aspect of the town, with its broad and grass-covered street, give it a peculiar appearance, unlike any other village in the valley.

Middle Street was laid out in 1683, and was originally twenty rods in width. It has however been reduced to about eleven rods. East Street was laid out in 1825.

In 1657, Edward Hopkins of Hartford, left a donation of about £400, which was appropriated to establish a school. In 1667, the town granted to the trustees of this fund a meadow in North Hadley, which now contains about 140 acres. Various other accessions have been made, the Legislature in 1816 granted an act of incorporation, and gave them a quarter of a township of land situated in what is now the State of Maine. A building was erected in 1814, on the middle lane which runs between East and West streets. From that time Hopkins' Academy became one of the notable institutions in this valley. The old building was burned in 1860, and the school held its sessions in rooms fitted up in the basement of the Congregational Church until 1865, when the fund was incorporated with that raised by the town, and a building erected for a High School. She can reckon many of the most distinguished men in New England among her graduates.

This town is celebrated as being the place of refuge of "the regicides," William Goffe and Edward Whalley, two of the judges who condemned Charles I. They had both occupied positions in Cromwell's army, the former being a major-general and the latter a lieutenant-general. After the restoration of the monarchy, an order for their apprehension as traitors was issued. They made their escape and reached Boston in 1660. They resided in New Haven, Conn., for three years and a half after their arrival, obliged all the while to use their utmost vigilance, frequently being compelled to resort to the woods and caves to elude their pursuers. At one time they secreted themselves under a bridge near New Haven, while the King's officers rode over on horseback.

In October, 1664, they came to Hadley and took up their abode with Rev. Mr. Russell, whose house was situated on the east side of West street, directly north of what is now the main road between Northampton and Amherst. Here they remained concealed fifteen or sixteen years. The dangerous secret was known to Peter Tilton and to a Mr. Smith, who lived at the north end of the village. Through Mr. Tilton, who was frequently a member of the general court, Goffe corresponded with his friends. By one of his letters, dated April 2, 1679, it appears that Whalley died some time previous at Mr. Russell's. He was buried in a tomb formed of mason work and covered with hewn stone, just without the cellar wall of the dwelling, where his remains were found by Mr. Gaylord in 1794, when he built a house on the site where Mr. Russell's stood. There is also a tradition that Goffe died in Hadley and was buried in the garden or near the house of Mr. Tilton.

On the 1st of September, 1675, while the people were assembled, on a fast day, at the church, the town was attacked by the Indians and thrown into the greatest confusion. A man of venerable aspect and commanding mien suddenly appeared among them, assumed command, arrayed the men in the best posture for defense, and by his example inspired them with new vigor. As soon as the enemy were repelled the stranger withdrew. Speculation concerning their deliverer was rife, but it only ended in the conjecture that the town had been saved by its guardian angel. The supposed angel was none other than General Goffe, who, seeing the danger of the town, rushed out to assist in the defense, and by his thorough knowledge of military tactics, enabled the town's people to withstand the assault. There seems to have been a suspicion in the minds of the cotemporaneous local historians that this officer was an important personage whom it was for the interest of the colony to conceal.

Hadley is also the birth place of Maj.-Gen. Joseph Hooker, for a time commander of the Army of the Potomac.

Here was manufactured, the first broom, of broom corn that was made in this country. About 1790 broom corn was introduced into the town and grown as an ornamental plant. At that time brooms were made of birch. A negro named Ebar commenced to manufacture the brush into brooms, and Levi Dickinson sold them. This was the origin of the broom business, which has now become one of the most important in this vicinity. At first Mr. Dickinson met with much opposition, there being great prejudice against what was regarded as an innovation. He predicted that it would become the leading business of the county, and if it has not been fully realized, the time has been when it was the most important in quite a number of the towns in this region. In Hadley alone there are manufactured nearly $200,000 worth of brooms and brushes annually. Formerly all the brush consumed in the town was raised in the valley; now much of it is grown in the West.

AMHERST AND ITS COLLEGES.

Seven miles east of Northampton is Amherst and its colleges. About a mile below, and about the same distance above, Northampton, the town is in full view, lying beyond Hadley and apparently at the base of the eastern range of hills, but really about two miles from them. Amherst College, though one of the youngest in New England, is already in the first rank of educational institutions. The college edifices are nine in number, grouped on the summit of a gentle eminence and commanding an unsurpassed view of the surrounding country, for miles on every side. Part of the buildings, dating back to the foundation of the college, are old and cannot boast much in the way of architectural beauty; but the most of them are of comparatively recent construction, and besides sustaining that great test of every building, adaptation to the use intended, are really fine edifices in themselves, and ornaments to the town. Among them may be mentioned the Library building, Williston Hall—

erected by the munificence of Hon. Samuel Williston, of Easthampton, who has been a liberal patron of the college—the Appleton Cabinet, the Observatory and Octagonal Cabinet, the Gymnasium, and the new Dormitory.

But the greatest pride of Amherst College is the cabinets; and any one who examines them even cursorily, will acknowledge that the pride is a legitimate and just one. On entering the college grounds, the first building that attracts the attention is the Observatory and the Octagonal Cabinet, so-called. The upper room of this building is entirely devoted to Prof. Charles U. Shepard's Mineralogical Cabinet, which comprises 6000 specimens of minerals of the rarest and choicest character, and fully arranged and labeled for study. Here is also the largest collection of meteorites in the world, gathered by untiring industry and at great expense by Prof. Shepard. The casual observer, and the man of science will alike love to linger long in this room; the uneducated attracted by the beautiful colors and unusual forms of the minerals, and their beautiful arrangement, and the educated to study the rare and costly specimens here exhibited. To those of a practical turn of mind, it may be interesting to know that the value of the whole collection is almost fabulous, and that single specimens cost thousands of dollars. In the lower room of the same building is the Wood's Geological Cabinet, containing 20,000 specimens of American and foreign rocks and fossils, offering unrivaled facilities for the students of this branch of science. Joined to the Octagonal Cabinet and opening from it, is the Nineveh Gallery, containing relics from Nineveh, and large sculptured slabs, arranged as they stood in the palace of Sardanapalus at Nimroud. Here, also is a collection of coins and medals, and a quantity of Indian relics. On the other side of the cabinet is the observatory, containing all the necessary instruments for taking observations of the celestial bodies.

Beyond the chapel, and on a lower terrace, is the Appleton Cabinet, in the upper room of which is the Adams Zoological

Cabinet, containing specimens of 5,900 species of animals, and 8,000 species of shells. Here also is an Herbarium containing more than 4,000 species of dried plants, with the seeds and cuttings of tropical plants and trees, besides a private collection of Lichens, consisting of 800 species. The lower room, one hundred and ten feet long, and forty-five feet wide is devoted entirely to the Ichnological Cabinet, presenting some 9000 examples of tracks in stone. This cabinet peculiarly belongs to Amherst, and more than any other one thing, perhaps has given a reputation to the College. There is no other cabinet like it in the world, in extent, and very few in kind. The science of Ichnology had its birth at Amherst; here lived its founder, Dr. Hitchcock, and here are gathered its richest specimens, "foot-prints on the sands of time," stone histories of the past. These tracks on the sand-stone of the Connecticut Valley tell queer legends of the animal life of long ago, and nothing can be more interesting than to spend an hour or a day in viewing these relics, now scientifically arranged and classified.

The Massachusetts State Agricultural College was located in Amherst in 1863, about a mile north of the village, and some 400 acres purchased as an experimental farm. The erection of the College buildings were commenced in 1866, and when in operation it is expected that this will be one of the best institutions of the kind in the country.

THE GREAT BEND IN THE CONNECTICUT.

Leaving Northampton, a mile north of the town the tourist comes to the great bend in the Connecticut—the river running seven miles to gain one. The broad meadows and the village of Hadley, extending across the peninsula from one bank of the Connecticut to the other, are in full view. It was at this place that the Farmington Canal from New Haven to Northampton terminated, when in operation. The patronage being insufficient it was abandoned about twenty years ago.

This is the last view had of the Connecticut until the tourist approaches South Vernon, nearly 30 miles distant. The river takes a more circuitous route, bearing further to the east.

HATFIELD.

Hatfield, four miles from Northampton, is a pleasant town, on the west bank of the Connecticut. Its inhabitants are chiefly engaged in agriculture, fattening cattle, and raising crops of tobacco and broom corn. The village is about two miles east of the depot. This, like many other towns in this region, suffered from attacks from Indians in its early days. May 30, 1676 some six or seven hundred Indians invaded the town, burnt twelve houses and killed a number of the inhabitants. A company of 25 men from Hadley crossed the river, attacked the Indians and succeeded in killing 25. Another attack was made Sept. 19, 1677 by 800 Indians, who killed 11 whites and carried 17 into captivity. Oliver Smith, the founder of the Smith Charities, lived in this town.

WHATELY,

Four miles from Hatfield, is a small agricultural town. The village will be noticed on the hill west of the railroad.

SUGAR LOAF MOUNTAIN.

Soon after leaving Whately, Sugar Loaf Mountain will be observed on the right. It is a conical peak of red sand-stone, 500 feet above the plain. It stands on the west bank of the Connecticut, within two hundred yards of the river, and rises almost perpendicularly from the meadows below. North of it is another peak somewhat higher, but seldom visited, as the view is less interesting. Sugar loaf stands as it were at the head of the valley, and the southern view is remarkable for its beauty. On the left, east of the river, and almost underneath the mountain, is the village of Sunderland, accessible from the the west side by a covered toll bridge. South, and on the

SUGAR LOAF MOUNTAIN.

same side of the river, are the villages of North Amherst, Amherst, Belchertown, North Hadley and Hadley. On the west side are South Deerfield, Whately, Hatfield, Northampton and Easthampton. Skirting the southern horizon are the lofty peaks of Mounts Holyoke and Tom, and between them, through the gateway to the ocean, glimmering in the sun-light, are the church spires in Holyoke and Chicopee.

Here lies before you a great basin, divided through its center by the Connecticut, and on either side the numerous villages and well cultivated fields, add beauty to the scene. At no other point is one more strongly impressed with the great wealth of the valley. Before you, on either side of the river, are thousands of dwellings and workshops, seemingly almost a continuous village. On this plain in years gone by, where peace and happiness now dwell, were enacted some terrible and bloody scenes. Here on this very mountain peak, it is supposed that King Philip, the terror of the early settlers, had his head-quarters and from which he kept watch over the movements of the whites below. At the southern face of the mountain was fought a great battle, and at the right, north of the village of South Deerfield, was one of the most terrible and heart-rending massacres ever perpetrated by Indians. The monument erected to commemorate the event, can be seen in front of the North Church.

Table Rock, on the eastern side, is a feature of great interest. It projects from the mountain side, and at a single leap one could strike the plain hundreds of feet below. By way of information it might be well to state that visitors are not expected to try that way of descending the mountain, as a source of amusement. It is feared that stopping so suddenly, would create an unpleasant sensation. Underneath Table Rock is King Philip's Chair, cut from the solid rock. Three excavations were made by the Indians, as is supposed, and one of them is a good seat. Some imaginative white man gave it the name, years ago, of King Philip's Chair, by which it is now known.

East of Sugar Loaf, on the opposite side of the Connecticut, is Mount Toby, twelve hundred feet above the river. In the north west can be seen Shelburne Mountain, and Haystack—the latter in Vermont.

The Mountain house, kept by Granville Wardwell, was built by him in 1864. It stands on the summit, near the southern point. Persons wishing to visit the mountain can leave the cars at South Deerfield, a mile and a half from the summit. A road has been constructed to the house.

SOUTH DEERFIELD—THE BATTLE OF BLOODY BROOK.

South Deerfield, a village in the town of Deerfield, at the base of Sugar Loaf Mountain, is chiefly noted for having been the scene of some of the most terrible Indian massacres recorded on the pages of history. Here was fought the battle of Bloody Brook, the history of which is familiar to every school-boy in the land.

The first conflict between the whites and Indians took place in August, 1675, at the south end of Sugar Loaf, where Captains Lathrop and Beers, who had left Hadley in pursuit of some Indians who were attempting to join King Philip, overtook them. In this engagement 26 Indians and ten whites were killed.

On the 18th of the following September a force of 80 soldiers, under command of Capt. Lathrop, who had been stationed at Hadley, was returning from Deerfield, acting as a guard to some teams that were transporting grain to Hadley, and while halting at a small stream north of where the village now stands, an attack was made. The stream was then bordered by trees on which the native grape clustered; and while the men were gathering them 700 Indians, probably under command of Philip fell upon them and most cruelly butchered almost the entire force. Only seven or eight escaped to tell the sad tale. Including Capt. Lathrop and the teamsters the number killed was about 90. Capt. Moseley, then at Deerfield, hearing the firing hurried to the spot, attacked the Indians, and after a most deadly strife put them to flight. Their loss was about 96 warriors.

Nearly all of the whites who were slain were buried in one common grave, a short distance south of where the massacre took place. A few years ago a monument 26 feet high was erected to commemorate the sad event. Edward Everett delivered an eloquent address, when the corner stone was laid.

DEERFIELD—INDIAN MASSACRES.

Passing Sugar Loaf Mountain, and the Bloody Brook Monument you soon come to Old Deerfield. Few towns in New England suffered so much in its earlier days from Indian depredations as did this. Within its borders, from King Philip's war to that waged by the French and Indians nearly 150 white settlers were killed, and many others carried into captivity. About 30 years after the massacre of Captain Lathrop and men at Bloody Brook, another, and if possible more heart-rending deed was transacted at the village of Deerfield. On the 29th of February, 1704, Maj. Hertel de Rouville, with upwards of 340 French and Indians, arrived at Petty's Plain, north of Deerfield meadows, which the traveler will notice towards the north-west previous to crossing the bridge over Deerfield river. Here he halted until the next morning, when he moved upon the village of Deerfield. The snow having drifted to the top of the palisades which had been constructed as a defense, the entire force entered the fortifications undiscovered, the settlers being in profound sleep. The houses were broken open, the frightened and defenseless inhabitants dragged from their beds, and such as offered resistance were killed and the others taken prisoners. Only a few escaped. Rev. John Williams, the minister of the town, was awakened from his sleep and rushed to the door and found the enemy entering. Calling to two soldiers who lodged in the house he sprang back and seized a pistol and attempted to fire at an Indian. It missing fire, he was seized and bound. Two of his children and a negro woman were taken to the door and butchered. Mr. Williams was kept standing in the cold for an hour before being permitted to dress. His savage captors meantime amused themselves by threatening his life and swinging their hatchets over his head. Mrs. Williams had recently given birth to a child, and still in a feeble condition was compelled to dress, and herself and five children taken captives.

An attack was made on the house of John Sheldon, which they found hard to enter. An attempt was made by the Indians to split the door down with their hatchets. Finally it was partly opened and a musket was thrust in and fired. Mrs. Sheldon, who had risen and was dressing, was hit and killed. The house was used as a place of confinement for the prisoners until all were gathered in from the other parts of the village. One house was defended by seven men, for whom the women cast bullets while the fight was in progress. When the sun was about an hour high, after the houses had been plundered and many of them set on fire, Rouville and his men started for Canada, halting at Petty's Plain, where they had left their packs and snow-shoes a few hours before.

Capt. Stoddard escaped from Mr. Williams' house during the attack, by leaping from the window. He tore up a cloak, which he had hurriedly seized, and bound about his feet, and ran to Hatfield. A son of Capt. Sheldon escaped the same way, and also went to Hatfield. A force left Hatfield in pursuit of the Indians, and they were overtaken north of Deerfield, where a skirmish ensued, but the pursuers being much the smaller party, were obliged to retreat—not, however, until they had lost nine of their number. The captives taken by Rouville numbered 180, and the killed 47. The enemy's loss exceeded 40.

Mrs. Williams, who had become weak and exhausted on the second day's march, was thrown down by the water while crossing a rapid stream, and her savage captor, thinking it impossible for her to continue the march, buried his tomahawk in her forehead, which soon caused her death. Mr. Williams was much of the time separated from his wife, and was in advance when she was cruelly butchered. She was the daughter of Rev. Eleazer Mather, the first minister of Northampton, and was an educated, refined, and noble woman.

At White River, Rouville divided his forces—one party going up that river to Canada and another up the Connecticut. Mr. Williams' party followed the White River route and most of his children the other, and they barely escaped death from famine.

After arriving in Canada the French treated Mr. Williams with great kindness, and finally he was redeemed by Gov. Vaudreuil. In 1706 Mr. Williams and four of his children, with other captives to the number of 57, embarked on board of a ship at Quebec, sent there by Gov. Dudley, and sailed for Boston. His daughter, Eunice, seven years old when captured, he was unable to procure, and she remained with the Indians. Arriving at womanhood she married an Indian, and by him had a family of children. From her descended Rev. Eleazer Williams, late missionary to the Indians at Green Bay, Wisconsin, the pretended Dauphin of France. A few years after the war she visited Deerfield with her husband and a number of other Indians. She was dressed in Indian costume, and all inducements offered her to remain were unavailing. A brother, who was taken to Canada with her, became the first pastor in Longmeadow. She subsequently twice visited him, but she could not be prevailed upon to remain, on the ground that it would endanger her soul, having become a convert to Romanism.

Mr. Williams, after his release from captivity, resumed his ministerial labors at Deerfield. His wife, who was killed on the way to Canada, was brought back to Deerfield, and her remains now lie interred by the side of her husband.

DEERFIELD RIVER BRIDGE.

Lossing states that one of the motives which led to the attack on Deerfield, was to recover a bell that had been sent from France to a Catholic Church in St. Regis, on the St. Lawrence, and which was captured by an English vessel while on the way, and sent to Salem and thence to Mr. Williams' church at Deerfield. The bell was carried off by the Indians and buried near where the village of Burlington is now situated, receiving the benedictions of the Catholic priest, who accompanied the expedition. In the spring it was taken to St. Regis and is still in use at the Catholic Cathedral at that place.

The "Old Indian House," known to former visitors and residents of Deerfield, showing the marks of the tomahawks upon the door, and perforations made by the balls inside, was the one in which Mrs. Sheldon was killed, and where the captives were temporarily confined. It was taken down a few years ago, but the door has been preserved, and is now in the possession of the Boston Museum.

Quite a number of distinguished men have been natives of Deerfield; among whom may be mentioned Gen. Epaphras Hoyt, author of Antiquarian Researches, the late President Edward Hitchcock, of Amherst College, and Maj. Gen Rufus Saxton.

The Deerfield Academy, still in existence, was formerly one of the most noted educational institutions in the country.

The meadows along the banks of Deerfield river are broad and fertile. Within a few years past Deerfield has had quite a number of summer visitors, where there is a good hotel.

Pocumtuc Rock, on the range of mountains east of the depot, is frequently visited. From it there is a fine view of the valley.

DEERFIELD BRIDGE.

Leaving Deerfield you soon come to the bridge over the Deerfield River. It is 750 feet in length and from 48 to 90 feet above the water. It was burnt on the morning of July 17, 1864, and before night half a dozen saw mills were employed sawing out lumber to be used in rebuilding it. Within three weeks the lumber was all on the ground and within six weeks trains were able to cross the bridge.

GREENFIELD—THE ROUTE TO HOOSIC TUNNEL.

After crossing the Deerfield River bridge the track of the Vermont and Massachusetts Railroad, will be seen on the right. At this place it curves to the east and follows the valley of the Deerfield River to the Connecticut, and then to Fitchburg, where it connects with the road to Boston. On approaching Greenfield, in the valley of Green River, west and below the railroad, the tourist will notice the various buildings of the Green River works, the first table cutlery manufactory established in this country, J. Russell & Co., proprietors. Mr. John Russell, the senior partner, commenced life as a blacksmith, but as all of our table cutlery was then made in England he conceived the plan of opening a shop in this country. In 1834, having sent to England for workmen who had been employed in the great establishments at Sheffield, he began operations, and from a small beginning he has built up a large and flourishing business, now giving employment to over 400 hands. There is no better cutlery made, and it is found on the tables of almost every dwelling, from the magnificent dining rooms of Fifth Avenue, to the rude hovel of the hardy pioneer on the Pacific slope.

Greenfield has a population of about 3,600 and is one of the many thriving towns in the valley. The streets are wide, and lined on either side by old and magnificent elms. It has long been a favorite stopping place for summer visitors, and in and about the town are some charming views of natural scenery. Its drives are numerous and pleasant, adding greatly to the interest of the town. Among the drives may be mentioned that to Leyden Glen, the Gorge Road, up Green River, to Still Water, in Deerfield, coming back by the Old Indian House, to Turner's Falls, to Shelburne Falls, and Hoosic Tunnel. On Rocky Mountain, about a mile east of the town are two other interesting localities—the Poet's Seat, and Bear's Den, from the former there are views of the Connecticut and the valley in the east, the locality of Turner's Falls, the town of Montague, and the valley lying to the west. From Bear's Den a view is had of Deerfield and the meadows around that town.

Greenfield is the shire town of Franklin County, and is the central point of a large agricultural community. Besides the Green River Works there are several manufacturing establishments,—the Greenfield Tool Company, just north of the town, and west of the railroad, where are manufactured carpenters' tools; the Greenfield Manufacturing Company, manufacturers of woolen goods, and several other smaller establishments.

Visitors to the Hoosic Tunnel, leave the cars at Greenfield and proceed by stage through the village of Shelburne Falls, and thence along the Deerfield River to the western end of the tunnel.

The principal hotel in Greenfield* is the Mansion House, where visitors will find good accommodations.

TURNER'S FALLS.

Some three or four miles east of Greenfield are Turner's Falls in the Connecticut. Here the river makes a descent of 70 feet in two and one half miles, and a company have purchased 700 acres of land in the vicinity with a view of building a manufacturing village. A dam 1,300 feet in length is to be built across the river, and several canals are to be constructed.

During King Philip's war a force, headed by Capt. Turner, marched to this place and attacked the Indians, who had gathered at the falls for the purpose of fishing. Three hundred were killed and drowned, but unfortunately Capt. Turner was himself shot in the latter part of the day.

The bird tracks of the Connecticut Valley which are of so much interest to scientific men were first found here.

BERNARDSTON.

Bernardston, seven miles from Greenfield, is a small village of several hundred inhabitants. Here is located Powers' Institute, an educational institution of some note. Soon after leaving the station, going north, the church spire in Gill can be seen several miles eastward. The railroad curves to the east, coming out upon the plateau above the Connecticut, where the first view of the river is had since leaving Northampton.

NORTHFIELD.

Before reaching South Vernon, the village of Northfield will be seen on the opposite side of the Connecticut. A branch of the Vermont and Massachusetts Railroad passes through the town, and the bridge over the Connecticut will be noticed northwest of the village. In the early part of September, 1675, the town was attacked by Indians, nine or ten persons killed, and the other settlers driven to the fort. Shortly after the pursuit and attack on the Indians south of Sugar Loaf Mountain, Capt. Beers was dispatched from Hadley—the headquarters of the English forces—to take provisions to the settlers at Northfield. Within two miles of the fort they were surprised, and Capt. Beers mortally wounded. The men saved themselves the best way they could, but out of a force of 37 men only 16 returned to Hadley.

SOUTH VERNON—THE STATE LINE.

At this place the traveler leaves Massachusetts and enters Vermont. The boundary line between the two States passes through the southern end of the passenger station house. Here the Vermont and Massachusetts Railroad, which intersects the eastern and western line at Grout's Corner, forms a junction with the other roads and extends to Brattleboro. The Ashuelot Railroad, extending to Keene, N. H., 23 miles distant, also comes into this place, crossing the Connecticut on a bridge just north of the station.

Leaving South Vernon the tourist is soon riding along upon the banks of the Connecticut, charmed with the beautiful scenery before him,—the extended view up the valley, with the mountain range opposite Brattleboro in the distance, and the beautiful island covered with forest trees, in the Connecticut, in the foreground.

MONADNOCK MOUNTAIN.

Just as the train approaches Vernon station, the summit of Monadnock, thirty miles eastward, in Jaffrey, N. H., can be seen through the valley of the Ashuelot. It is 3,450 feet above the sea, and is the first land seen by sailors entering Boston harbor from European ports. In clear weather Bunker Hill Monument can be seen with the aid of the glass. From the summit forty lakes and a large number of villages are in full view, and the scenery around the mountain is grand and beautiful. A large hotel has been erected half way to the summit, and is under the management of George D. Rice. To reach it from the Connecticut Valley, the tourist should leave the train at South Vernon, proceed to Keene by the Ashuelot Railroad, and thence to Troy on the Cheshire Railroad, from which place a stage runs to the hotel, five miles distant. Boston people can leave the city by the early morning train, visit the mountain and return home the same day.

VERNON—THE CAPTURE OF MRS. HOWE BY INDIANS.

In the early settlement of Vernon, Forts Bridgman and Sartwell, built to protect the inhabitants from Indians, were the scenes of bloody massacres. The former was attacked and destroyed June 24, 1746, and on July 27, 1755, the latter was entered and its occupants carried into captivity. These forts stood west of the railroad, nearly a mile north of the depot. Among those captured were Mrs. Jemima Howe and her seven children. Her husband, Caleb Howe, had been previously killed in the field while returning from work. Mrs. Howe's youngest child was torn from her breast, and it perished with hunger. Herself and other children, after a long march, reached Canada. She spent a number of years there, but by her own heroism she procured her release, and with five children returned to Vernon. Her oldest daughter was taken to France, and marrying a Frenchman, never returned to America. Mrs. Howe had been twice married, and both husbands had been killed by Indians. After her return she married a third time, Amos Tute. A son by this husband, Jonathan Tute, died from the effects of inoculation, and was buried in the cemetery in Vernon. Rev. Bunker Gay of Hinsdale, N. H., more noted for eccentricity than education, wrote an epitaph, which is still legible upon the tombstone, that has caused many a stranger to pause before Jonathan's grave and contemplate his unfortunate end. A few of the more remarkable lines are copied below:

"Here lies cut down, like unripe fruit,
A son of Mr. Amos Tute.
* * * * *

To death he fell a helpless prey,
On April V and Twentieth Day,
In Seventeen Hundred Seventy-Seven,
Quitting this world, we hope, for Heaven.

Behold the amazing alteration,
Effected by inoculation;
The means empowered his life to save,
Hurried him headlong to the grave."

FORT DUMMER—THE FIRST SETTLEMENT IN VERMONT.

Leaving Vernon you soon come to Fort Dummer, a mile south of the village of Brattleboro, where the first settlement in Vermont was made, and here was born the first white child in the State, John Sargent, whose descendants still reside in Brattleboro. Fort Dummer was built in 1724 by the Colonial authorities of Massachusetts, and named in honor of Sir William Dummer, then Lieut. Governor. The site of the fort was near the river, where a dwelling house now stands directly east of the large farm house which can be seen near the wooded hills west of the railroad. When the fort was built it was supposed to be within the limits of Massachusetts, and at that time was the northern outpost of civilization.

BRATTLEBORO.

Distance from New York, 194 miles; Montreal, 250; White Mountains, 125; Lake Memphremagog, 168; Quebec, 330.

Of the many beautiful towns on the banks of the Connecticut, none present more attractions to the summer tourist than Brattleboro. Situated on an uneven surface, and surrounded by hills and mountains, the scenery is grand and picturesque, and it is said, bears a striking resemblance to that of Switzerland. The view from Cemetery Hill, a high point just south of the town, is particularly fine. From it is seen the Connecticut on the right, sweeping around the base of Wantastiquet Mountain in a graceful curve, while the mountain itself, rises abruptly from the east bank of the river to the hight of nearly 1,100 feet. To the north and west lies the village, nestling among the shade trees, while further in the distance are numberless hill-tops, outlined on the deep blue sky beyond. Main Street extends north and south, parallel with the river, and is one hundred feet above it. Further west are terraces upon which are situated many of the private dwellings. The highest point in the village is nearly three hundred feet above the river. A mile north of the village is West River which rises among the Green Mountains, and flows into the Connecticut. In the southern part of the village is Whetstone Brook

VIEW IN BRATTLEBORO LOOKING NORTH FROM CEMETERY HILL.

which furnishes power for the various manufactories along its banks. Here in Brattleboro, in 1845, was established by Dr. Robert Wesselhœft, a distinguished German, the third Water-Cure in this country, and which for a long time received extensive patronage, some of the most eminent men in the country coming here for treatment. Late years Brattleboro has been a favorite resort for summer visitors and frequently there are from 600 to 800 strangers in the town. The drives in and around the village are remarkable, winding along the banks of impetuous little streamlets, through beautiful groves, and over high hills. A new drive can be taken every day for nearly a month, without going outside of a radius of four miles, and all of them have peculiar features of interest.

The Vermont Asylum for the Insane is located in the north part of the town, and is said to be one of the best conducted institutions of the kind in the country. It was founded in 1834 by Mrs. Anna Marsh of Hinsdale, N. H., who died leaving by will, $10,000 for that purpose. The Asylum was incorporated and is managed by a board of trustees in accordance with the provisions of the will. The State of Vermont has contributed at various times $23,000 to assist in establishing the institution, and rebuilding the main edifice which was destroyed by fire in 1862. The Asylum owns 600 acres of land in one body, adjoining the grounds on which the buildings are located, and about as many more of woodland. The labor on the farm is mostly done, voluntarily, by the patients, who are greatly benefitted by it. The property of the Asylum is now valued at $150,000, all but $33,000 of which has been accumulated by the good management of the institution. Dr. Wm. H. Rockwell, the present Superintendent, has served in that position since the Asylum was first opened, coming here from the Insane Retreat at Hartford, Connecticut, where he was assistant physician.

The village is the residence of Ex-Gov. Frederick Holbrook, who was Governor of Vermont during the first two years of the Rebellion, and to whom much is due for the quick response Vermont made to the call for troops; Gen. J. W. Phelps, a graduate of West Point, a participator in the Florida, Mexican and Utah wars and also in the Great Rebellion, serving with Gen. Butler in the Department of the Gulf; and Charles C. Frost, the Scientific Shoemaker, who, besides conducting his usual business, has acquired several languages and become one of the most noted botanists in the country. Brattleboro is also the home of Larkin G. Mead, Jr., the Vermont Sculptor, who, for several years, has resided in Italy. Mr. Mead, when a lad, modeled a statue in snow in the last night of the year, at the head of Main street, and when the villagers went forth to their labor New Year's morning, they beheld the "Recording Angel," with tablet in hand, apparently in the act of recording the events of the opening year. This first attempt at sculpture gained him notoriety at once, and his first patron was the late Nicholas Longworth, the Cincinnati millionaire. Subsequently the State gave him a commission to execute in marble a full length statue of Ethan Allen, which has been placed in the vestibule of the State House at Montpelier. It was eminently fitting, as well as quite poetical, that Vermont should give a commission to a gifted son to perpetuate the outward semblance of her greatest hero, in her greatest product—marble.

Many distinguished people have made Brattleboro a summer resort. Daniel Webster, when United States Senator, from Massachusetts, used frequently to visit the place, and it is said that the policy to be pursued in Congress, which led to his great debate with Hayne, was originated here, while stopping with the late Hon. Jonathan Hunt, then member of Congress.

The population of Brattleboro is not far from 4,000.

THE BRATTLEBORO HOUSE.

The hotels at Brattleboro furnish good accommodations for the tourist. The Brattleboro House on Main Street has long been known as one of the best kept houses in Vermont, and its proprietor, Chas. G. Lawrence, has no superior as a caterer to public taste.

The Wesselhœft House, by P. B. Francis & Co., is one of the oldest and best summer houses in the Connecticut Valley,

BRATTLEBORO HOUSE.

and none have had so many patrons. It was formerly the Wesselhœft Water-cure, but of late years it has been opened for the accommodation of summer guests.

DISCOVERY OF AN ELEPHANT'S TUSK.

In 1865 a workman, while digging muck on a farm in Brattleboro, found, about five feet below the surface, a part of the tusk of an elephant, forty-four inches in length, eighteen in circumference at the largest, and eleven at the smallest end. It was in a fair state of preservation, and was taken to Montpelier and placed in the historical rooms at the State House. It belonged to a species of elephant long since extinct, that inhabited the northern part of North America, having wandered across the Siberian plains to the Arctic Ocean and Behrings Strait, and beyond, to this country, south, to about the parallel of 40 degrees. Their bones show them to have been about twice the weight and one-third taller than the modern species. The tusk teeth and some bones of one of these elephants were found in a muck bed at the summit of the Green Mountains, in Mount Holly, in 1848, by workmen who were building the railroad from Bellows Falls to Rutland.

WANTASTIQUET AND MINE MOUNTAINS.

Opposite Brattleboro, on the east side of the Connecticut, are Wantastiquet and Mine Mountains, the former rising from the river to the hight of 1,061 feet. The latter extends eastward from Wantastiquet, and is only separated from it by a narrow gorge. During the latter part of the last century, a party sunk a shaft many feet into the solid rock on Mine Mountain, in search of silver, which they had incredulously been led to believe existed there, but after the expenditure of large sum of money the enterprise was abandoned.

WEST RIVER.—GEN. STARK.

Leaving Brattleboro, the railroad continues along the bank of the Connecticut, and for some distance the mountain scenery on the opposite side is exceedingly beautiful. About a mile north of the village you cross West River on a bridge at its mouth.

Its Indian name is Wantastiquet, signifying straight, or arrowy. It rises among the Green Mountains, and is a very rapid stream.

A little way north of West River, near the dwelling seen on the opposite side, Gen. Stark crossed the Connecticut with an Aid, on his way from Manchester, to fight the battle of Bennington. The gallant General was taken across the river by the ferryman, in a little old canoe, and soon afterwards achieved a great victory over the invaders of our country.

DUMMERSTON, PUTNEY, AND EAST PUTNEY.

Continuing north, the small stations of Dummerston, Putney, and East Putney are passed. Just north of Putney, the village will be seen west of the railroad. Opposite East Putney is the village of Westmoreland, in New Hampshire, one of the churches standing upon the hill north-west of the village. Above the church can be seen the track of the Cheshire railroad, curving eastward.

WESTMINSTER—THE FIRST BLOOD OF THE REVOLUTION.

About twenty miles from Brattleboro and four from Bellows Falls, is Westminster. This is a place of great historic interest, as here begun the opening scenes of the American Revolution. A bitter quarrel had sprung up between the royal authorities in New York and the people who had purchased land in Vermont under the New Hampshire grants—the latter not wishing to acknowledge the illegitimacy of the authority under which they held their titles. It was finally determined that the New York royal court should not hold its approaching session at Westminster, and after trying to dissuade the judge from holding the court, who gave some equivocal promises, the people, unarmed, seized the court house on the afternoon of the day that the court was to be held. The royal authorities, not liking to be put down by what they considered a mob, attempted to enforce their rights by arms. At eleven o'clock at night, while the people of Westminster had possession of the court house, the royal authorities fired into it, mortally wounding William French and Daniel Houghton. This occurred March 13th, 1775. French was only 22 years of age, and was a resident of Brattleboro. Previous to the attack on the court house, he went from Brattleboro to Dummerston, where he joined the Dummerston Rangers. He was buried in Westminster, and the grave is still seen in the village cemetery. The original grave stone is in existence, and is kept in the old church. The court house stood at the top of the hill in the highway, about a mile south of the depot. The principal men of the royalist party were seized and carried under escort of Col. Benjamin Bellows, the founder of Walpole, to Northampton, Mass., and lodged in jail. The New York authorities however, afterwards procured their release.

It is claimed that the Westminster massacre so enraged Gen. Gage, at Boston, the British commander, showing as he thought the determined spirit of the people to resist British authority, that he was induced to march to Lexington and inflict the blow which opened the Revolution. If so, Westminster is entitled to the honor of being the birth place of American liberty.

The oldest church now in Vermont is still standing in Westminster, and can be seen from the cars—the only one in the village having a spire. It was erected in 1770. It is now used as a shop and town hall.

The legislature of Vermont held some of its first sessions in the town, and the first printing office in the State was established here in 1778, and the first paper, the Vermont Gazette, in 1781.

The village lies about a mile south of the depot, upon broad table land, and is very pleasantly situated.

WALPOLE—THE HOME OF THE BELLOWS FAMILY.

Opposite Westminster, lying above the river, is the pleasant village of Walpole, one of the prettiest and neatest in the valley of the Connecticut. The streets are wide, and the dwellings large and elegant. There is little business in the town, and it is chiefly noted as the home of the Bellows family, descendants of Col. Benjamin Bellows, the founder of the town, who came here from Lunenburg, Mass., more than a hundred years ago. The members of the famlly who have been abroad and secured wealth, have usually come back to the old home to spend the remainder of their days. Among those who have summer residences here is Rev. Dr. Henry W. Bellows, of New York, a great grandson of the founder of the town. His cottage can be seen just south of the village, near a large brick dwelling.

The descendants who wished to honor their distinguished ancestor, gathered from all parts of the country in 1854 and erected a marble monument in the village cemetery to his memory. An address was delivered by Rev. Dr. Bellows, giving an account of the early settlement of the place.

Col. Bellows received a grant of the township of Gov. Wentworth, and came to Walpole in 1752, where he built a fort upon an impregnable point, overlooking the Connecticut, a mile north of the village, near the house now owned by Thomas Bellows. He organized a town government, and seems to have been moderator, town clerk, and selectman—all in one. He was a marked man, and rendered great service in enlisting and equipping men for the Revolution.

Before Col. Bellows built his mill, he was obliged to carry his corn to Northampton, Mass., to have it ground, going down in boats in the Spring, and returning with meal and other stores.

Within the last few years Walpole has become quite a place of resort during the summer, and there is a large boarding house on the hill, and a hotel in the village, where good accommodations are provided.

Two miles north of the village is a mineral spring, where bathing houses have been built. It has been named Abenaquis, after the Indian tribe who inhabited this region.

Travelers who have been abroad state that the scenery around Walpole bears a striking resemblance to that around Berne, in Switzerland. From Derry Hill can be seen Saddle-back, Monadnock, Ascutney, and the whole Green Mountain range. Blanchard and Ravine Falls, near the village, have many admirers among those stopping in the town.

AN INDIAN ATTACK—THE HEROISM OF JOHN KILBURN.

John Kilburn was another of the early settlers of Walpole. When Col. Bellows came to the town he found Kilburn in a garrisoned house, near Cold River, about two miles north of Walpole. In the summer of 1755 two men were shot by Indians. "Shortly before this," says Dr. Bellows in his address, "an Indian by the name of Philip had visited Kilburn's house in a friendly way, pretending to be in want of provisions. He was supplied with flints and flour and dismissed. It was ascertained that this same Indian had visited all the settlements on the river, doubtless to procure information of the state of their defenses. Word came from Governor Shirly that 500 Indians were collecting in Canada whose aim was the butchery and extinction of the whole white population on the river.

Col. Benj. Bellows had at this time about 30 men at his fort, about half a mile south of Kilburn's, but too distant to afford him any aid. About noon on the 17th day of August, 1755, Kilburn and his son John, in his eighteenth year, a man by the name of Peak and his son, were returning home to dinner from the field, when one of them discovered the red legs of the Indians among the alders, 'as thick as grasshoppers.' They instantly made for the house, fastened the doors and prepared for an obstinate defense. Kilburn's wife Ruth, and his daughter Hetty, were already in the house. In about fifteen minutes, the savages were seen crawling up the bank east of the house, and as they crossed a foot path, one by one, 197 were counted;

about the same number it afterward proved had remained in ambush, near the mouth of Cold River, but joined the attacking party soon.

The savages appeared to have learned that Col. Bellows and his men were at work at his mill, about a mile east, on what is now called the Blanchard Brook, near where it was crossed by the Drewsville road, and they intended to waylay and murder them before attacking Kilburn's house. Col. Bellows and his men were now returning home, each with a bag of meal on his back, when the dogs began to growl and betray the neighborhood of an enemy. The Colonel, knowing the language of the dogs and the wiles of the Indians, instantly adopted his policy. He directed his men, throwing off the meal, to crawl carefully to the rise of the land, and on reaching the top of the bank to spring together to their feet, give one whoop and instantly drop into the sweet fern. The movement had the desired effect to draw the Indians from their ambush. At the sound of the whoop, fancying themselves discovered, the whole body of the savages rose from the bushes in a semi-circle round the path Col. Bellows was to have followed. His men, fired upon the Indians, and they were so disconcerted that they darted into the bushes and disappeared. The Colonel, sensible of his unequal force, hurried his men off by the shortest cut to the fort, and prepared for its defense.

The Indians then determined to take vengeance upon a weaker party, and soon appeared on the eminence east of Kilburn's house. Here the same treacherous Philip, who had visited him and partaken of his hospitality so short a time before, came forward under the shelter of a tree, and summoned the little garrison to surrender. 'Old John, Young John,' was his cry, 'I know ye, come out here. We give you good quarter.' 'Quarter!' vociferated old Kilburn, in a voice of thunder, 'You black rascals, begone, or we'll quarter you.' It was a brave reply for four men to make to four hundred!

Philip returned, and after a short consultation, the war-whoop rang out, as if, to use the language of an ear-witness, "all the devils in hell had been let loose." Kilburn was lucky and prudent enough to get the first fire, before the smoke of the battle perplexed his aim, and was confident he saw Philip fall. The fire from the little garrison was returned by a shower of balls from the savages, who rushed forward to the attack. The roof next to the eminence from which the attack was made, was a perfect "riddle-sieve." Some of the Indians fell at once to butchering the cattle; others to a wanton destruction of the grain, while the larger part kept up an incessant fire at the house. Meanwhile Kilburn and his men—aye, his women—were all busily at work. Their powder they poured into their hats for greater convenience; the women loaded the guns, of which they had several spare ones—all of them being kept hot by incessant use. As their stock of lead grew short, they suspended blankets over their heads to catch the balls of the enemy, which penetrated one side of the roof and fell short of the other. These were immediately run by these Spartan women into bullets, and before they had time to cool, were sent back to the enemy from whom they came. Several attempts were made to force the door, but the unerring aim of the marksmen within sent such certain death to their assaliants, that they soon desisted from their efforts. Most of the time the Indians kept behind logs and stumps, and avoided as they best could, the fire of the little Gibraltar. The whole afternoon, even till sundown, the battle continued, until, as the sun set, the savages unable to conquer so small a fortress, discouraged and baffled, forsook the ground, and as was supposed, returned to Canada, abandoning the expedition on which they had set out. It is not unreasonable to suppose that their fatal experience here, through the matchless defense of those Walpole heroes and heroines, was instrumental in saving hundreds of the dwellers on the frontier from the horrors of an Indian massacre.

Seldom did it fall to the lot of the early settlers to win a more brilliant crown than John Kilburn earned in this glorious exploit. Peek got the only wound of his party, receiving a ball in the hips, from exposure at a port-hole, which unhappily, for lack of surgical care, caused his death on the fifth day. The Indians never again appeared in Walpole, although the war did not terminate until eight years afterward. John Kilburn lived to see his fourth generation on the stage and enjoying the benefits of a high civilization on the spot he had rescued from the savages. A plain stone in Walpole burying ground commemorates his departure, and speaks his eulogy in a brief, expressive phrase.

His son John last visited the scenes of his youthful exploits in 1814, and died at Shrewsbury, Vt., in 1822.

What amount of destruction Kilburn made among the savages it was impossible to tell, as they carefully carried off and concealed their dead."

MOUNT KILBURN—THE GOVERNOR'S CALF PASTURE.

Opposite Bellows Falls village, in New Hampshire, is Mount Kilburn, formerly known as Fall Mountain. It is little over 800 feet high, and from the summit a fine view of the village and the distant mountain peaks, is had. The early settlers gave it the name of Fall Mountain from the fact that at its base are the Great Falls in the Connecticut. In 1856 President Hitchcock and the Students of Amherst and Middlebury Colleges met at Bellows Falls and christened it Mount Kilburn, in honor of the hero who fought the Indians so gallantly from his little fort, just below the south end of the mountain. This mountain is situated in Walpole, and was included in the grant to Col. Benj. Bellows, the founder of the town. Quite an amusing anecdote is related concerning it, which is given below:

" Gov. Wentworth, in his grants of land reserved 500 acres in each township, and in making his selection in Walpole, consulted Colonel Bellows, as to what was the most favorable portion to lay claim to,—expressing his own decided preference for five hundred acres in the immediate neighborhood of the Great Falls as the probable site of the future settlement. The Colonel very honestly told him that the land thereabout would make a very good calf pasture, but nothing better. The Governor, perhaps imagining that the Colonel wished to appropriate these lands to himself, and so discouraged his own selection of them, at once resolved to lay his claim there, and his 500 acres on the rocky sides of Fall Mountain were for some time jocosely called 'the Governor's calf pasture.'"

Almost worthless when selected, portions of the 500 acres have become exceedingly valuable, owing to the superior pine timber found there.

BELLOWS FALLS.

Distance from New York, 220 miles; Montreal, 225; White Mountains, 101; Lake Memphremagog, 171; Quebec, 311.

In approaching Bellows Falls the attention of the tourist will be called to the river and the many objects of interest in the vicinity. For a considerable distance below the falls, the river is very rapid, and presents a beautiful appearance, and at no place along its whole course is there so much wild grandeur. Above the village the river curves to the eastward and passes close to the base of Mount Kilburn, which rises precipitously to the hight of 828 feet. It then curves slightly towards the west and rushes wildly over the rocky bed, down through a narrow gorge, and out into a broader channel below. A large rock divides the stream into two channels, each about 90 feet wide. In low water, the river flows into the western channel and is contracted to about 16 feet in width. The river in passing over the several rapids makes a descent of 42 feet. The toll and railroad bridges cross the river over the falls, and from the former a good view of them is had. Below the bridge numberless pot-holes will be observed of various dimensions, worn in the solid rock. West of the station rises a high hill, and beyond it is a valley, only a few feet above the river bank. It is supposed by geologists that this was once the bed of the Connecticut, and the many terraces in the vicinity strengthen this opinion. It is also claimed that the region above the falls was once a vast lake, and that its outlet flowed eastward into the Merrimac, from a point further north.

Bellows Falls received its name from Col. Bellows, the founder of Walpole, and it was formerly a great fishing place with the Indians, who came here to catch shad and salmon. The latter were so numerous, even after the whites settled in this region that workmen in making yearly contracts for their labor stipulated that they should not be obliged to eat salmon oftener than twice a week—a condition, which at the present time they would hardly be so particular to require.

The first bridge across the Connecticut was built at this place in 1785, and was 365 feet in length. For eleven years it was the only bridge across this river.

A canal, nearly half a mile in length, was constructed many years ago around the falls on the western side, and it was thought that a large manufacturing village would at some future day be built here. Its growth, however, has been quite slow, although there are now a number of firms extensively engaged in manufacturing.

Summer tourists have, of late years, spent considerable time here. The drives in the vicinity are extensive and very pleasant. A favorite one with old residents is to Warner's Pond, in Alstead, N. H., where picnics are held.

THE ISLAND HOUSE.

This hotel, kept by Mr. Charles Towns, is one of the best in the State, and has long been a favorite with tourists. It is pleasantly situated on the eminence east of the station and overlooks the river and valley. The rooms are large and con-

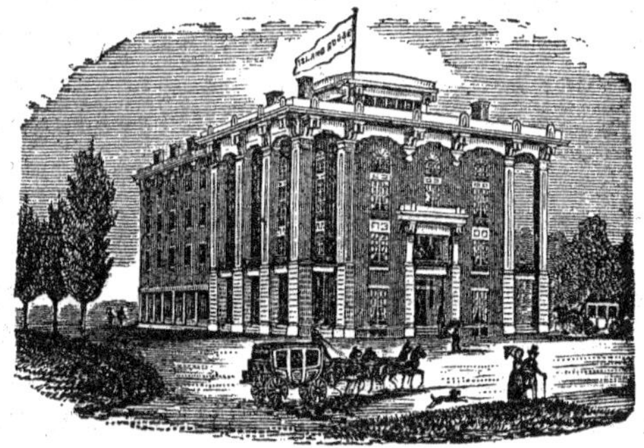

THE ISLAND HOUSE.

veniently arranged. A livery stable is kept in connection with the hotel.

REFRESHMENT ROOMS.

Tourists who do not remain over can get warm meals at the extensive refreshment rooms in the station, very neatly kept by Mr. F. A. George. The trains going north stop here long enough to give passengers time for dinner.

The Rutland and Burlington, and the Cheshire Railroads intersect the Valley line at this place.

A MRS. PARTINGTON ON THE CARS.

One of those ridiculous incidents, which are sufficient to produce a smile at a funeral, occurred on the Cheshire Railroad, early in the winter of 1865. A lady of venerable aspect appeared on the platform at the depot in Bellows Falls, with the inevitable band box and bundle. She paced up and down the platform in a very happy frame of mind, beguiling herself in humming a cradle song, and to all appearance was at peace with herself and the "rest of mankind." In due season Conductor H. H. Stone appeared and shouted "all aboard." The old lady not heeding the admonition, he inquired her proposed destination. "Going to Fitchburg, sir," was her reply. "Well, madam, you had better get into those cars if you want to go to Fitchburg." "What! doesn't this whole consarn go?" alluding to the depot. "Not to-day, madam; you had better get into that car." "Wall, now, Mister, is that so? Jist carry this bundle—I never rid a rod on the railroad in my life." The old lady was escorted on board and the train departed. Passing the summit and descending into the Ashuelot Valley, near Keene, the passenger train overtook the freight, out of steam and "stalled" in the deep snow. It moved up to the freight train and was about to give it aid, when down came an engine under full headway. A severe snow storm was raging, and so completely obscured the track that the signal man who had been sent back was not seen. It thundered on at a fearful rate down the grade, and in an instant had run its whole length completely inside of the rear passenger car. Several persons were instantly killed, and others were groaning horribly from injury and fright. The passengers leaped out of doors and windows, and for a while great consternation prevailed. The conductor as he saw nothing of the old lady, thought it more than probable that she had been killed. He entered the car in search of her, and to his great astonishment found her sitting quietly alone. Notwithstanding she had made a complete somersault over the seat in front, and her bundle had gone unceremoniously down the aisle, she maintained a wonderfully placid expression upon her countenance, exhibiting neither fear nor astonishment. "Are you hurt?" inquired the conductor. "Hurt, why?" said the old lady. "We have just been run into by an engine, two or three passengers have been killed and several others severely injured," replied the conductor. "La me; I didn't know but that was *the way you always stopped*."

GOING NORTH.

Leaving Bellows Falls, you cross the Connecticut River into New Hampshire, and continue on the east side of the river until you reach the bridge at Windsor, 26 miles distant.

CHARLESTOWN.

Passing the small station at South Charlestown, you come to Charlestown, eight miles from Bellows Falls. The village, which will be seen east of the railroad, is one of the oldest in western New Hampshire. It was formerly known as Number Four, and in 1747 a garrison of 30 men, commanded by Capt. Phineas Stevens, was attacked by 400 French and Indians, who, after making three days siege were obliged to abandon the project and return to Canada. When commanded to surrender by the French General, who boasted of his superior numbers and of the probable massacre that would take place when the fort was captured, Capt. Stevens very coolly replied: "I can assure you my men are not afraid to die." Sir Charles Knowles, a British naval officer at Boston, when he learned of Capt. Stevens bravery presented him an elegant sword, and from this circnmstance, when the township was incorporated it was named Charlestown. The village is very pleasant, and for several years quite a number of city people have spent the summer here.

Passengers for Springfield, Vermont, which is six miles west, leave the railroad at this place. Springfield is a large manufacturing town, and is one of the most picturesque places in Vermont. The scenery along Black River, in and around the town, is remarkable for its beauty and wildness.

NORTH CHARLESTOWN.

At this station, five miles from Charlestown, a fine view of Ascutney Mountain is had, west of the Connecticut. The scenery, on the west, in the valley is exceedingly picturesque.

CLAREMONT.

Twelve miles from Windsor, and fourteen from Bellows Falls is Claremont Station. The village is two miles east of the railroad. It contains some four or five thousand inhabitants, and there is a large manufacturing interest in the place.

SUGAR RIVER BRIDGE.

Soon after leaving Claremont Station, you come to the bridge over Sugar River. This stream furnishes water power for the manufactories at Claremont. The bridge is 600 feet long and 105 above the river. On the west bank of the Connecticut, from this place, will be seen Ascutneyville, a small village in Wethersfield.

ASCUTNEY MOUNTAIN.

This mountain which is seen on the west side of the Connecticut is 3,320 feet high and is situated in Windsor and Wethersfield. It is an isolated peak, and its bold and rocky summit forms a prominent feature in the landscape for many miles around. Three deep valleys course their way down the western side of the mountain, and from this fact it is stated that the Indians called it Ascutney, signifying, "Three Brothers." The view from the summit is the most grand and extensive of any in Eastern Vermont. Below is the beautiful Connecticut, winding itself among the hills and forests, while hundreds of farm houses and villages are scattered seemingly over a vast plain. A road has been constructed from Windsor to the summit, a distance of five miles, and horses and guides can be obtained of Mr. Cushing of the Windsor House at Windsor. There is a rude house on the mountain, to protect the tourist in case of storm.

WINDSOR.

Distance from New York, 246 miles; Montreal, 199; White Mountains, 75; Lake Memphremagog, 145; Quebec, 285.

From Sugar River Bridge to Windsor the scenery is grand and beautiful. Below, on the west, is the Connecticut, while still beyond rises the lofty summit of Ascutney, the grim sentinel of the valley. Crossing the bridge over the Connecticut, which was carried away by ice in the spring of 1866, you again enter Vermont. Here nestling among the shade trees upon the hillside is the ancient and beautiful town of Windsor. West of the depot, fronting on Main Street, which extends north and south, is seen the United States Court House, built several years ago by the Government at great expense. It is also occupied as a Post Office. The Vermont State Prison is located at this place, on a street west of Main. The average number of convicts is about 80, and they are employed in manufacturing scythe snaths. Is not Vermont setting a bad example by teaching her "crooked sticks," who are sent to prison to be made straight, to make straight sticks crooked?

The constitution of Vermont was formed and adopted in this town, and the building in which the convention was held is still standing on Main Street, occupied as a shop.

Hon. Wm. M. Evarts and E. W. Stoughton, distinguished members of the New York bar, have summer residences here. Mr. Evarts owns a large farm north of the village, the extensive buildings on which are seen just after leaving the depot, west of the railroad.

Formerly there was considerable manufacturing in the town, and during the rebellion Lamson & Goodnow were employed to make guns for the Government. This firm is now engaged on other work.

Cornish hills in New Hampshire, opposite Windsor, rise to considerable hight, and the view from them is very extensive.

HARTLAND.

Four miles north of Windsor is Hartland. Before reaching the depot you cross Lull's Brook, which is seen coursing its way down a narrow valley, and from the cars can be seen a beautiful waterfall. This stream received its name from Timothy Lull, of Dummerston, the first settler of the town, who, with his wife and children, came up the Connecticut in a canoe, in 1763, and landed at the mouth of the brook. Taking out a bottle and breaking it in presence of his little family, he gave his own name to the little stream, by which it has since been known. The valley in this vicinity is rich in alluvial deposits, but after passing the depot the aspect of the country is soon changed, the soil now being light and sandy.

NORTH HARTLAND.

This station is four miles from Hartland, and six from White River Junction. Passing North Hartland you come to the valley of Otta Quechee River. Here the railroad crosses that stream on a bridge 650 feet long and about 80 feet above the water. As you pass over the bridge you will notice the beautiful waterfall west of the railroad, where the Quechee makes a perpendicular descent of about fifteen feet. This river is of Indian origin, and was formerly called Ottageechee, taking its name from the manner in which the water tumbles and whirls down the rocks at the falls.

WHITE RIVER JUNCTION.

Distance from New York, 260 miles; Montreal, 185; White Mountains, 61; Lake Memphremagog, 105; Quebec, 271.

Before reaching the station the village of Lebanon, in New Hampshire, on the east bank of the Connecticut, will be seen in full view. The most prominent building is Tilden Female Seminary, a flourishing institution, under the management of Hiram Orcutt, Esq., of the Glenwood Seminary, at West Brattleboro.

White River Junction is one of the most important railroad stations on the line. From this point trains from the North, South, East, and West, meet. The Vermont Central Railroad here passes into the valley of White River, and pursues a more westerly course, while the Northern New Hampshire Road, forming a junction with it, crosses the Connecticut and connects at Concord, N. H., with other roads leading into Boston. The Connecticut and Passumpsic Rivers Railroad extends from this place in a northerly course, crossing White River at its mouth, just north of the station, to Newport, on Lake Memphremagog, passing through the rich and fertile valleys of the Connecticut and Passumpsic Rivers. Travelers to the White Mountains take this railroad to Wells River where they connect with the railroad to Littleton and thence by stage to the various points in the mountains.

In going either to the White Mountains, or Mount Mansfield there is no change of cars at White River Junction. If the tourist is going to the White Mountains he should take a seat in the forward car before reaching the Junction, and if to Mount Mansfield, in the rear, or one of the Vermont Central cars.

For a description of the route from White River Junction to White Mountains, Lake Memphremagog and Quebec, see page 171.

THE EATING HOUSE AND HOTEL.

The trains stop at White River Junction for dinner, and in the depot can be procured good meals. A table is spread in the dining hall adjoining the refreshment rooms, and here the wants of the inner man are abundantly supplied. Early fruits and vegetables are furnished in their season, and at few places on the line can so good a dinner be obtained.

The proprietors, the Messrs. Barrons, also keep the Junction House, a few rods west of the depot, where the tourist can remain over night and take the morning train for the White Mountains, if he prefers.

WHITE RIVER.

Tourists for Mount Mansfield and points on the Vermont Central Railroad, on leaving White River Junction enter the valley of White River, keeping close upon the bank of that stream. The Indian name of the river is Kaskadnac, signifying white pebbles, with which the bottom is strown. This is the largest river in Vermont, on the east side of the mountains. At its mouth it is quite broad, but very shallow.

WOODSTOCK.

This is a small station, three miles from White River Junction. Passengers for Woodstock, the shire town of Windsor County, leave the cars at this place. The scenery continues picturesque and beautiful and a short distance west of the station, White River is crossed on a bridge 650 feet in length.

WEST HARTFORD.

Eight miles from White River Junction is the station of West Hartford. The village is small and lies between the railroad and the river. The high, steep hills, and green pastures give a pleasant aspect to the surrounding scenery. The river is more narrow than at its mouth, and assumes a torrent like character.

SHARON.

Before reaching this station White River is crossed on a bridge 400 feet long. The depot is on the south side of the river and the village on the north. The town was settled in 1765 by emigrants from Connecticut.

SOUTH ROYALTON.

Here is a quiet, pretty village, situated in a valley of considerable extent. A large hotel fronts the village green upon the south, a short distance from the railroad. This station is 18 miles from White River Junction, and is the first stopping place for express trains going west. Soon after leaving the station the river is crossed on a bridge 600 feet long, built in 1865.

ROYALTON.

The village is south of the depot, and contains several stores. In 1780 this town was attacked by Indians, who burnt twenty houses, killed two whites, and took twenty-five prisoners. The

Indians were on their way to make an attack on Newbury and capture Lieut. Whitcomb, who had wantonly shot Gen. Gordon, a British officer, between Chambly and St. Johns, and robbed him of his watch and sword. Meeting some whites in the woods, they misled the Indians by stating that there was a large force at Newbury, which had the effect to turn their attention to Royalton.

BETHEL.

North of the village, and directly in rear of it, the hills rise abruptly to the hight of nearly 500 feet. There is a bank and several stores in the town. This township was the first one in the State, granted by the government of Vermont. All express trains stop at this station.

WEST RANDOLPH.

This is one of the largest and most thriving places on the route east of the summit. The buildings, many of which have recently been erected, are tastefully built, and the whole place has the appearance of prosperity. Passengers for Chelsea, the shire town of Orange County, leave the railroad at this station. The old village of Randolph is three miles north of here, where is located the Randolph Grammar School.

BRAINTREE.

Upon reaching Braintree, the general aspect of the country is changed from beautifully rounded hills and luxuriant vegetation to a rocky and mountainous region. The narrow valley and general wildness of the view give beauty and grandeur to the scene.

ROXBURY—THE SUMMIT OF THE GREEN MOUNTAINS.

Passing on through the deep, narrow gorge, you at last come to Roxbury station, at the summit of the Green Mountains. Here in the same swamp, and only a few feet apart, are the head waters of White and Dog Rivers—the former flowing east into the Connecticut, and the latter west into Lake Champlain. Near the summit is a quarry of American verd antique marble. West of the station a bridge 400 feet long is crossed.

NORTHFIELD.

Sixty-four miles from White River Junction, and ten miles from Montpelier is Northfield. Here were located the shops of the Vermont Central Railroad, which are seen south of the depot. They are quite extensive, but since the removal of the principal business formerly done in them, to St. Albans, they are occupied only for making repairs. Gov. Charles Paine, who was the projector of this railroad, and whose father made the first clearing in the town, is buried in the cemetery at this place. There are some eight or ten slate quarries in this town, some of which will be noticed upon the hillside north of the railroad.

MONTPELIER JUNCTION.

From this place a branch railroad extends easterly a mile and a half to the village of Montpelier, the capital of the State.

MONTPELIER.

Distance from New York, 324 miles; Montreal, 122; Quebec, 302; White Mountains, 125; Lake Memphremagog, 169.

Leaving the Junction by the train on the branch road, in a few minutes you are landed at Montpelier, the capital of Vermont. The village, which contains some three or four thousand inhabitants, is situated in the valley of the Winooski, on the north bank of the river. Fine views are had of the village from the hills which overlook it.

The capitol, which is the pride of the town, stands in rear of the square, at the west end of the village, fronting on State Street. The building is of granite, of the Grecian Doric order, and in point of beauty has no superior in the New England States. In the portico stands a life size statue of Vermont's greatest hero, Ethan Allen, carved in Vermont marble by a Vermont Sculptor, Larkin G. Mead, Jr., of Brattleboro. The old hero stands with uplifted hand, and as you look upon his massive brow and stern features, fancy runs back to the command of surrender in the name of the Great Jehovah and Continental Congress. In the State House can be seen the regimental flags, which were triumphantly borne over the battlefields of the Rebellion by stalwart hands, fresh from their Green Mountain homes. The visitor after looking upon these sacred relics should not fail of visiting the geological and historical rooms, where are deposited many rare and curious specimens.

There are two banks of issue, two fire and one life insurance company in the town. Of manufacturing establishments there are several doing an extensive business. James R. Langdon, the wealthiest man in the place is largely engaged in manufacturing flour. He is said to be worth three quarters of a million dollars.

There are six churches, Congregational, Baptist, Independent, Episcopal and Catholic. Within a few years several new edifices have been erected, and no town in the State has more neat and commodious places of worship.

MIDDLESEX.

Leaving Montpelier Junction, the tourist enters the valley of the Winooski, and the views along the banks of the river are grand and beautiful. Before the train reaches the station, the rapids, over which the water flows with great rapidity, will attract attention. Middlesex Narrows, a channel through the solid rock, made by the Winooski river, is an object of interest. For about 80 rods the river has worn a channel in the rock 60 feet wide and 30 feet deep. Passing westerly, Camel's Hump, the second highest peak in the State, is seen towering far above the neighboring summits.

WATERBURY.

At this station, 73 miles from White River Junction and 31 miles from Burlington, the tourist leaves the railroad to visit Mount Mansfield, going ten miles north by stage to Stowe, where there is the largest and most complete summer hotel in the State. This village is situated in quite an extensive valley, surrounded by beautiful hills and lofty mountain peaks, and for a quiet summer resort it has few equals. The Waterbury Hotel, kept by Mr. N. P. Keeler, capable of accommodating 100 guests, was recently built, and has no superior for the accommodation of tourists. It is situated in a pleasant locality, a short distance from the railroad, and the rooms are large and airy. The drives to Bolton Falls, three miles west, where there is a natural bridge over the river, and eight miles to Camel's Hump, as well as the many others, are pleasant and charming. Gov. Paul Dillingham is a resident of this town.

THE ROUTE TO STOWE AND MOUNT MANSFIELD.

The tourist should not fail to visit Mount Mansfield, from which is had the most extensive view in New England, except from the White Mountains. To do so you will leave the railroad at Waterbury and take the stage to Stowe, ten miles northward. The ride is charming indeed, with Mr. Durkee on the box. Take a seat with him, and he will point out to you the many places of interest along the route. Before reaching Stowe, Old Mansfield looms up in the distance, the Nose and Chin rising above the neighboring peaks.

Stowe is a quiet, pretty country village, lying in the valley between Mansfield and Worcester mountains, and no lovelier spot can be found for a summer residence, if one wishes to be in close proximity to extensive mountain scenery. The summit of Mansfield is eight miles from Stowe, but this is the headquarters of mountain visitors, as here is the spacious Mansfield House, and here horses and carriages are provided for those going to the mountain.

THE MANSFIELD HOUSE—THE WALKS AND DRIVES.

This spacious and elegant hotel, in the village of Stowe, was built by a stock company, and opened to visitors in 1865. It is 200 feet long, three stories high, and has a wing in rear 45 by 90 feet. It will accommodate 300 guests. In the rear wing, on the first floor, is the dining room, and on the second there is a dancing hall, each 45 by 60 feet. Mr. W. H. H. Bingham is President of the Hotel Company, and Mr. Leonard Love is principal manager. There are billiard tables and a bowling alley connected with the house. A livery stable, with nearly a hundred horses, is also owned by the company.

The walks and drives in the vicinity are unsurpassed by those of any other summer resort in New England. Sunset Hill, east of the hotel, is a favorite with all. From here is seen the village at your feet, and the valley for many miles north and south. East is the Worcester mountain range. South, Camel's Hump, and West Old Mansfield in all its grandeur.

7

The principal drives are, to Mt. Mansfield, eight miles; Smugglers' Notch, eight miles—one of the most wild and romantic places in the country; Bingham's Falls, five miles; Moss Glen Falls, three and a half miles; Gold Brook, three miles; West Hill, two miles; Morrisville Falls, eight miles; Johnson Falls, 12 miles; Nebraska, six miles.

During the summer the stages from Stowe to Waterbury connect with all the principal trains.

MOUNT MANSFIELD.

Before reaching the village of Stowe, or from the observatory of the Mansfield House, the tourist can get a good view of Mount Mansfield. The outline of the summit resembles the human features. Old Mansfield, as is imagined, is in a reclining posture, his face turned upward. The north peak represents the chin, the middle the nose, and the southern the forehead. This mountain is the highest in Vermont, and from it can be seen elevations in every county in the State. The Chin is 4,348 feet above the sea, 3,800 feet above the village of Stowe, and 340 above the Nose. The Nose is 160 feet above the Forehead.

Having surveyed the outline of this grand old mountain, the tourist will take a seat in the Mountain Coach, or upon the back of a trusty pony, and set out for the summit. For several miles the road extends along the valley by the side of a small river. Coming to the base of the mountain you turn to the left and commence the ascent. The road soon winds along through the forest, and you are finally brought to the door of the Half-Way House. Here is a clearing of a few acres, and to the left of the house, which is somewhat primitive in appearance, is a magnificent spring, gushing in great volume from the mountain side. You will want to stop here a few minutes and drink of its pure and refreshing waters, and gaze upon the extensive and lovely landscape in the valley below. As the coaches do not go beyond this point, you who have come hither in them will mount one of the sure footed ponies in waiting at the door, and continue the trip to the summit. Entering the forest again, your faithful animal walks slowly up the mountain, seemingly conscious of the task before him. From the Half-Way House to the summit the distance is two miles; but if this is your first trip you will be ready to affirm that it is at least six. As you approach the summit, the trees are of the more hardy kinds, stinted in growth and quite unlike those in the valley. Reaching the eastern face of the Nose, you halt here for a few minutes to take a view of the valley in the east. Turning westward to your right, you look down into Smugglers' Notch, which seems near enough to reach at a single bound over the tree tops. It is a deep gorge, winding between the mountains, and received its name from the fact that in former years a contraband trade was carried on by early settlers with Canada, the participators in it going and coming by this unfrequented route. The scene is wild and beautiful in the extreme, and you are inclined to linger here in contemplating its sublimity. As you leave the spot you proceed towards the Summit House, which is only a short distance off. On your left rises the Nose some two or three hundred feet, like a massive wall. Looking upward and towards the summit, farther west, you catch the first view of the "Old Man of the Mountain." His features are quite well formed, and are decidedly Websterian in appearance. Proceeding forward you at last reach the Summit House, a large and commodious hotel, capable of holding a hundred guests. Resting a few minutes, and then leaving your ponies at the stable, you walk to the western face of the Nose, a few rods distant, which you ascend. Reaching the summit, you involuntarily exclaim,—Eureka! what a view! Neither the pencil of the artist, nor words of the poet, have adequately described it. Its grandeur and sublimity surpass description. Here you are, nearly 4,000 feet above the valley, which lies at your feet. The Winooski is hardly seen, except here and there, resembling the smallest possible rivulet. On either hand, as far as you can see, the eye rests upon hundreds of mountain peaks, stretching away into the thick, dark haze which surrounds them.

West lies the great valley of the Champlain, and still beyond, 16 miles distant, is the lake itself, the whole length of which comes under the eye. A few miles from its western shore rises the lofty peaks of the famous Adirondacks.

North is the wide spread valley of the St. Lawrence, and in favorable weather, with the aid of the glass, steamers can be seen upon its waters. Montreal Mountain, with the city at its base, Jay Peak, and Owl's Head, the latter rising from the west bank of Lake Memphremagog, form prominent features in the landscape.

In the east the Franconia range and the White Mountains, sixty miles distant, limit the vision, while the intervening space is covered with numberless hills and mountains.

South can be seen Camel's Hump, Killington Peak and Ascutney.

Indeed, as one contemplates this sublime landscape he is inspired with reverence for the Great First Cause, who has shaped all so beautifully and so majestically.

On leaving the Nose, you will want to visit the Chin if the day is not too far advanced. You will think it is only a short distance to it, and will be surprised to learn that it is two miles. About one-third of the way from the Nose to the Chin you will notice the "drift scratches" upon the rock, and the identical bowlder which made them. These reveal to man the fact that even this lofty summit was once beneath the ocean, and that icebergs sailed over it.

Having visited all the interesting localities, and feasted upon the wonders found in this great book of nature, you will retrace your steps to the Mansfield House at Stowe, with a more perfect idea of the immensity and grandeur of Green Mountain scenery.

BOLTON FALLS.

Leaving Waterbury, going west, you cross a bridge over Winooski River, 425 feet in length. The scenery along the river increases in interest as you approach the mountain range. A few miles below Waterbury you come to Bolton Falls, seen north of the railroad. The high bluffs on either side of the river were evidently once united, forming a natural bridge. Through it the river has finally worn a deep and narrow channel. Perpendicular and overhanging rocks form the gorge, while huge bowlders, piled together, nearly bridge the river at low water. Just after passing the falls the tourist can get a good view of them from the car window, where he will notice the foaming stream and the projecting rocks above. The highest peaks of the Green Mountains are nearly in line with these falls, and but a few miles distant.

RIDLEY'S STATION.

At this place, where the tourist is less than 350 feet above the ocean, he is passing through a gap 4,000 feet below the summit of Mount Mansfield. Visitors to Camel's Hump leave the cars at this station.

CAMEL'S HUMP.

Leaving the railroad at Ridley's and going south, you can reach the summit of Camel's Hump, six miles distant, by private teams. A good carriage road has been constructed three miles up the mountain, and the remainder of the way is accomplished on horseback. Not far from the summit is a spring of excellent water, and also a house for the accommodation of visitors. The view from the summit is similar to that from Mount Mansfield. The hight above the sea is 4,083 feet, and some over 3,800 above Winooski River. The peculiar outline of its summit, which suggests its name, and its comparatively isolated position, make it a conspicuous object for many miles around.

JONESVILLE.

Three miles west of Bolton is Jonesville. East of the station the valley is narrow, and in full view from the cars is a beautiful cascade with a lofty rock near it. This, with the wild scenery, gives the place an unusually picturesque appearance.

RICHMOND.

Before reaching Richmond the valley becomes broader and more fertile. The village lies principally north of the station. Passing westward you cross Clark Bridge over the Winooski, 600 feet long.

WILLISTON.

Passing through Williston, which is an excellent agricultural region, you get good views of Mansfield and Camel's Hump. Here is seen the profile of old Mansfield, outlined on the sky beyond. West of the station you cross Bradley Bridge, 400 feet long.

ESSEX JUNCTION.

Here passengers for Burlington change cars, taking the train which runs to that place, eight miles distant.

FROM ESSEX JUNCTION TO BURLINGTON.

Soon after leaving Essex Junction, the view of Mansfield and Camel's Hump is exceedingly beautiful, and one is greatly impressed with their magnitude and grandeur. Passing from the sandy table lands you enter the more fertile valley of the Winooski River. The scenery along this stream is highly interesting. The river has made deep gorges through the limestone rock, and as one passes over the two railroad bridges he will behold the perpendicular and overhanging walls of rock, which rise on either side to the hight of nearly one hundred feet. North of the railroad, in the river, a rocky island, with high, perpendicular walls, will be noticed, crowned with fir trees.

Continuing towards Burlington, you soon come to Winooski Falls, where is situated the manufacturing village of Winooski. South of this place, upon the bluff beyond, can be seen the granite column, 42 feet high, erected by the State of Vermont, at the grave of Ethan Allen, in the Burlington cemetery.

THE TUNNEL.

Leaving Winooski, you soon come to the tunnel, which extends through a high sand bluff, a distance of 350 feet. Passing through it you come out upon the shore of Lake Champlain, within the limits of the city of Burlington.

The mode of constructing this tunnel was unlike that of any other in this country. Sharpened stakes were driven into the sand in the form of an arch, when an excavation was made below them. In this space was built an arch of masonry, and when completed the stakes were driven further into the bank, and another section of masonry constructed. This process was repeated until the whole work was finished. In the lower portions of the tunnel there were occasionally alternations of clay and sand, and beneath a thin stratum of clay, at the depth of 80 feet from the surface a live toad was found, occupying a small cavity in the sand. When first taken out he was in a torpid state, but upon exposure to the air soon showed signs of life, and became as active as others of his species that are found in localities supposed to be more favorable to longevity. He lived six months, and his skin is now in the possession of a Burlington gentleman.

BURLINGTON.

Distance from New York, 364 miles; Montreal, 97; Quebec, 277; White Mountains, 165; Lake Memphremagog, 209.

Situated upon an eminence, sloping westward down to Lake Champlain, which it overlooks, Burlington is truly one of the most beautiful places in Vermont. The tourist will ascend College Street to the University, and from the observatory of the main building look out upon the grand panorama of nature spread before him. From here, beyond the lake is seen the wild mountain region of Northern New York—numberless peaks rising far above the lake and forming a landscape of remarkable beauty. Close to the beholder lies the city of Burlington, covering the hillside with its dwellings, stores and workshops. Beyond is Champlain itself, with its islands and bays. At this point the lake is ten miles wide, but one unaccustomed to measure distance upon water with the eye, would hardly think it was more than five or six. Juniper Island, with its light-house, and comprising some eleven acres of land, is a conspicuous object in the foreground, while at the left the dark mass seen peering above the water is Rock Dunder. Further towards the middle of the lake are the Four Brothers—little gems of islands arrayed in green. North and south the dark waters of Champlain extend beyond your vision.

Rock Dunder is a black mass of naked slate rock, nearly three miles from shore, a little south of the city. It rises twenty feet above the water, and one might easily suppose it to be a fort. It is stated that when the British fleet approached Burlington in the war of 1812, the commander, imagining it to be some infernal Yankee invention to blow his ships to atoms, opened fire upon it, and after an ineffectual attempt to sink it in the lake, he concluded that it was a useless undertaking, and gave it up.

Opposite Burlington, in New York, is the village of Port Kent, and near it, on the road to Keeseville, is some remarkable scenery on the Ausable River—places where that stream has worn a deep and narrow channel through the solid rock. Still further west are the Adirondack mountains, whose peaks tower majestically heavenward; and conspicuous among them are Mt. McIntyre, White Face, and Mt. Marcy—the latter 5,467 feet above the sea, and the highest point between the White Mountains and the Alleghanies.

Plattsburg, on the west side of the lake, north of Port Kent, can be seen in favorable weather. During the summer steamers run between that place and Burlington.

Turning eastward you will behold a view of unusual interest, although not equal to that just surveyed. In the distance are the lofty summits of Mansfield and Camel's Hump, while the space between you and them resembles a vast plain dotted with patches of forest and cultivated fields.

The Vermont University, from the observatory of which the tourist has looked upon the surrounding scenery, is the oldest educational institution in the State, it having been chartered in 1791. It received from the State a grant of land containing 29,000 acres. In the war of 1812 the United States Government occupied the University as a depository of arms. In 1824 the buildings were destroyed by fire, and in 1825 the erection of new ones was begun. The north-west corner stone, which bears an inscription, was laid by Gen. Lafayette. There is a medical department connected with the University, and in 1865 the Vermont State Agricultural College, endowed by grants of land from the general government, was also united with it. Both institutions now have a joint fund of $300,000, mostly in real estate. Before leaving the University the tourist will find it worth while to examine the specimens of natural history belonging to the institution. He will also notice with interest, near the entrance to the grounds, the huge bowlder, about three feet in diameter, worn perfectly smooth and as round as a cannon ball while in a pot-hole at Northfield, where it was found several years ago.

The Vermont Episcopal Institute, under the patronage of the Episcopal Church, is located north of the city, fronting upon Lake Champlain. It is an elegant structure, and can be seen from the University buildings

There are some elegant private residences in the city, a number of which are occupied by gentlemen who have retired or are still doing business in New York.

East of the University is Burlington Cemetery, where are the graves of Ethan Allen and others distinguished in the history of Vermont. The Tuscan column of granite, 42 feet high, four and one-half feet in diameter at its base, standing upon a pedestal six feet square, which was erected by the State in 1857 to the memory of the hero of Ticonderoga, is an object of interest, and is in keeping with the character of him whose memory it is intended to perpetuate. On the sides of the pedestal are inserted four marble tablets, suitably inscribed.

Burlington has a population of 8,000, and is still increasing. The mercantile business of the place has for many years been large, a number of firms being engaged in the wholesale trade. Its lumber interest, however, is the most extensive, the annual sales amounting to sixty million feet. Burlington is the fourth lumber mart in this country—only Chicago, Albany and Bangor doing a larger business. The lumber companies are, L. Barnes & Co., the Hunterstown Lumber Company, and C. Blodgett & Son. The Hunterstown Company own large tracts of timber land, and saw mills on the Ottawa River, in Canada.

Among the business enterprises, are the Burlington Manufacturing Company, who have rolling mills and a nail factory, and are about to engage in manufacturing railroad iron of Bessemer steel; flouring mills, a sash and blind factory, a pottery, woolen mills, the Mechanic Pioneer Shops, a chair factory, and coffee and spice mills.

In the war of 1812 some 4,000 American troops were stationed here, under Gens. Macomb and Wade Hampton. Fortifications were thrown up in the north part of the city, the outlines of which are still visible.

GOING NORTH.

Leaving Burlington the tourist will return to Essex Junction and proceed northward. The surface of the country is generally level, and void of interest.

COLCHESTER.

Just before reaching the station you come in sight of Lake Champlain, but taking a more northerly course you leave it on the left.

MILTON.

The village, which lies west of the station, contains several mills, situated on Lamoille River. South-east of the village and not far from the railroad, are the Great Falls in the Lamoille, which, in running fifty rods, makes a descent of 150 feet. Near the middle of the cataract is a small island, upon each side of which the water rushes down with great force, tossing the spray into the air, and making an incessant roar.

GEORGIA.

Before reaching Georgia you cross a high bridge, 450 feet in length, over Lamoille River. You are now ten miles from St. Albans, and are descending towards the lake, which comes in view several miles north of the station. Here the country is level and has the appearance of a good agricultural region.

ST. ALBANS.

Distance from New York, 381 miles; Montreal, 65; Quebec, 245; White Mountains, 181; Lake Memphremagog, 225.

Approaching St. Albans from the south the village is seen spread out before you upon a broad plain and a gently sloping hill which faces the west. East of the village, and about a mile from the depot, there is quite an elevation, upon which are some extensive and neat dwellings. A little to the north-east of the village is Aldis Hill, and to the south-west, Bellevue. From either the scenery is grand and beautiful. Almost at the feet of the tourist is the village. To the west and beyond are broad, green fields, reaching down to Lake Champlain, two and a half miles distant. North and south, as far as can be seen, is Champlain with its innumerable islands, and beyond are the lofty summits of the Adirondack range. Almost directly north is Montreal, seen with the aid of a glass, and east are the Green Mountains, clothed with their summer verdure. It is stated that some years ago four Americans met in Italy, three of whom agreed that from no point, with the same altitude, was there so fine a view to be had as from Aldis Hill. The fourth had not ascendid its summit, but on returning to this country he went to St. Albans for that purpose, and was so charmed with the scenery that he settled and finally died in the town. There is something so magnificent and enchanting in the scenery from the hights about St. Albans—so broad and so beautiful—that one feels, as he gazes off upon the distant lake and the dark mountain range beyond, himself lifted far above the low and sordid in life—an inward yearning towards the good and the true.

South of the village is an elevation known by the very unpoetical name of Johnny Cake Hill. It received this appellation from a stranger, who, many years ago, chanced to pass that way just at night, in the early settlement of the place. Applying at a farm house for supper, Johnny Cake was offered as the principal dish. Not choosing to partake of it, he declined and went to another house in search of supper. Here he met with no better success. Traveling on, from house to house, wherever he applied the inevitable Johnny Cake was sure to turn up. From this circumstance he gave to the locality the name of Johnny Cake Hill, by which it has since been known.

Jesse Welden was the first white man to reside within the limits of the town. He went from Bennington to St. Albans before the Revolution, and on the breaking out of the war he retired to a locality in closer proximity to civilization. In 1784 he returned and erected a log house near the southern end of Main Street. Here he remained for quite a number of years, but as others began to come in and make settlements, he plunged again into the wilderness, to become the pioneer of other localities. At one time he owned all the land upon which the village of St. Albans is situated. The first framed house in the town was built by Eldad Butler.

The principal business of the town was formerly done at St. Albans Bay, at the lake, two and a half miles distant. Since the opening of the railroad the Bay has become a mere hamlet, while the village at the center of the township has grown to stately proportions.

Main Street, running north and south, and upon which the stores are mostly located, is one of the finest streets in New England. It is unusually broad and very straight for a mile. On either side are rows of shade trees, mostly maple. North of the stores, at various points on Main Street, are some elegant and spacious dwellings—as fine as any seen in much larger places. East of the business part of the village, and fronting on Main Street, is a large and handsome park, containing four acres. It is covered with shade trees, and in a few years will be a very beautiful and inviting spot. Above the park, and facing it on the east side, are the Congregational, Episcopal and Methodist Churches, the Court House and the High School building. At the north end is the Welden House.

Franklin County, of which St. Albans is the shire town, is one of the most productive in the State. It is especially adapted to butter and cheese making. A butter market is held at St. Albans every Tuesday, and thousand of dollars are paid to the farmers by the agents of Boston merchants—frequently as high as $30,000 in a single day, and in one day in 1865 $60,000 were paid out. No other town in Vermont has a stated market day. Ice cars, loaded with butter, are sent every Tuesday night in the summer from St. Albans to Boston. In 1865 3,035,257 pounds of butter were shipped from St. Albans, which, at an average of 40 cents per pound, the market price that year, was worth $1, 214,102.80. In the same year were shipped 1,174,261 pounds of cheese, valued at 15½ cents per pound, making a total of $182,010.48. In the last fifteen years there were shipped 33,603,044 pounds of butter, valued at 33 cents per pound, and which sold for $10,091,093.20. For the same period there were shipped 16,628,097 pounds of cheese, which, valued at 9 cents per pound, would bring $1,496,527.73.

St. Albans is the headquarters of the Vermont Central Railroad. Here live its principal officers, and here are located its various shops for the manufacture and repair of locomotives, passenger and freight cars. Nearly all the locomotives and cars used on the road are made by the company, and they are fully equal to the best running upon the New England roads. The shops, which are all new and are provided with the best machinery, are the most extensive of any in the eastern States. The machine and car shops are each 600 feet long and from 60 to 75 feet wide. The engine houses, one of which has recently been erected, are also very extensive. A new passenger house three hundred feet long, and sufficiently wide for four tracks, was built in 1866. The upper stories are used for offices by the company.

THE WELDEN HOUSE AT ST. ALBANS.

St. Albans was for a long time deficient in hotel accommodations. In 1865 the Welden House, built by a corporation at a cost of $118,000, and named in honor of the first settler of the town, was opened to the public, and it is acknowledged to be one of the finest hotels in the country. Pleasantly situated at the north end of the park, and overlooking the village and the lake, it is one of the most desirable stopping places to be found. The proprietors are Cool & McDonald, and under their management the Welden will ever be a favorite with summer tourists.

A sulphur spring has been discovered in the town, which has been secured for the guests of the Welden House. Water from the Alburgh and Highgate sulphur springs, and from the mineral spring in Sheldon, will also be kept at the hotel. The Sheldon spring has been purchased by a New York gentleman,

THE WELDEN HOUSE AT ST. ALBANS.

and some remarkable cures have been made by using its waters.

St. Albans is the residence of Ex-Governor Smith, one of the ablest men in the State. His residence and grounds, on the eminence east of the village, which it overlooks, are very fine. There are between 4,000 and 5,000 inhabitants in the town, and no place of its size has better churches or high school building. They have all been built within a few years—the Congregational Church at a cost of $27,000, the Catholic at $25,000, the Episcopal at $15,000, and the High School building at $18,000.

Ten passenger trains arrive and depart from St. Albans daily, thus affording excellent opportunities to visit the place. The distances from it to the large cities and prominent places of interest are: To New York, 332 miles; Boston, 260; Saratoga, 149; Burlington, 32; Ogdensburg, 142; Montreal, 65.

THE ST. ALBANS RAID.

Not even a thunder storm from a cloudless sky could have astonished the people of St. Albans more than did the famous rebel raid on Wednesday afternoon, Oct. 19th, 1864, under the leadership of the so-called Confederate, Lieut. Bennett H. Young. Nothing unusual had happened to excite suspicion, and the people of the town were quietly pursuing their accustomed vocations, when soon after three o'clock the squad of ruffian robbers, calling themselves Confederate soldiers, left their hiding places and went forth with the deliberate purpose of committing great crimes—robbery at all events, and murder if necessary. All at once the town was in great commotion. A band of armed men appeared in the streets, maddened to desperation with liquor. The banks were entered and robbed, shots were fired at unoffending citizens, horses seized and ridden off, and all without meeting hardly a shadow of opposition, so complete the surprise and so illy prepared were the people to resist. There were twenty-one raiders in the town, five of whom entered the St. Albans Bank, four the Franklin County, and three the First National Bank. The others remained in the street to prevent a capture. About $200,000 in all were taken; $75,000 from the St. Albans Bank, $50,000 from the First National, and the balance from the Franklin County Bank. Less than half of this amount, about $90,000, is all that was afterward recovered.

When the raiders entered the St. Albans Bank, the teller, Mr. C. N. Bishop, stepped to the counter to wait upon them, supposing that they had some ordinary business to transact. Instantly they presented their revolvers at him, and taking them to be robbers he sprang into the rear room, where the acting cashier, Mr. M. A. Seymour, was engaged. The robbers followed and seized both by their collars, at the same time threatening to shoot them if resistance was made. They then announced that they were Confederate soldiers, come to retaliate for the doings of Sheriden in the Shenandoah Valley. Mr. Seymour requested the privilege of taking an inventory of the property about to be carried away, so that a claim might be made upon the government. "D—n your government," was the reply. "Hold up your hands and take the Confederate oath." To save their lives Mr. Seymour and Mr. Bishop complied, and they are the only ones who had the Confederate oath administered to them in New England.

At the Franklin County Bank the raiders found the cashier, Mr. Marcus W. Beardsley, and a wood sawyer. Both were seized and locked up in the vault, where they remained until released by the citizens of the town after the raiders had left. They came out nearly exhausted and pale as ghosts.

Several of the raiders were stationed near the corner of Lake and Main Streets, and as fast as any came up either street they were ordered upon the park at the peril of their lives. Here some 25 or 30 citizens, unarmed, were herded together, and kept there until the raiders departed.

Further up Main Street the Confederates were busy in securing horses. Those in the streets and livery stables were seized. Mr. Fuller, seeing his led out by his hostler, at the command of one of the raiders, demanded him to return them to the stable. Young, the leader, drew his pistol and fired. Mr. Fuller stepping behind a tree, the ball passed him and hit Mr. E. J. Morrison, the contractor of the Welden House, who was standing on the steps of the store north of the Messenger newspaper office. He was taken home, and died on the 21st, two days after. Other shots were fired and two persons were wounded, but both recovered.

In a short time the raiders had seized their plunder and were galloping up Main Street, on their way to Canada. As soon as possible they were pursued by some forty citizens of St. Albans, and followed so closely that they gave up the plan of robbing the Sheldon Bank. Still pursued they were driven into Canada. The local authorities there assisted in arresting all that could be found, fourteen of them, and took them to St. Johns. From here they were transferred to Montreal under the plea of a want of suitable accommodations for conducting the trial. They were taken before Judge Coursol, and about $90,000 of the stolen money found in their possession was placed in the hands of Lamothe, the Chief of Police. The Judge, after some delay, decided that he had no jurisdiction in the case, as the writ had not been issued by the Governor General, and ordered the raiders to be discharged and the money found in their possession restored to them. Another writ was obtained, and finally four of the party were arrested at Point Levi, near Quebec. They were brought before Judge Smith, and he decided that the case did not come under the Ashburton treaty, and so here ended Canadian justice.

A claim was made upon the Canadian Government for the return of the $90,000 given up to the raiders by Judge Coursol, and Parliament passed an act for that purpose; $50,000 in gold, equal then to $90,000 in currency, was given, pro rata, to the Banks.

ROUSE'S POINT.

Rouse's Point, named in honor of an early settler on the adjoining lands, is twenty-four miles from St. Albans. Here a bridge one mile long has been constructed across Lake Champlain by the Vermont Central and the Ogdensburg Railroads. It has a draw or boat-bridge, 300 feet in length, which is opened by a steam engine for the purpose of permitting vessels to go up and down the lake. The scenery here is quite interesting. Fort Montgomery, a work for national defense, some 200 rods above the bridge, will be seen jutting into the lake from the New York shore. The site of the old fort was some 20 or 30 rods south of the present one. After work on the new fort had progressed for some time, it was ascertained that it had been located north of the 45th parallel, and the British authorities notified our Government that it was within the limits of their territory. When the line was subsequently run under the Ashburton and Webster treaty, concessions were made in the State of Maine by our Government, as a proper compensation.

HIGHGATE AND ALBURGH SULPHUR SPRINGS.

These springs have long been resorted to for the cure of cutaneous and scrofulous diseases, and in many cases have proved efficacious. The Highgate Spring is in the western part of Highgate, twelve miles from St. Albans. The railroad from St. Albans to Montreal, passes between the hotel and the spring house. The Franklin House, large and commodious, is a delightful summer retreat. In rear of the hotel on a gentle eminence is a grove of native trees, which add greatly to the beauty of the place.

The Alburgh Springs are seventeen miles from St. Albans, on the railroad to Rouse's Point. These springs have been a place of resort since 1816, and the number of visitors is gradually increasing. Here are two hotels for the accommodation of visitors—the Missisquoi and the Mansion House. Each will accommodate a hundred guests. Pleasure seekers come here to enjoy fishing, hunting and rowing on the bay. Here the railroad crosses the bay on a bridge 4,200 feet long.

FROM ST. ALBANS TO MONTREAL.

The scenery from St. Albans to Montreal, a distance of 65 miles is without special interest. The country is generally level and the villages are small. The stations are: Junction, East Swanton, Highgate Springs, Province Line, St. Armand, Moore's, Stanbridge, Des Riveires, St. Alexandre, Stanstead, Shefford, and Chambly Junction, St. Johns, Lacadie, Brosseau's, St. Lambert, and Montreal. At the Stanstead, Shefford and Chambly Junction you connect with that road, and the Montreal and Champlain Railway, operated by the Grand Trunk. At St. Johns you cross the outlet of Lake Champlain, which flows into the St. Lawrence. St. Lambert is opposite Montreal, at the entrance to Victoria Bridge. The country for some distance, in Canada, before reaching Montreal is mostly inhabited by the French.

MONTREAL.

The tourist before reaching the Victoria Bridge, when approaching Montreal, will notice Lachine on the north side of the St. Lawrence, and further east the city of Montreal, with the Mountain in the rear. On reaching the Victoria Bridge across the St. Lawrence, the train passes under the Grand Trunk Railway and thence eastward until it reaches the grade of that road, when it proceeds toward the bridge. Six or eight minutes are occupied in crossing it, and you then pass the offices and shops of the Grand Trunk, curve to the right, cross the Welland Canal, and thence to the depot in Montreal, having made a circuit of four miles since leaving the bridge. Here your trunks are examined by the Custom House officers, and you then proceed to your hotel.

The Canadians are not a fast people, and if, in your pursuit of pleasure, you should encounter, occasionally, a vexatious delay, you will do well to remember the maxim of one who has lived long among them, and has the happy faculty of maintaining his good nature under all circumstances: "Keep your patience—remember you are in Canada!" Forgetting for the time the prompt, direct, and off-hand way of doing business in the States, practice this maxim and your happiness will be complete.

In your perambulations about the city, should you find it desirable to ask some simple question of a plain, laboring man, and he should answer in your mother tongue as distinctly as words ever fell from the lips of man, that he "can't speak English," do not threaten to flog him for lying. This, beyond the gibberish imbibed with his mother's milk, is all he has had ambition to master.

Should gold be above par, you will do well to provide yourself with specie, which you can obtain of any broker, before leaving the hotel to visit the objects of interest in the city. It will save you much trouble in making change with those not acquainted with the state of the money market. The Canadian's stand point in financial matters seems a little singular to you at first, although you may not be able to controvert it. He will tell you, perhaps, that greenbacks have *gone down*, while you feel that he is mistaken. With you greenbacks are all right, but the mischief is in gold—that has *gone up!*

Montreal has a population of 110,000, and its age dates back more than three hundred years, to 1542, when a European settlement was begun here. Jacques Cartier, however, looked upon the spot with delight in 1535, when an Indian village existed under the name of Hochelaga. He gave it the name of Mont Royal, and a century after its first settlement it was christened Villie-Marie. In 1760 the British took possession of it, and it has since continued to increase in importance, until it is now the metropolis of British North America. The city is situated on Montreal Island, which is thirty miles long by ten in the extreme breadth. This island is formed by a branch of the Ottawa on the north and the St. Lawrence on the south. North-west of the city is a mountain of considerable hight, from which there is an extensive prospect. The view from it is exceedingly picturesque. The roofs and domes of the buildings in the city are covered with tin, which, glittering in the sun-light, present a peculiar contrast with the grey limestone walls and towers.

The many elegant buildings of cut limestone give Montreal that substantial and permanent appearance which no city in the States possesses. The streets, however, are generally narrow, and less attractive than they would have been had they been made wider when laid out, and in this respect they do not bear comparison with the streets of other important American cities.

The city has a frontage on the St. Lawrence of about three miles, and no where are there such splendid wharves as are found here. They are made of cut limestone, and show a greater extent of masonry than can be found elsewhere upon this continent.

THE VICTORIA BRIDGE.

One of the principal objects of interest to strangers visiting Montreal is the Victoria Bridge, which spans the St. Lawrence and is used only by the Grand Trunk Railway, giving Montreal an unbroken railway communication of 1,100 miles in one road, from Portland to Detroit. The bridge which is built of iron on the tubular principle, is 9,194 feet in length—nearly two miles, and cost $6,300,000. There are two long abutments and 24 piers of solid stone masonry. The water in passing under the bridge, runs at the rate of seven to ten miles an hour, and it is calculated that each pier will stand a pressure of seventy thousand tons of ice, which at the opening of the river comes sweeping down the current with great force. The blocks of stone in the piers are bound together with cement and iron rivets, and the face towards the current is beveled off to a sharp pointed edge so as to present as little resistance as is possible. The bridge rises from the shores to the center, at the rate of one foot in every 112, or nearly 48 feet to the mile. The object of this is to give sufficient hight in the center so that steamers and vessels can pass under the bridge without difficulty. The distance from the water, in summer, to the bridge is 60 feet. The engineers of this noble structure were Robert Stephenson and A. M. Ross. Trains cross it in about six minutes. The tourist can visit the interior of the bridge by applying at the office of the Grand Trunk Railway for a pass, near their shops, a short distance west of the bridge.

The tourist will notice, in visiting or crossing Victoria Bridge, north of the railroad, on the Montreal side of the river, at Point St. Charles, near the abutment, a massive stone resting on a huge rock, the whole about eighteen feet high, and enclosed with a white railing. This was erected by the workmen of the bridge to commemorate the spot where 6,500 Irish emigrants were buried in 1847, who died of ship fever.

OTHER OBJECTS OF INTEREST.

The public buildings of Montreal, built of cut limestone, have no equals in this country, and are worthy a visit. The Cathedral of Notre Dame is said to be the largest building in this country. It is 255 feet long, 135 wide, and its two towers each 220 feet high. In the north-west tower is a bell which weighs 29,400 pounds, and is named "Gros Bourdon," from its deep bass tone. In the other tower is a chime of bells. The view from these towers, one of which is always open to the public, is magnificent; the city and country many miles around can be seen. Ten thousand people can be seated in this cathedral—8,000 on the first floor and 2,000 in the galleries. Its cost was £100,000.

The Court House, on Notre Dame Street, opposite Nelson's

monument, is of cut limestone, in the Grecian Ionic style, and is one of the most elegant buildings in the city.

The Bank of Montreal, at Place d'Armies, of the Corinthian style of architecture, built of cut stone, is an elegant building. Among the other bank buildings worthy of note may be mentioned Molson's Bank, corner of Great St. James Street; City Bank, near Bank of Montreal; Bank of British North America, and Ontario Bank.

The Post Office, on Great St. James Street, is of beautiful cut stone, and one of the finest buildings in that locality.

The Bonsecours Market, on St. Paul and Water Streets, is a magnificent edifice in the Grecian and Doric style. It cost about $300,000, and has a front of three stories on Water Street and two stories on St. Paul. The city occupy the upper part of the building for offices. In the east wing is Concert Hall, capable of seating 4,000 persons.

Mount Royal Cemetery, two miles from the city, on the east side of the mountain, and the water works which tap the St. Lawrence at the Lachine Rapids, west of Montreal, are objects of interest, and no one should fail to visit them.

The various churches and convents will claim the attention of the tourist, and he will find them worth visiting.

"Shooting the Rapids," to those fond of daring adventure, would round off a visit to Montreal, and pleasantly increase one's recollections of his summer's tour. Take the early morning train from Montreal to Lachine, a few miles west of the city and there wait the coming of the steamer. About eight o'clock you go on board, and at Caughnawaga she will lie to for a few minutes for the Indian pilot. The steamer will then start to make the run down the Lachine Rapids. As soon as they are reached steam is shut off, and you are carried down by the force of the current alone. Presently you are running at lightning speed through the breakers, over the whirling, bubbling waters. The waves are lashed into spray, and the scene becomes one of wild and fearful grandeur. The faithful Indian is still at his post, and the steamer is taken safely through the danger. At times you pass within a short distance of huge rocks, and to touch one would crush the steamer into an utter wreck. After passing the rapids the steamer proceeds to Montreal, going under Victoria Bridge before arriving at the wharf.

Before leaving Montreal the tourist should visit Notman's photographic rooms, on Bleury Street. Here you will find some rare specimens of the photographic art. Mr. Notman is one of the best photographers in the world, and was awarded a gold medal at the International Exhibition in London in 1862, over all other European and American competitors. His views of objects of interest in Montreal and Canadian scenery are exceedingly beautiful.

THE HOTELS.

Montreal is well supplied with first-class hotels. Among them may be mentioned St. Lawrence Hall, Donegana Hotel, and the Ottawa House. The Donegana Hotel is situated on Notre Dame Street, the Broadway of the city, and is elegantly furnished. The rooms are large and airy, and from them are good views of the city. The landlord, Daniel Gale, is an American, and will direct strangers to places of interest about the city. The cars of the street railway pass the hotel every ten minutes.

The St. Lawrence and Ottawa are on Great St. James Street.

OTTAWA, CANADA WEST.

Ottawa, the seat of the Canadian government, 164 miles by railroad from Montreal, is situated on Ottawa River, 90 miles above the confluence with the St. Lawrence. It was formerly called Bytown, from its founder, Col. John By, who assisted in constructing Rideau Canal between Kingston, on Lake Ontario, and the Ottawa River. This work was commenced in 1826, and opened for navigation in 1832, at a cost to Great Britain of £803,774 sterling. The city of Ottawa is well laid out, and the scenery in the vicinity is not surpassed by any in America. In addition to railroad facilities for travel a line of steamers run up and down the lake during the summer months.

HOTELS.

The Russell House, James A. Gouin, proprietor, is situated in Center Town, near the Parliament Buildings, Post Office, Custom House, etc. Within five minutes' walk from this hotel is the Suspension Bridge, where views may be obtained of the celebrated Chaudiere Falls, second only to those of Niagara in imposing grandeur. This hotel is large and commodious, and the tourist will find it a pleasant stopping place.

TO WHITE MOUNTAINS, LAKE MEMPHREMAGOG, AND QUEBEC.

At White River Junction the tourist, going to the White Mountains, Lake Memphremagog, or Quebec, continues up the Connecticut River, crossing White River at its mouth. The scenery along the river is rich and beautiful.

NORWICH AND HANOVER.

Five miles from the junction you come to Norwich and Hanover, the former in Vermont and the latter in New Hampshire. The villages are about three-fourths of a mile from the station.

The bridge at this place is the only free bridge across the Connecticut.

DARTMOUTH COLLEGE.

In the beautiful village of Hanover, N. H., a short distance from the depot, on a plain considerably elevated above the Connecticut, is Dartmouth College. This is one of the oldest colleges in New England, only Harvard, Yale and Brown preceding it chronologically. Founded in 1769, it is nearing its centennial. The only college in New Hampshire, it has trained most of the eminent men in the State, and from its high reputation has drawn students from all parts of the country. It has been well said that it is on the intellectual landscape of the State, what Mount Washington is on the physical. In every section of the land, and in every walk of life, its sons have attained distinction. Thirteen of them have been Governors of six different States, thirty-one have been Judges of the Supreme Court in various States, or of the Federal Courts; four have been members of the Cabinet at Washington; and five have occupied diplomatic stations abroad. The contributions of the college to the cause of education have been especially large. Twenty-two of its alumni have been Presidents of twenty-one different colleges; seventy-eight have been College Professors, twelve of them in various Medical chairs; and thirteen have been Professors of twelve different Theological Seminaries. It has educated more than 800 men for the pulpit. On the roll of its alumni, among other honored names, we note those of Daniel Webster, Rufus Choate, George P. Marsh, and Salmon P. Chase. In addition to the Classical, it has a Scientific and a Medical Department. It has, besides the President, Rev. Asa D. Smith, D. D., L. L. D., twenty Professors, and, for the present year, 298 students. The war drew heavily upon the classes—a large number of the students serving in every capacty, from that of a private to that of a Major-General. The Freshman Class numbers 50, which, with the present large attendance, shows the College to be in a flourishing condition. There are four halls for the Classical department, a Scientific building, a Medical college, and an observatory. The latter commands a delightful view down the valley of the Connecticut, the vista ending with Mt. Ascutney. A gymnasium, 47 by 90 feet, has been erected at a cost of $24,000, the gift of Geo. H. Bissell, Esq., of the city of New York, a graduate of the college; and measures are in progress for the erection of an imposing Alumni Hall. The tourist would greatly enjoy a few days in Hanover and vicinity. The rides, in every direction, are pleasant, and during the summer season there is a great influx of agreeable company from the cities.

Among the students there have always been some dependent, mainly, for the means of prosecuting their studies on their own exertions. Such men have usually spent a portion of the winter in school-teaching. In Whittier's last beautiful poem,—"Snow-Bound," there is a picture of the Dartmouth Schoolmaster, which will awaken pleasant memories in many minds:

"Brisk wielder of the birch and rule,
The master of the district school,
Held at the fire, his favored place,
Its warm glow lit a laughing face,
Fresh-hued and fair, where scarce appeared
The uncertain prophecy of beard.
He played the old and simple games
Our modern boyhood scarcely names,
Sang songs, and told us what befalls
In classic Dartmouth's college halls.
Born the wild northern hills among,
From whence his yeoman father wrung
By patient toil, subsistence scant,
Not competence, and yet not want,
He early gained the power to pay
His cheerful, self-reliant way;
Could doff at ease his scholar's gown
To peddle wares from town to town;
Or, through the long vacations reach,
In lonely lowland districts teach,
Where all the droll experience found
At stranger hearths in boarding round;
The moonlit skater's keen delight,
The sleigh-drive through the frosty night,
The rustic party, with its rough
Accompaniment of blind man's buff,
And whirling plate, and forfeits paid,
His winter task a pastime made.
Happy the snow-locked homes, wherein
He tuned his merry violin,
Or played the athlete in the barn,
Or held the good dame's winding yarn,
Or mirth provoking versions told
Of classic legends, rare and old,
Wherein the scenes of Greece and Rome
Had all the commonplace of home,
And little seemed at best the odds
'Twixt Yankee peddlers and old gods•
Where Pindus-born Araxes took,
The guise of any grist-mill brook,

And dread Olympus, at his will,
Became a huckleberry hill.

A careless boy that night he seemed;
But at his desk he had the look
And air of one who wisely schemed.
And hostage from the future took
In trained thought and love of book.
Large-brained, clear-eyed,—of such as he
Shall Freedom's young apostles be,
Who, following in War's bloody trail,
Shall every lingering wrong assail;
All chains from limb and spirit strike,
Uplift the black and white alike;
Scatter before their swift advance
The darkness and the ignorance,
The pride, the lust, the squalid sloth,
Which nurtured Treason's monstrous growth,
Made murder pastime, and the hell
Of prison torture possible.
The cruel lie of caste refute,
Old forms remould, and substitute
For Slavery's lash the Freeman's will,
For blind routine, wise-handed skill;
A school house plant on every hill,
Stretching in radiate nerve lines thence
The quick wires of intelligence,
Till North and South together brought,
Shall own the same electric thought,
In peace a common flag salute,
And, side by side, in labor's free
And unresentful rivalry,
Harvest the fields wherein they fought."

THE DARTMOUTH STUDENT AND THE CHELSEA CLERK.

Several years since one of those students at Dartmouth, who, as Whittier says in the above lines,

"Could doff at ease his scholar's gown
To peddle wares from town to town,"

entered the village store at Chelsea, Vt., in search of a customer for some of the books that he was selling. Inquiring of the clerk, one of those over-smart, self-sufficient young men sometimes met with, who resembled an Indian in complexion, if he would like to purchase, the following colloquy took place, in the presence of the usual number of country store loungers: *Clerk*—"Well, yes, I should like to trade with you if you have a particular work that I am desirous of obtaining." *Student*—"I do not know that I have it, but I presume I can get it for you—what is it?" *Clerk*—"It is Davis' treatise on the Androscoggin River." *Student*—"I am sorry to say, sir, that I haven't it; but I have here a work which I think is of some importance to you. It is an elaborate treatise on the North American Indians, and I am authorized by the publishers to sell it to *any remnant of the several tribes at half price!*"

NORWICH UNIVERSITY.

This institution is located about three-fourths of a mile from the Norwich and Hanover depot, and about a mile and a half from Dartmouth College. It was established in 1820 by Capt. Alden Partridge, under the name of the American Literary, Scientific and Military Academy, and continued in a flourishing condition until Capt. Partridge removed the school to Middletown, Conn. The Middletown school at length was discontinued, and the principal returned to Norwich. In 1834 a charter was obtained for the Norwich University, and among those who have graduated at this institution, are, Hon. Thomas H. Seymour, Ex-Governor of Connecticut; Rev. Theophilus Fisk; the late Hon. Henry W. Cushman; Hon. Mr. Morse, of Louisiana, formerly member of Congress; Hon. Horatio Seymour, Ex-Governor of New York; Hon. William L. Lee, late Chief Justice of the Sandwich Islands; Hon. Caleb Lyons, L. L. D., Governor of Idaho; Rev. C. H. Fary; Rev. D. S. C. M. Potter; Rev. Josiah Swett, D. D., Professor in the Episcopal Theological Institute, at Burlington; Robert Frazer, Esq.;

Professor Alonzo Jackman, L. L. D.; Gen. Robert Millroy; Gen. T. G. Ransom; Gen. Dodge; Col. Clark, of New Hampshire; Col. Jesse A. Gove; Col. F. Farrar; Col. Thomas H. Whipple; Col. Simon Preston; Col. Burton; Col. G. A. Brearex; and Col. T. B. Ransom, who fell at Chepultepec, Mexico, and who succeeded Capt. Partridge as President of Norwich University, after Capt. Partridge's resignation. Capt. Partridge, who was a native of Norwich, died and was buried in the town.

The main building was burned in 1866, and efforts were then made to rebuild it, but without success. The school has since been removed to Northfield, Vt. Norwich is a beautiful place, surrounded with high hills and romantic scenery. Among those who have lived in the town was Hon. Paul Brigham, for twenty-four years Lieut. Governor of Vermont.

POMPANOOSUC.

Following close upon the bank of the Connecticut you come to Pompanoosuc station. This was formerly called Ompompanoosuc, an Indian name given to the little stream that you cross before reaching the station, and signifying a river where onions are found. From this station is shipped large quantities of copperas ore, taken from a mine several miles west in the town of Strafford. It is sent to Philadelphia and England, and from it is made sulphuric acid.

A few miles north of the station the first view of the summit of Moose Hillock is had, opposite Newbury, in New Hampshire. Eastward will be seen the rounded form of Bald Mountain.

THETFORD AND LYME.

This station, fifteen miles from White River Junction, accommodates the residents of the two towns—Thetford lying on the west side of the river, and Lyme on the east side, in New Hampshire. The village of Thetford is about a mile west of the station.

NORTH THETFORD.

The scenery along the Connecticut continues picturesque and beautiful. From this station is shipped copper ore from Vershire. The Corinth Copper Company, now working mines at Vershire and Corinth, are getting out 250 tons of ore per month. It is shipped to Portsmouth and thence to Baltimore by water, where it is smelted. A considerable quantity of the ore is loaded upon the cars at Bradford.

FAIRLEE AND ORFORD.

Approaching the station the village of Orford will be seen on the opposite side of the river, in New Hampshire. Here is located a female seminary, seen a short distance east of the river. Passing the station a ledge of rocks, rising to the hight of two or three hundred feet, will be noticed on the left, resembling a massive wall. Still further north, about five miles from the station, is another, equally as interesting. To the right is a beautiful view of the valley.

BRADFORD.

This is the second most important town on the route from White River Junction to Newport. St. Johnsbury alone exceeding it in point of business. There is considerable manufacturing done here—Waite's River, which is crossed before reaching the station, furnishing the water power. Three thousand fish kits are manufactured weekly by a single firm, and are sent to Boston. Passengers for Topsham, Corinth, Orange, Washington and Piermont stop at this station.

In the north-west part of the town, in Wright's Mountain, is a cave with several apartments, called Devil's Den. It is thought to have once been the abode of human beings.

In this town, in 1812, was manufactured, by James Wilson, the first artificial globe made in the United States.

HAVERHILL—MOOSE HILLOCK.

After leaving Bradford you come in sight of Haverhill, N. H., situated upon a hill overlooking the valley. Formerly this was the headquarters of the stage lines extending through Northern New Hampshire, and in those days was a place of considerable note. As you proceed north from Haverhill the valley is wide in extent, and the meadows broad and fertile.

In New Hampshire, east of Haverhill, you will notice Moose Hillock, rising to the hight of 4,636 feet, the summit of which is the first point seen from this region to indicate the approach of winter. Sugar Loaf and Black Mountain are nearer to you, further up the river.

NEWBURY.

Distance from New York, 295 miles; from White Mountains, 25; Lake Memphremagog, 70; Montreal, 184; Quebec, 235.

Before arriving at Newbury you will notice the village on the left, standing on a terrace nearly a hundred feet above the meadows. The railroad passes through a tunnel, made in the narrow terrace, extending eastward from the village. Newbury is one of the oldest towns on the upper Connecticut, and few places present greater attractions for a quiet summer residence. The village, which lies upon high table land, overlooking the broad meadows, contains several stores, two hotels, and the Wesleyan Academy, a Methodist institution. Here are the celebrated Newbury Sulphur Springs, long known to invalids in New England. They are in the valley, east of the depôt, where a bath house has been fitted up. An analysis of the water has been made, and it is highly recommended by able physicians.

The scenery in and around Newbury combines the grand and the beautiful. Here you have broad meadows, lofty mountain peaks, and a majestic river, and the view from the adjacent mountains resembles that from Mount Holyoke, in Massachusetts, more than any other point in the Connecticut Valley.

Directly in rear of Newbury is Mount Pulaski, an elevation easy of access, and from it can be seen a wide extent of country. The tourist should ascend its summit, and look upon the almost matchless scenery spread before him. To the right is the valley of Haverhill, with its long street, and directly east is Moose Hillock. To the left of it are Sugar Loaf and Black Mountains. Further beyond, in the north-east, are the Franconia Mountains, and in a pleasant day Franconia Notch can be seen, through which tourists pass to the White Mountains. The Profile House is only about 25 miles from Newbury.

Below, and almost underneath you, is the village of Newbury, the green fields resembling a beautiful carpet. Above the town is the Great Ox-Bow, and the magnificent meadows lying along the river.

Among the distinguished residents of Newbury in earlier days were Gen. Jacob Bayley and Col. Thomas Johnson, both of whom took active part in the French and Revolutionary wars. Col. Johnson was in the British service at Crown Point, where, for want of provisions, horse-beef was dealt out to the men. At the opening of the Revolution he entered the army and was finally taken prisoner and sent to Canada. He was paroled and permitted to return home on condition that he would not again take up arms, and would return when called upon.

Gen. Bayley was an important man to the inhabitants of this region, and the British determined upon his capture. June 17, 1782, Capt. Pritchard and a force of British troops came to Newbury to take him prisoner. Reaching the hights west of the Ox Bow, they signaled Col. Johnson, and he went to them. He learned the object of the expedition, and on giving them some trifling information returned home. Gen. Bayley and two sons were in the meadows plowing, near the Ox Bow. Johnson wrote a message and directed his wife's brother to leave it in the field where the General would find it. Dudley Carlton, the bearer of the message, dropped it in the furrow, and on coming to it Gen. Bayley took it up and read, "The Philistines be upon thee, Samson." That was enough for him. He turned out his team and escaped. That night an attack was made on his house, but he was not there to be captured as his enemies had expected.

There is now a house standing in the Johnson village, south of the Ox Bow and east of the railroad, that was built in 1775 by Col. Johnson. The frame was raised on the day that news reached Newbury of the battle of Lexington. Three of the men who were at the "raising" enlisted and were at the battle of Bunker Hill. One of the number, Peter Johnson, a brother of the Colonel's, was wounded in the arm.

THANKSGIVING POSTPONED FOR WANT OF MOLASSES.

As ludicrous as it may seem at the present time, in the early settlement of the town Thanksgiving Day was actually postponed two weeks in Newbury, for want of molasses. Communication with the larger towns was then difficult. Thanksgiving was appointed by the Colonial authorities having jurisdiction over this region, and as it happened the proclamation did not reach Newbury until after the appointed day had passed. The minister, on the following Sabbath, read the proclamation and said that, inasmuch as the day had gone by, he would suggest that the following Thursday be observed by the people of the town as a day of Thanksgiving and prayer. A worthy deacon, who enjoyed the good things of life as well as things spiritual, rose and said that as there was no molasses in town, and his boys had gone to Number Four (Charlestown, N. H.) to get some, he would move that Thanksgiving be postponed one week. The "boys" not returning, the day was again postponed, and, finally, the good people of Newbury were obliged to go without their molasses altogether. As it is inferred from this that there was no "sweetning" in the place, a thoughtful housewife wonders what they did for pumpkin pies.

THE GREAT OX BOW.

The Great Ox Bow, just north of the village of Newbury, is an object of interest to tourists. In its southern course the Connecticut bears off to the east and thence back to the west, making a circuit of four and a half miles, while across the neck it is only a hundred rods.

WELLS RIVER.

Leaving Newbury and passing the Great Ox Bow you soon come to the pleasant village of Wells River, in the town of Newbury, 40 miles from White River Junction. Here White Mountain tourists change cars for Littleton, it being the junction of the Boston and Montreal and White Mountains Railroads. It is 20 miles to Littleton, from which travelers go by stage 11 miles to the Profile House and 22 to the Crawford House. The view at this point is magnificent. The Franconia range skirts the eastern horizon. Leaving the station you cross Wells River, a small stream which furnishes power for the mills along its banks. For full description of White Mountains, see page 237.

MC INDOE'S FALLS.

The Connecticut is narrower and more rapid as you approach its source. Several miles below McIndoe's you pass Dodge's Falls, where the river makes a considerable descent. At McIndoe's the falls are still higher, and furnish excellent water power. The two saw mills at this place, and the one at Dodge's Falls, are owned by Mr. Stephen Barker, who manufactures two million feet of lumber annually. The logs are put into the Connecticut many miles further north, and are floated down in rafts in high water. After passing the station you will notice a cove in the river, formed by a huge rock extending from the bank. The river is only about 75 feet wide, and so rapid that an iron bar thrown into it would not sink. Mr. Barker keeps his logs in this cove until they are wanted at the mills. The fall in the Connecticut from Hartford to this place is 449 feet, and from here to Lake Connecticut, 100 miles, 1,140 feet.

BARNET.

Passing McIndoe's you soon come to Barnet. The village is west of the railroad, mostly upon the hill. The four story woolen mill, owned by the Caledonia Manufacturing Company, occupies a conspicuous position. The members of the firm are Ex-Governor Buckingham, Amos King, Edward Chappell, Charles King, and Edward Carew, all of Norwich, Conn. They contemplate erecting another factory, nearer the railroad. Heavy fancy woolen goods are made by the company. This town was granted to two sons of Phineas Stevens, who so gallantly defended the fort at Charlestown against the French and Indians. It was settled principally by Scotch.

PASSUMPSIC RIVER.

Soon after leaving Barnet you come to the mouth of the Passumpsic River, which empties into the Connecticut. The Indian name is Bassoomsuc, signifying a stream where there is much medicine. It is so tortuous that Dix says it resembles a gigantic cork-screw, liqufied. Indeed it is so crooked that it is a very smart bird that can fly from one side of the river to the other. In a distance of 25 miles the railroad crosses the river twenty-three times.

ISLANDS IN THE CONNECTICUT—DIGGING FOR GOLD.

In the Connecticut River, just below the mouth of the Passumpsic, there are no less than fifteen islands. The most prominent one is Gold Island, covered with spruce and cedar. Many years ago some persons, who had been led to believe that the Indians had buried gold there, dug the island over in search of it, but their efforts were not rewarded with a yield of the precious metal excelling a California placer. Between this place and Lunenburg, Vt., are the famous fifteen miles falls in the Connecticut.

MC LERAN'S AND PASSUMPSIC.

A short distance above the mouth of the Passsumpsic you come to McLeran's. Before the railroad was built from Wells River to Littleton, this was the starting point for stages to the White Mountains. The falls in the Passumpsic will be noticed on the right. Four miles from here you pass Passumpsic station.

ST. JOHNSBURY.

Distance from New York, 311 miles; White Mountains, 44; Lake Memphremagog, 44; Montreal, 148; Quebec, 211.

Leaving Passumpsic you soon come to St. Johnsbury, the most important station on the line. Here are the offices of the Connecticut and Passumpsic Rivers Railroads. Main Street, where most of the business is done, is upon the hill west of the railroad. This is the shire town of Caledonia County, and the large and neat Court House, built of brick, will be noticed upon the eminence west of the depot. The view from Main Street is extensive and pleasing. The towering hills, covered with a luxuriant vegetation, the distant eastern mountain range, and the valley of the Passumpsic, form a beautiful landscape. The village has an unusually neat and thrifty appearance, and the elegant and costly school houses, which have been erected within the last few years, speak well for the industry and intelligence of the people. There are about 4,000 inhabitants in the town.

THE FAIRBANKS SCALES—GOVERNOR FAIRBANKS.

The life of St. Johnsbury is the Fairbanks Scale Manufactory, where are employed nearly 400 hands. It is situated on Sleeper's River, west of Main Street. With a small beginning this establishment has grown to mammoth proportions, and at the present time the Fairbanks Scales are used almost throughout the civilized world. Indeed, they have become so general that it is much easier to tell where they are *not* used than where they are. They are the invention of Mr. Thaddeus Fairbanks, the only surviving member of the original firm composed of three brothers, Erastus, Thaddeus and Joseph P. Fairbanks. Like most great inventions, this had its origin in almost a trifling circumstance, and has far surpassed even the intention and expectation of the inventor. In 1829 there was an excitement among the farmers in Vermont and New York concerning the cultivation of hemp. Erastus and Thaddeus Fairbanks were then engaged in manufacturing plows, stoves, etc., and a company in Lamoille County applied to them to build a hemp dressing machine. After completing it they built one for themselves, having determined to carry on the business of hemp dressing, in addition to that which they were already doing. When the farmers began to bring in their hemp, there was at once a want of some arrangement to determine its weight while upon the wagon, so as to save time and labor. The active brain of Thaddeus was called in requisition, and he finally succeeded in perfecting a rude contrivance for weighing the hemp, but containing essentially the principles now used in the scales. At that time transactions by weight were confined essentially to the use of the Even Balance, the Dearborn Beam, and the Roman Steelyards. Erastus, who, with his quick discerning eye, saw its importance, advised his brother to obtain a patent. Application was made, and a patent granted, bearing date of the year 1830. At this time it was not intended to apply the principle to scales only for weighing hemp, hay and other agricultural products; but there being a demand for them in other branches of business, their modifications have been multiplied until they now number 125—from the neat letter balance of a fractional ounce to the ponderous weighlock scale of 500 tons. This was the origin of the Fairbanks Scale, and, although the hemp excitement was of short duration, it produced one of the most important inventions to the business world that has ever been perfected. A patent was taken out by them in England,

and a Liverpool firm engaged in the manufacture of the scales, but subsequent improvements and great accuracy have made those of American manufacture the most popular, even in England and throughout all Europe.

Before the opening of the railroad to St. Johnsbury, all their freight was carried by teams to Portland and Burlington. Since the construction of the road, of which Governor Erastus Fairbanks was one of the principal movers, and for several years its President, the business has greatly increased. In 1865 their in-coming and out-going freight amounted to 5,228 tons. They use about twelve tons of iron daily in their foundry, and in a single year they consume about a million feet of lumber in packing boxes. Their freight bills amount annually to about $50,000, and their monthly pay-roll $15,000 to $17,000. Their business, for a single year, amounts to a million of dollars. The members of the firm are now Thaddeus, Horace and Franklin, the two latter sons of Erastus. Joseph P., the youngest brother, died in 1855, and Erastus in 1864. Charles Fairbanks, another son of the Governor's, who was for a time a member of the firm, retired from it several years ago, on account of ill health.

Ex-Governor Erastus Fairbanks, the senior partner, was a man of more than ordinary ability, although his advantages for an early education were quite limited. He was born at Brimfield, Mass., Oct. 28, 1792, and was a son of a poor farmer. His father being unable to give him an education, he attended only the district school, from which he "graduated" at the age of 17. In May, 1812, he left the parental home and went to St. Johnsbury to reside with Judge Ephraim Paddock, a maternal uncle, and in whose office it was his intention to study law. His eyes being too weak to admit of his pursuing a course of study, he abandoned the plan, and the two subsequent winters taught the district school on the plain in St. Johnsbury. In the summer of 1813 he was clerk in a store at Windsor. In

1814 he opened a store at Wheelock, two towns north of St. Johnsbury, in connection with Mr. Frederick Phelps, of St. Johnsbury, who furnished the goods—Mr. Fairbanks' only capital at this time being a horse and wagon which his father had given him, and which he subsequently sold to a hatter for $75, taking his pay in hats. He finally purchased the goods of Mr. Phelps for $800, giving a note for them, to be paid the following winter in ashes. In 1818 he sold his store in Wheelock and removed to East St. Johnsbury, where he opened another. In the autumn of that year he went to Barnet, where he remained in the mercantile business until 1824, when he removed to St. Johnsbury and commenced business with his brothers, who, with their parents, had removed from Brimfield to St. Johnsbury in 1815. They commenced the manufacture of stoves and plows. It was, however, with great difficulty that they found a sale for the plows, as the farmers considered cast iron as too brittle a material to successfully take the place of the rude ones made of wrought iron and wood. They were obliged to take them to the farmers, where they were left on trial. Finally these plows became quite popular and had a large sale.

Governor Fairbanks represented St. Johnsbury in the Legislature in 1836–7–8. In 1844 and 1848 he was chosen Presidential elector on the Clay and Taylor tickets. In 1852 he was elected Governor of Vermont, and in 1864 he died, lamented and loved by all who knew him.

The Messrs. Fairbanks have done much to beautify and adorn St. Johnsbury, and their residences are models of neatness and good taste.

ST. JOHNSBURY CENTER.

Three miles north of St. Johnsbury you come to St. Johnsbury Center. The Passumpsic River lies between the village and the railroad. Here is a paper mill and several manufacturing establishments. Above the depot is a pretty fall in the river.

LYNDON.

At Lyndon there is considerable business, and in the village is a large flouring mill. West of the depot is Minister Hill, receiving its name from the fact that it was donated to the first minister of the town. Before reaching the village you pass, on your right, another of those charming little waterfalls in the Passumpsic. The southern village is Lyndon Corners, and that seen further north is Lyndon Center.

WEST BURKE—LAKE WILLOUGHBY.

Passing Folsom's, where the stage route from Lyndon to Island Pond crosses the railroad, you come to West Burke, 16 miles from St. Johnsbury. Before reaching the station you pass Burke Mountain on your right, 2,000 feet high, and from which there is a magnificent view.

Here passengers leave the railroad for Lake Willoughby, six miles distant. Mr. David Trull, proprietor of the West Burke Hotel, near the station, will furnish the tourist conveyance to that place on the arrival of the trains. Willoughby is one of the most remarkable lakes in this country. It lies between two mountains, which rise abruptly from its shores to the hight of nearly 2,000 feet. The lake is from half a mile to two miles wide, and is six miles long. The water is so deep, in places, that no bottom has been found. Mr. Alonzo Bemis has erected a large hotel at the south end of the lake, where tourists can get good accommodations. It is a wild and romantic spot, and to the lover of nature it presents many attractions. Mr. Robert Van Arsdale, of Newark, N. J., has built a summer residence at the south end of the lake, and spends the summer months here. A good view of Willoughby Mountain, rising from the east shore of the lake, is had before you reach West Burke Station. For a fuller description of Lake Willoughby see page 210.

SOUTH BARTON—THE SUMMIT—JAY PEAK.

Leaving West Burke you soon reach the summit dividing the valleys of the Connecticut and St. Lawrence. You will notice the little rivulet as you proceed north, running southward, and presently you come to another running north into Crystal Lake, Barton River, Lake Memphremagog, St. Francis River, and thence into the St. Lawrence.

Jay Peak, 4,018 feet high, and one of the most lofty summits of the Green Mountain range, will be seen in the north-west. A carriage road has been constructed from the base to the summit, and it can be easily reached from Newport, 14 miles distant. All the villages near its base, and the mountain peaks for nearly a hundred miles around it, can be seen. See Page 236.

BARTON.

Continuing north you pass along upon the western shore of Crystal Lake, a small but beautiful sheet of water, and finally come to Barton, at the outlet of the lake, where there is excellent water power. The lake is about a mile wide and two miles long. Barton was named in honor of its first proprietor, Gen. William Barton, who will be remembered as the intrepid Lieut. Col. Barton of Revolutionary fame. When Lieutenant-Colonel of Rhode Island militia, he, with forty soldiers and a negro, surprised and captured the British Maj.-Gen. Proctor while in bed at his headquarters at Newport, R. I. The town was granted to Gen. Barton Oct. 28, 1781, under the name of Providence, as a reward for this daring exploit. In 1789 its name was changed to Barton.

RUNAWAY POND.

About seven miles south-west of Barton depot, in the town of Glover, is the old bed of Runaway Pond, through which the stage road from Barton to Montpelier now passes. It was formerly known as Long Pond, and was the source of the Lamoille River, which flows into Lake Champlain. It was about a mile in length, three-fourths of a mile wide, and 150 feet deep, with an outlet at the southern end. About 100 rods north of it was Mud Pond, the outlet of which flowed into Barton River, and thence north into Lake Memphremagog. In dry seasons Barton River being insufficient to supply the mills along its banks with water, is was determined to change the outlet of Long Pond by digging a channel from it to Mud Pond. In June, 1810, the inhabitants of Glover and adjacent towns assembled in great numbers for that purpose. It was commenced within a short distance of Long Pond and completed to Mud Pond. The small barrier at the head of the Pond was then removed, and insfead of following the channel the water descended into the sand beneath. The stream continued to increase and finally the whole body of water rushed with great force towards Mud Pond, carrying every thing before it. Passing through Mud Pond and into the Barton River, it gathered force as it went. A path thirty or forty rods wide and from twenty to sixty feet deep was hollowed out by the water. Trees, mills, and even rocks of many tons weight were carried away. So powerful was the current that after having gone seventeen miles, a rock weighing a hundred tons was moved several rods. It kept on its course until it finally passed into Lake Memphremagog. No lives were lost, but the workmen barely escaped. It seems that beneath the surface at the head of the pond was a bed of quick-sand and once opened there was nothing to prevent the water from wearing a channel deep enough to drain the whole pond. A similar occurrence took place in Switzerland in 1818.

BARTON LANDING.

Here are several stores and a saw mill. The village received its name from the fact that smuggled goods were brought up the river from Canada and landed here. A daily stage runs from this place to Irasburg, three and a half miles westward, and which is one of the prettiest villages in Northern Vermont. The Irasburg House, kept by Rufus B. Richardson, will accommodate about a hundred guests.

COVENTRY.

Leaving Barton Landing you soon reach Coventry Station. The village lies several miles west of the railroad. Continuing northward you come to a bay connected with Lake Memphremagog. Passing along its eastern bank you cross it on a spile bridge, and in a few minutes are landed in front of the Memphremagog House at

NEWPORT,

upon the southern end of Lake Memphremagog. For several years this was the terminus of the Connecticut and Passumpsic Rivers Railroad. In May, 1867, the road having been extended, was opened to

DERBY,

at the Canada line, five miles further north, where it connects with coaches for steamboat and the Grand Trunk Railway, passengers going through the same evening to Quebec.

LAKE MEMPHREMAGOG.

NEWPORT.

Distance from New York, 365 miles; Springfield, 229; White Mountains, 85; Montreal, 104; Quebec, 167.

Newport, not Newport down by the sea, but Newport, Vt., on the shore of Lake Memphremagog, close to the Canada line, where years gone by smuggling was counted among the virtues—it doesn't pay as well now—is a thriving, pleasant country village, destined to be a place of considerable importance in the future. The scenery around it is grand and inspiring, and the breezes from the lake are cool and refreshing.

South of the village, rising to the hight of two or three hundred feet is Prospect Hill, overlooking the lake and the country for miles around. From it is seen Owl's Head, Mt. Elephantis, Mt. Orford, Jay Peak and Willoughby Mountain. The view of the lake, with its islands and bays is remarkably fine, especially at sunset, when all nature is tinged with a golden hue.

The attractions around Newport are many. The tourist of course will first want to take a sail down the lake to Magog, 30 miles distant, with Capt. Handyside, on the new iron steamer Orford. It leaves at 7.30 A. M., and returns about 6 P. M. At Magog you can dine at the Parks House, visit Mount Orford, five miles from the village, the highest mountain in Lower Canada, and return the next day, stopping, if you choose, at the Mountain House, at the base of Owl's Head, 12 miles from Newport, on the return trip. From here you can ascend to the summit of Owl's Head, which is nearly 3,000 feet above the lake, and from which you can get a magnificent view—the valley of the St. Lawrence and Montreal conspicuous among the objects seen. Fourteen miles west of Newport is Jay Peak. This mountain is 4,018 feet high, and from it can be seen the whole range of the Green Mountains, including Mount Mansfield, Camel's Hump, and Killington Peak. The other objects of interest to be seen are Ascutney Mountain, near Windsor, White and Franconia Mountains, Kearsarge, Moose Hillock, Lake Champlain, the Adirondacks and Montreal.

About 25 miles south of Newport, and six from West Burke station, is Lake Willoughby, a most remarkable and charming place. East, about ten miles distant, is Stanstead Plain, in Canada. The country in that region is rich and fertile, and the drive is one of much interest.

MEMPHREMAGOG HOUSE.

The Memphremagog House, at Newport, is on the shore of Lake Memphremagog, at its southern end. The iron steamer,

Orford, Capt. D. W. Handyside, commander, will be seen lying at the dock, steam up, and ready for a trip to Magog, at the outlet of the lake. The hotel is pleasantly situated, and from its balconies there is a splendid view of the lake and Owl's Head. It will accommodate 300 guests. The landlords, Buck & Pindar, are well known to tourisis.

THE LAKE.

Over-shadowed by lofty mountain peaks which rise to the hight of nearly 3,000 feet, and bordered by dense forests and grassy slopes, in Northern Vermont and Lower Canada, is Lake Memphremagog—the Beautiful Water. In general appearance it resembles Lake George, in Northern New York. It is 30 miles long and two miles wide, and lies in a deep and narrow basin. About one third of the lake is in Vermont and the remainder is in Canada. There are no marshes or ponds of stagnant water along its banks, and its rock bound shores and wooded islands give it a picturesque appearance.

THE LAKE TROUT.

Fed by mountain streams, pure and cold, it is the home of the prince of the finny tribe, the speckled trout, which here attain unusual proportions. It is no uncommon thing to catch those that weigh from ten to fifteen pounds, while old fishermen, who are posted on favorite localities, will occasionally show you one weighing from 30 to 40. Ask him how it was done, and he will tell you, with a twinkle in his eye, that he "spit on his hook." The best fishing places are near the Mountain House, at the base of Owl's Head, where the water is the coldest and deepest. Mr. Jennings will furnish you with boats should you like to try your hand at it.

These trout are served, fresh from the lake, at the Memphremagog and Mountain Houses.

9

DOWN THE LAKE.

Refreshed with a night's sleep in this cool and bracing mountain region, the tourist will prepare for a trip on the steamer Orford, with Capt. Handyside, formerly of Lake Superior, where he has seen long service. He will point out to you many of the interesting places on the lake, now familiar to him.

The plank is in, and you have waved your last "good-bye" to friends on shore, and the little steamer, like a thing of life, is walking the water. To your right is Indian Point extending into the lake, and long since the abode of the red man. Directly ahead is Bear Mountain, and beyond, further up the lake, is Owl's Head, twelve miles from the Memphremagog House. It towers far above its neighbors, and its peculiarly rounded summit, riven seemingly into immense fisures, will attract your attention.

Leaving Newport you pass Adams' Bay on the west, and soon afterward Potton Bay on the same side of the lake, named after the township in which it is situated.

THE TWIN SISTERS.

Gliding smoothly over the water past Indian Point, you come in sight of the "Twin Sisters"—two beautiful islands covered with evergreens, and standing near the eastern shore. Looking between these islands, as the steamer comes abreast of them, you will notice the village of Stanstead, in Canada, ten miles distant.

PROVINCE ISLAND.

Straight ahead is Province Island, containing about 100 acres, most of which was formerly cultivated by a Frenchman, who, with his family, lived here in seclusion. Mr. Carlos Pierce, a

Boston dry goods merchant, and who has a summer residence and an extensive farm at Stanstead, is now its proprietor. Here he intends to raise blooded stock.

THE CANADA LINE.

The new steamer is making good headway, and you begin to feel the exhilarating influence of the pure air and the grand mountain and lake scenery. You are now approaching the Canada line and presently will pass into British waters. In Vermont the farms and farm houses indicate thrift and enterprise, but beyond, in Canada, the country is wild and poorly cultivated. Near the lake shore you will notice a clearing extending westward up the mountains. An iron post marks the dividing line, and it will be pointed out to you by Capt. Fogg. Eastward, extending across the southern end of Province Island, on the crest of the hill, you will observe a gap in the woods which shows the course of the line on that side of the lake. The steamer's bell is tolled and soon you will pass from the United States to the dominions of Queen Victoria.

TEA TABLE ISLAND.

East of Province Island, and close in shore, is Tea Table Island. It is a charming little spot, covered with cedar, and is just the place for a rural pic-nic.

CEDARVILLE.

Beyond, on the eastern shore, is Cedarville, in the town of Stanstead. A cedar grove comes down to the lake, and the place has a quiet, rural aspect. The bay extends north of the landing, and terminates in a sharp point.

FITCH'S BAY.

Steaming along you are soon off Fitch's Bay, which extends north-east about seven miles inland.

WHETSTONE ISLAND.

Near the entrance to Fitch's Bay is Whetstone Island, which is remarkable for a quarry of Novalculite or Magog oil stone, as it has been called. This quarry of Novalculite, which made capital whetstones, was worked some years ago by a company from Burke, but the British government finally put a stop to it.

MAGOON'S POINT.

On the east side of the lake you soon pass Magoon's Point, the grassy slope of which reaches down to the water. Excellent lime is burnt here, said to be the best in the country.

An unexplored cavern exists in this locality, and it has been believed that a large amount of treasure stolen from a Roman Catholic Cathedral was secreted there. Indeed, there are persons who claim to have *seen* two massive gold candlesticks which were found buried in the road near the cave.

ROUND ISLAND.

As the steamer nears the base of Owl's Head, you pass Round Island on your right. It is only half a mile from the Mountain House, and is frequently visited by tourists, who hire

Mr. Jennings' boats for the purpose. It is covered with cedars and its rounded form, and rock bound shore give it an interesting appearance.

THE MOUNTAIN HOUSE.

Heading in shore, the Orford glides swiftly up to the wharf of the Mountain House, which is situated at the base of Owl's Head, in a sheltered nook, is completely shut out from the outside world, except by lake communication. This is twelve miles from Newport, although you can hardly believe it, the time has passed so pleasantly. A. C. Jennings, a veteran hotel keeper, is proprietor of the Mountain House. North of the house is a little bay, and from it rises almost abruptly the mountain to a great hight. Tourists ascending Owl's Head leave the steamer at this place, but before viewing the scenery from so elevated a position you will continue the trip with Capt. Handyside.

The lake and the Islands in this vicinity present a picturesque appearance, and you never tire in beholding the view.

MINNOW ISLAND.

East of the Mountain House and nearer the eastern shore is Minnow Island, named from its diminutive size. It is a favorite fishing place in that region, and some of the famous lake trout are caught there.

SKINNER'S CAVE.

East of the Mountain House will be noticed Skinner's Island, close to the water. On the north-western side, near the end, is Skinner's Cave. It is an interesting locality, and is frequently visited by the guests of the Mountain House. It is about ten feet wide at the entrance, twelve to fourteen feet high, and extends into the rock a distance of some thirty feet, narrowing from the entrance until the two walls meet.

SKINNER'S CAVE.

There is a legend connected with it which Dix has told in verse, but before giving you his story we will state that it concerns one Uriah Skinner, the bold smuggler of Magog. In the war of 1812 smuggling was extensively carried on between persons residing in Canada and Vermont, and Uriah was the most successful of them all. He, however, was caught at last, as will be seen:

WHAT BECAME OF THE BOLD SMUGGLER OF MAGOG.

"Fancy a fellow; brawny and brown,
With very black hair that hangs shaggily down,
With whiskers remarkably bushy and black,
With fists which might give a most terrible thwack;
With very fierce eyes under dark heavy brows,
That flashed like a cat's when it springs on a mouse,

Or like coals in a cavern that gleam fiery red,
With a great Roman nose, so uncommonly red,
That whenever he washed it ('twas seldom) I wis,
The water would certainly bubble and hiss!
With a mouth, firm, compressed, and much prone to a sneer,
With a purple scar stretching from chin unto ear;
With a huge dagger stuck in the belt round his waist,
And five or six pistols beside it placed;
With a heavy cutlass not long nor pliant,
Such as little "Jack" used when he slaughtered the "Giant,"
With great heavy boots—and as heavy a purse,
With a tongue that scarce wagged but it uttered a curse!
Fierce as a tiger—as cruel as Nero—
Fancy all these, and you'll picture my hero;
Whose name, for fame has preserved the same,
Was Uriah Skinner, who'd always on hand
Plenty of articles contraband.

Of all the smugglers who plied on the lake,
Uriah Skinner was hardest to take;
The officers hunted him often, and yet
Uriah Skinner they never could get!
For *if* his boat they e'er chanced to have sight of,
He vanished, as 'twere, and was speedily right off,
Like the Flying Dutchman, he seemed to melt
Into mist; so that some who pursued him, felt
Inclined to believe he had something to do
With a certain dark gentleman—you know who!

The pitcher may often go to the well
Yet at last be broken. so it befell
In the case of Uriah—for that bold chap
Was caught at last like a rat in a trap!

* * * * *

Night on the lake, so clear and calm,
The night breeze sings in the pines its psalm;
Stars shine bright in the dark blue sky,

And the crescent moon sails in her glory on high:
Above and below, it is all serene,
Who, as he gazed on the peaceful scene
At that moment, would fancy that nine or ten
Very keen sighted, and well armed men,
Motionless, and still as the dead,
Were ambushed under the great Owl's Head?
And their ears were open as well as their eyes,
Listening and looking alike for a prize;
There they watched to catch the first glimpse or note
Of Skinner, expected that night in his boat.

"Look—don't you see!
That, Skinner must be!"
Oh, Skinner! bold smuggler! there's peril for thee!
For down to the shore with leap and bound,
The officers rush—as goes a blood-hound
On a fugitive's track when the scent is found!
The boat is manned, and they're off the next minute,
They see Skinner's boat, and Uriah S. in it;
Now the chase grows eager and hot,
And Skinner himself thinks so too, I wot,
For his boat speeds over the waters blue,
Swiftly as flieth an Indian's canoe,
And he has an Indian's craftiness too;
Now they near him—now they are on
His heels as it were—and now—HE IS GONE!

But where?
How they stare
And rave and swear!
And how—here, there, and everywhere,
The island they search—for they think, like the deer
Who leaves the forest and takes to the floods,
The smuggler has quitted the lake for the woods!
But all they find is the empty boat,
Which one of the officers pushes afloat:
The fruitless search they at length give o'er,

And Uriah Skinner was never seen more!
'Tis said, that one of the officers swore,
A strong brimstone odor pervaded the shore!
And another averred that he saw Skinner go
In the clutch of old Nick, to the regions below.

Nearly six years had passed away,
When a fisherman out in a storm one day,
Was very near making an awful plunge
To become a meal for the pickerel or longe;
But through the mist, gazing eager-eyed,
In the side of an island, a cave he spied,
And in less than a minute, was safe inside.

Very soon passed the storm, and then,
Ere he prepared to go fishing again,
He looked above, beneath, and around,
And what do you think the fisherman found?
Neither a golden nor a silver prize,
But a skull with sockets where once were eyes;
Also some bones of arms and thighs,
And a vertebral column of giant size:
How they got there, he could't devise,
For he'd only been used to common place graves,
And knew nought of "organic remains" in caves;
On matters like *those*, his wits were dull,
So he dropped the subject as well as the skull.

'Tis needless to say
In this later day,
'Twas the smuggler's bones in the cave, that lay:
All I've to add is—the bones in a grave
Were placed, and the cavern was called 'SKINNER'S CAVE.'"

LONG ISLAND—BALANCE ROCK.

North of Skinner's Cave is Long Island. It is about a mile and a half long, and half a mile wide. It has a bold and rocky

BALANCE ROCK.

shore, and near its northern end, on the western side, are some perpendicular rocks, named the Palisades.

On the southern shore of the island is the famous Balance Rock, so frequently visited by tourists. Capt. H. will point it out to you, but you would do well to row over to it in a skiff while at the Mountain House. It is a huge granite rock of many tons weight, resting upon another close to the water's edge and poised upon a single point, as seen in the illustration. How it got into its present position is a matter of speculation.

MOLSON'S ISLAND.

Further north is Molson's Island, on the eastern side of the lake. It is owned by Mr. Molson, a Montreal broker, whose summer residence will be noticed eastward upon the hillside, from which there is indeed a picturesque view.

THE SCENERY—CANADIAN RESIDENCES.

At this point there is some of the best scenery on the lake. From the west shore, Owl's Head rises abruptly to a great hight and its cone-like shape will attract your attention. Further north is Mount Elephantis, and in the distance, between the two mountains is Jay Peak.

The eastern shore which rises to the hight of several hundred feet above the lake, is adorned with the summer residences of the wealthy business men of Montreal. Among them are Judge Day's, Mr. Molson's and Mr. Chapman's.

MOUNT ELEPHANTIS.

You are now past Mount Elephantis or Sugar Loaf, as it is sometimes called. The upper point bears resemblance to an elephant's head and back. As you proceed north, you will observe that this mountain is in the shape of a horse shoe. Within the curve is some excellent farming lands, situated upon an elevated plain above the lake. Capt. Fogg has given this locality the name of "Sebastopol," from its impregnable position.

CONCERT POND.

West of the most elevated point of Mount Elephantis, lying between that and Ridge Mountain, is Concert Pond. It is several hundred feet above Lake Memphremagog, and abounds in brook trout. It is a favorite fishing place for tourists. The Pond is two miles long and half a mile wide, and the view of it from Mount Elephantis is exceedingly beautiful.

GEORGEVILLE.

Upon the eastern shore of the lake, about twenty miles from Newport, and seven and a half from the Mountain House, is Georgeville. It contains two hotels and several stores, and is the most important place along the lake. Capt. Fogg resides here, and in the bay south of the village the Mountain Maid was built.

KNOWLTON'S LANDING.

At Georgeville Capt. Fogg takes in the mail and heads towards Knowlton's Landing, on the west side of the lake. This is the crossing place for the inhabitants in the eastern townships when going to Montreal. For nearly thirty years Capt. Fogg has carried the mail across the lake at this place, commencing first with a canoe. The lake is three miles wide, and will average 300 feet in depth, from one shore to the other. Stages run regularly from Knowlton's to Waterloo, 20 miles distant, where they connect with the Stanstead, Shefford and Chambly Railroad, for St. John's and Montreal.

Sergeant's Bay extends some five miles inland, northeast from Knowlton's.

GIBRALTAR POINT.

Leaving Knowlton's you pass Gibraltar Point on your left. The rocks rise perpendicularly from the lake, presenting a magnificent appearance. On the summit, near the southern point, is the boundary corner of four towns—Potten, Bolton, Stanstead and Magog.

LORD'S ISLAND.

Turning Gibraltar Point and coming into the lake again, you get an extensive view. In the distance you will notice

Lord's Island, the last one of any importance before reaching Magog.

MOUNT ORFORD.

For some time, in looking north your eye has rested upon an elevation, peering above the distant hills. As you approach the northern end of the lake its elevated summit is more distinctly seen. This is Mount Orford, 3,300 feet high, and the most extensive mountain in Lower Canada. It is five miles from Magog, and a carriage road has been constructed to its summit.

MAGOG.

The whistle of the Mountain Maid is blown and you will notice that she is heading in shore. Ahead is the village of Magog, at the outlet of the lake. Coming up to the wharf, the steamer is made fast and you go on shore. A few minutes walk will take you to the Parks House, kept in *true Canadian style.* The village is somewhat antidiluvian in appearance and you wonder if some of the early settlers did not come over in the ark. Here the water in the outlet makes a great descent, furnishing excellent power for the many saw mills. Beyond the town, towards the base of Mount Orford is a wide belt of forest, and for many miles around there is an unlimited supply of the best of timber, principally spruce.

A stage runs from Magog to Sherbrook, on arrival of the steamer, 16 miles distant, where the tourist can proceed by the Grand Trunk Railway to Quebec or to Montreal. The distance from Sherbrook to Quebec is 121 miles. Another stage runs to Waterloo, 21 miles distant, where you can connect with the Stanstead, Shefford & Chambly Railroad. By this route to Montreal it is 84 miles.

THE RETURN TRIP.

Having spent a few hours at Magog, the steamer's whistle is blown and you go on board to make the return trip. The view up the lake, towards the south is exceedingly beautiful. In the dim distance, lying between Owl's Head and Mount Elephantis, is Jay Peak, and the Green Mountain range. The Mountain Maid steams on through the water, making here and there an occasional stop until you finally reach the Mountain House. Leaving the steamer to spend the night with Mr. Jennings, you wave a "good-bye" to Capt. H., and pass up the steps to the hotel.

OWL'S HEAD AS SEEN FROM THE NORTH.

OWL'S HEAD AS SEEN FROM THE NORTH.

Up with the sun, after a night's sleep, you step out upon the high point of rocks south of the house to enjoy the view. Here you watch sunlight and shadow until summoned to breakfast. The morning meal over, you commence to fit out for a trip to the summit of Owl's Head. Staff in hand you leave the hotel. For a little way the course is tolerably level, but after about ten minutes walking, the ascent commences in earnest. On either side the path is bounded by woods, where the wild bird sings and the squirrel gambols undisturbed. Before long, you perceive before and above you, a singular rock of very large size, projecting over the path from the right hand side. This is called Shelter Rock; a name not altogether inappropriate, as a large party might find refuge from a shower beneath its overhanging portion. Not far beyond "Shelter," is High Rock—a huge mass of stone crowned with plumy ferns, and half clad with the greenest moss. A little brook of the purest water is soon reached—it is this stream which supplies the fish pond below. The rivulet crossed, after a rather steep "grade," you hear the tinkle of cow-bells, and suddenly enter a large open space, almost circular in shape and nearly level. After the brisk climbing, the pathway through the Old Field, as it is termed, is a pleasant change enough. You may, if you choose, loiter and pick berries and wild flowers, which are very abundant. A maple grove is next passed, and then you arrive at a circular sort of basin named Fern Hollow. Still ascending, you reach Fern Rock, where a botanist might long luxuriate. The way now becomes pretty steep, but if you halt occasionally to recover breath, you may use your eyes as well as rest your lungs, for there are plenty of objects worthy attention. For here is Birch Rock. On the steep hill-side above you are two large, oblong granite rocks—their ends being placed so close together that there does not appear room to place a finger's point between them. Yet in that fissure is sufficient earth to nourish a fine birch tree, which seems to rise from, and grow out of the lower stone. Onward and upward we go, until we are brought to a stand at the Toll-Gate, where it is by no means an unusual thing to find a toll-keeper also. This Toll-Gate is formed by two large rocks, from whose upper surface trees spring upwards, and between which, there is just room for one very stout, or two very slim persons to walk abreast. Hoops have no chance here, unless the circles are changed into ovals, or elipses. Occasionally a lady has been compelled to retire to a leafy bower, hard by, called Crinoline Chamber, and divest herself of all "hindrances," for a Camel may as well attempt to go through the eye of a needle as a fashionably dressed lady to get through the Toll-Gate. This perilous "pass" having been accomplished, the next object of attraction is Chair Rock, from whose summit the first view of the lake during the ascent, is obtained.

Passing along you come to Breakneck Stairs. Next come Jennings' and Winding Staircase, and then Refreshment Hollow, where your little tin can will be found useful in conveying water from the spring to your lips. Somewhat refreshed, you press forward and soon stand on the summit of Owl's Head—nearly 3,000 feet above the waters of Memphremagog.

The prospect is magnificent beyond description. Looking south you see Clyde, Barton and Black Rivers, Newport, all the islands on the lake, and the lake itself from end to end. To the north, Durham's Point, Dewey's Point, Knowlton Bay, the Outlet, Orford Mountain, and countless other objects. To the east, Seymour Lake, Stanstead Plain, Rock Island, Salem Pond, Charleston Pond, Derby Center, Derby Line, Willoughby Lake, White Mountains, Little Magog, Massawippee Lake, Georgeville, &c. To the west, the continuation of the Green Mountain Range. To the north-west, the Sugar Loaf and Ridge Mountain, Broome Lake and North and South Troy. In a clear day Montreal can be distinctly seen in the north-west.

The summit itself, as might be expected from its appearance from below, is all split up or riven into gorges and ravines, from which four distinct peaks ascend. In one of these ravines is the Freemason's Lodge, so named from the fact that the Golden Rule Lodge of Stanstead, hold a lodge there once a year, on the 24th of June. It is a spot well calculated for exercising the mysteries of the craft. On a triangular rock are painted the compass and square, and below that masonic emblem, other inscriptions.

THE NEW IRON STEAMER ORFORD.

Montreal and Boston capitalists purchased in 1867, the steamer Mountain Maid, so long commanded by Capt. Fogg, and the interests of the company. The Lake Memphremagog Steam Navigation Company, with Mr. Allen, of Montreal, as President, was then organized. The hull of an iron steamer, built on the Clyde at Glasgow, Scotland, was purchased and taken to Magog, where it was completed and placed upon the Lake. The steamer is 170 feet long, 45 wide on main deck, and is divided into four water-tight compartments. It has two boilers and a beam engine, (36-inch cylinder) that were made at Montreal. It is neatly and conveniently fitted up, with dining saloon and ladies' cabin, and everything that is possible has been done to make it a first-class pleasure boat. It has been named the "Orford," and is commanded by Capt. Wm. D. Handyside, late of Lake Superior, with George C. Merrill, formerly of the Mountain Maid, as Purser. The speed of the steamer is 17 miles per hour, and will make close connections with stages and trains for Montreal, Quebec, and Lake Champlain.

WILLOUGHBY LAKE.

WHERE SITUATED—GENERAL APPEARANCE.

In Northern Vermont, in the town of Westmore, little more than 20 miles from the Canada line and 350 from New York, is Willoughby Lake, bordering which there is some of the most wonderful and sublime scenery found in New England. The Lake is six miles long, the northern end curving a little to the east, and from half a mile to two miles wide. Its depth is so great that no reliable measurement of it has been made. Between the mountains, in the narrowest place, where the water is the deepest, it has been sounded to the depth of 600 feet, and no bottom was found.

On either side rises a huge mountain to more than 2,000 feet —Mount Willoughby, on the east side, according to a barometrical measurement made in 1860 by the Vermont State Geologist, to 2,638 feet above the lake and 3,800 feet above the sea.

SINGULAR APPEARANCE OF MOUNT WILLOUGHBY FROM THE CARRIAGE ROAD.

A carriage road was constructed several years ago along the eastern shore of the lake, from which you get a better view of the mighty grandeur of Mount Willoughby than from any other point near its base. For nearly two miles a perpendicular wall of granite rock, intermingled with silicious limestone, rises to the hight of 600 feet, while below, between it and the lake, the side of the mountain for more than a thousand feet in hight, which is covered with huge rocks, is little less than perpendicular.

WILLOUGHBY LAKE.

A VIEW FROM THE SUMMIT.

Leaving the hotel just south of the lake, you enter the woods, and after a walk of two miles through the forest of maple, beech and spruce, passing two springs of the purest and coldest of water, you reach the summit very little fatigued. From here you get a magnificent view. East are the Franconia and White Mountains—the summit houses of Mount Washington being easily seen with a glass in a clear day. West you have before you the entire range of the Green Mountains, among which can be seen the summits of Killington Peak, Camel's Hump, Mount Mansfield and Jay Peak. Between these two great mountain ranges, and within your vision, are ponds, wide forests, cultivated fields, farm houses and villages, forming a magnificent scene.

Having beheld the distant view, you walk further to the west and approach close to the mighty precipice, where you look down upon the lake, 2,500 feet below. At first your nerves may betray signs of weakness, but shortly overcoming all fear you are absorbed in the grandeur of the scene. The purity and transparency of the water of the lake is here observed. Along its shores for several miles, every rock and sunken log, and almost the little fishes, can be seen. From here you have a view of the entire length of the lake, the eastern shore of which seems almost in a straight line. Mount Hor, on the west side, and Mount Willoughby on the east, have the appearance of once having been united, and you wonder what mighty agency in years long past were employed to rend them asunder. Some geologists are of the opinion that during the drift period a northern current rushed through here and wore away the calcareous rock, which had become partially decomposed. However this deep and narrow gorge was formed, it is a place of rare interest to the student of nature and the lover of the sublime.

The tourist will now descend to the valley below, well paid for the time it has taken to ascend the summit.

THE WILLOUGHBY LAKE HOUSE.

To reach this most charming place, the tourist will leave the cars at West Burke, 77 miles from White River Junction, and 28 miles south of Lake Memphremagog. At the depot you will find a carriage in readiness to take you to the Lake House, six miles distant. The Hotel is kept by Mr. Alonzo Bemis, and is situated in a delightful place, south of the lake, which it overlooks. There is always a good breeze through the valley, and even in the warmest of weather you will find this a cool and delightful resort. The Hotel will accommodate about a hundred guests, and under the management of Mr. Bemis it has become widely known. Horses and carriages are kept for guests who may wish to visit the neighboring places of interest, and on the lake you will find row-boats for those who may desire to fish for lake trout, or sail along the shores. There is also good trout fishing in the streams in the immediate vicinity of the Hotel.

Excepting the farm-house and other buildings connected with the Hotel, and the summer residence owned by Mr. Robert Van Arsdale of Newark, N. J., there are no other buildings in the vicinity. The quietness of the place and the beautiful scenery, are in refreshing contrast with the stirring, bustling scenes of city life which the tourist has just left behind.

The accompanying engraving of the lake and mountains is from a photograph by Mr. B. F. Gage, of St. Johnsbury, and it will give the tourist a good idea of the place, but no picture can give you a correct representation of its sublimity and grandeur.

Looking down the lake towards the north from the Hotel, you will observe the summit of Owl's Head in Canada, thirty miles distant.

The Hotel is supplied with pure, cold spring water, brought in pipes from the hillside. From the Hotel it runs north into the lake, and thence into Lake Memphremagog and the St. Lawrence. About twenty rods in rear of the Hotel is a little lakelet, which discharges into a small stream running south into the Passumpsic and thence into the Connecticut. It is situated so near the water-shed between Long Island Sound and the St. Lawrence, that a few hours work would change its outlet from the Connecticut to the St. Lawrence.

THE WALKS AND DRIVES.

The walks and drives around Willoughby are numerous and pleasant. That down the lake shore, under the frowning walls of Mount Willoughby will first claim your attention. You enter the forest which overhangs the road and pass along under the grateful shade. Presently you come to a huge granite rock, at least twelve feet high, which at some time came from the mountain above. Passing along you come to another granite rock lying in the lake. You climb down the bank and walk out upon it, and from which you have a magnificent view. Don't be alarmed—but below you is the "Devil's Den." The rock contains a cavern, and in it the "old fellow" is supposed to have held court in times past. Above you, at the foot of the perpendicular wall, is the "Flower Garden," where many rare plants are found. It is visited by botanists who have discovered varieties of plants found in no other place north of southern Pennsylvania. Continuing north you come to the "Silver Cascade," where a little stream leaps down the rocks from the mountain. A short distance north is "Point of Rocks," where the mountain approaches close to the lake, and once filled the road at this place.

The scenery down the entire length of the lake is grand and beautiful, although not so rugged as it is before reaching "Point of Rocks." On the opposite side is Mount Hor, Sugar Loaf and Bear Mountain, covered with a maple and spruce forest.

The distances from the hotel to other places of interest are: Island Pond, where there is a good hotel, 20 miles; Newport by team, 20; Derby Line, 22; Stanstead Plain, 23; St. Johnsbury, 22; Barton, 11; West Charleston, 10; Burke Mountain, 10; West Burke, 6; Newark, 6.

In going to Barton, about a mile and a half east of the depot, you come to the "Flume." The stream from May's Pond passes through it, descending into Crystal Lake. In the solid granite rock is a passage way for the water 140 feet long, 10 feet wide, and from 20 to 30 feet in depth. The walls rise almost perpendicularly, and are as smooth as if cut by the hand of man. Some utilitarian has constructed a saw-mill over it and turned it to practical account, thus greatly marring its beauty. It is, however, in its present state well worth visiting.

Plunket Falls, in Clyde River, in Charleston, twelve miles from Willoughby Lake House, are exceedingly beautiful. Here the river makes a descent of a hundred feet in half a mile, and at one point below the saw-mill it makes almost a perpendicular fall of thirty feet.

Another favorite ride from the hotel is to Newark Hill, from which can be seen the White and Green Mountain ranges.

There are other drives in this vicinity none the less interesting than these, and the tourist will find Willoughby one of the most charming and home-like resorts found in this interesting region. Should he stop only for a single day he will have no occasion to regret the visit.

MOUNT HOLYOKE.

WHERE SITUATED.

Mount Holyoke, which is situated two miles from Northampton, Mass., is part of a mountain ridge of greenstone, commencing with West Rock, near New Haven, and extending northerly across the State of Connecticut, and finally terminating in Belchertown, Mass. It is on the east side of the Connecticut River, and its summit forms the boundary line between the towns of Hadley and South Hadley. Its hight is 1,175 feet above the sea, and about 1,000 above the river.

THE VIEW.

It is probable that there is no other mountain of the same hight in this country, from which the view is so extensive and beautiful. Thousands visit it annually and are enraptured with the magnificent landscape spread before them. N. P. Willis has written enthusiastically of it, and "in point of cultivation and fertile beauty," he truly remarks, "it is probably the richest in America." The late Edward Hitchcock, formerly President of Amherst College, in his work on the Geology of Massachusetts says:

"In the view from Mount Holyoke we have the Grand and the Beautiful united, the latter, however, greatly predominating. The observer finds himself lifted up nearly a thousand feet from the midst of a plain, which northerly and southerly, can scarcely be less than one hundred and fifty miles; and so comparatively narrow is the naked rock on which he stands, that he wonders why the winds and storms of centuries have not broken it down. He soon, however, forgets the mountain beneath him, in the absorbing beauties before him; for his eye rests on a rich alluvial valley, geometrically diversified in the summer with grass, corn, grain and whatever else laborious industry has there reared. Mount Tom is higher than Holyoke, yet most of the interesting group of objects around the base of Holyoke, is wanting around that of Tom. Hence Tom is not much frequented, while during the summer months Holyoke is a place of great resort. The "Prospect House" is situated, undoubtedly, on the most commanding spot on the mountain."

MOUNTS HOLYOKE AND TOM FROM THE NORTH-EAST.

The above view shows Mounts Holyoke and Tom, as seen from the north-east—Holyoke on the left and Tom on the right.

WHAT CAN BE SEEN FROM THE SUMMIT.

The view from Mount Holyoke extends more than a hundred miles up and down the valley of the Connecticut, and mountains in four States can be seen, viz: Monadnock, N. H., Green, Vt., East and West Rock, New Haven, Conn., Greylock, Wachusett, Sugar Loaf, Norwottuck, Toby, Tom, and Nonotuck, Mass.

Thirty-eight towns and villages can be seen with the aid of the telescope, nearly all of which are visible to the naked eye, thirty-one in Massachusetts, and seven in Connecticut, as follows:—Northampton, Haydenville, Williamsburgh, Goshen, Hadley, Hatfield, Whately, South Deerfield, Greenfield, Shelburne, Sunderland, North Hadley, North Amherst, Amherst, Pelham, Belchertown, Granby, South Hadley, Wilbraham, North Wilbraham, Springfield, Chicopee, Holyoke, Longmeadow, West Springfield, Agawam, Southampton, Easthampton, Montgomery, Blanford, Ludlow, in Massachusetts; Thompsonville, Windsor, East Windsor, Enfield, Hartford, Suffield and Somers, in Connecticut.

Among the objects of special interest that can be seen are: State Lunatic Hospital and Round Hill, at Northampton; Williston Seminary, Easthampton; Amherst College and Massachusetts State Agricultural College, Amherst; Mount Holyoke Female Seminary, South Hadley; Wesleyan Academy, Wilbraham; United States Armory, at Springfield; Manufacturing Town of Holyoke; Old Hadley, with her beautiful streets; Ox-Bow Island; Shepherd's Island in the Connecticut River &c.

MOUNT HOLYOKE FROM SOUTH-WEST.

Looking at Mount Holyoke from a point north of Smith's Ferry, you have the view, sketched by the artist, as shown in the above illustration.

WHO NAMED IT.

Mount Holyoke was named in 1654 after Capt. Elizur Holyoke, one of the first proprietors of Northampton, and it is stated that Mount Tom, on the opposite (west) side of the Connecticut River, received its name from one Rowland Thomas. There are various traditions concerning this matter, but the following, as stated by Dr. Holland in his History of Western Massachusetts, is the most probable, as well as quite poetical: "A company of the first settlers of Springfield went northward to explore the country. The party headed by Elizur Holyoke went up on the east side of the river, and another headed by Rowland Thomas went up on the west side. The parties arriving abreast, at the narrow place in the river below Hockanum, at what is now called Rock Ferry, Holyoke and Thomas held a conversation with one another across the river, and each, then and there, gave his name to the mountain at whose feet he stood. The name of Holyoke remains uncorrupted and without abbreviation, while Mount Thomas has been curtailed to simple and homely 'Tom.'"

THE DIFFICULTY OF VISITING MOUNT HOLYOKE IN FORMER DAYS.

It is probable that Mount Holyoke has been frequently visited since the first settlement of Northampton, more than two hundred years ago, but its summit, on which the Prospect House is situated, and the most sightly place on the mountain, has not been easy of access until within the last eight or ten years. A number of old people have visited the Prospect House within a few years, who used to make pilgrimages to the spot on which the house now stands, upwards of three-quarters of a century ago, when there was scarcely a foot-path to that locality. In those days and at subsequent periods, it was customary for parties who visited the mountain, to take with them an ample supply of provisions for an all-day trip. A wood-road led up the mountain, near the place where the north road was located; but instead of running southerly to where the stable now stands, it bore off easterly to the gorge in the mountain east of the Prospect House, known then as "Taylor's Notch," from which place a foot path led to the summit.

THE FIRST HOUSE AND HOW IT WAS BUILT.

The mountain becoming so much of a place of resort, it was deemed desirable to have a house erected on the summit, where shelter and refreshments could be provided when needed. In the early part of 1821, a public meeting was held in Northampton for the purpose of devising a plan for the erection of a suitable building. A committee of five was appointed to solicit subscriptions, of whom Samuel F. Lyman, Nathaniel Fowle, Robert H. Thayer, were members. Mr. Lyman, who was a law student in Northampton at that time, now Judge of Probate, was the leading spirit in the enterprise. He was appointed chairman of the committee, and succeeded in procuring subscriptions in materials to the amount of $120, besides a considerable amount in labor. The 17th day of June, the anniversary of the Battle of Bunker Hill, was the time fixed to erect the building. The church bells in Northampton and Hadley were rung at six o'clock in the morning, and a large number of people in those towns, turned out and started mountainward with tools, lumber and provisions. Before noon there were nearly three hundred people present on the mountain, to assist in the erection of the house. The lumber was taken up the wood-road to Taylor's Notch, and thence carried by hand to the summit. The timber for the frame of the building was cut on the mountain, and the work was laid out and conducted by Thomas Pratt and Ebenezer Eaton, who were the "boss" carpenters. The building was fifteen by twenty-two feet, and was covered with rough boards.

A NIGHT ON THE MOUNTAIN.

The house not being completed, quite a large number of the young men, some of whom had volunteered in the enterprise, more for the sake of having a "jolly time" than from any particular love of mountain scenery, or the benefit the house would be to the public, remained on the mountain over night, sleeping in buffalo robes carried there for that purpose. As water was scarce and liquor abundant, some of the "manifestations" of that night would bear the interpretation that the party had consumed during the day a little water with a good deal of brandy in it. Among those who remained on the mountain during the night, were Samuel F. Lyman, Nathaniel Fowle, Robert H. Thayer, Josiah Dickinson, Thaddeus Russell and William Tower—all of Northampton.

THE HOUSE COMPLETED—ORATION BY HON. ELIJAH H. MILLS.

The building was completed on Saturday, the following day after it was commenced. Then came the dedication. A large number of people from the adjoining towns participated, including the venerable Dr. Woodbridge, of Hadley. An eloquent oration was delivered by Elijah H. Mills, of Northampton, in which he portrayed the beauties of mountain scenery described in sacred and profane history, and then instituted a comparison with the grandeur of Holyoke. The address produced a great sensation, and a Hadley man, who was one of Dr. Woodbridge's parishioners, declared quite emphatically that there was a good deal more Bible in it than in any of the Doctor's sermons.

This being before the days of temperance societies, there were no pledges to break, and as they had drawn inspiration from something more powerful than romantic scenery and eloquent words, all were jubilant in the highest degree over what had been accomplished, and it is presumable that a more "jolly" party has never left the mountain since, than did on that Saturday. Among those present, either on the first or last day, including those previously mentioned, were Samuel F. Lyman, Nathaniel Fowle, Robert H. Thayer, Elijah H. Mills, Dr. David Hunt, Josiah Dickinson, Ansel Wright, Sylvester Bridgman, Thomas Pratt, Thaddeus Russell, Ebenezer Eaton, William Tower, George Parsons, all of Northampton, and Dr. Woodbridge, and Cotton White, of Hadley, besides many others from those and neighboring towns. It is a memorable fact that this was the first house built on any mountain in New England.

THE HOUSE LEASED.

During that summer the house was visited by a very large number of people, and from the time the house was built to the first of October, upwards of 6,000 names were entered in the register kept on the mountain for that purpose. In a single day that season there were visitors at the Mountain House who recorded their names from no less than twenty-three towns. Willis Pease, of Florence, then residing at the foot of the mountain, was the first person who kept refreshments in the new house. Mr. Pease states that an agreement was made with him in August to lease the house for three years by paying $21, the amount then due on the house, for material, &c. He was to meet the persons who then had charge of it at the Warner House on the following morning, when he was to pay over the money and take the lease. But when the individuals who had made the verbal agreement to lease the house to Mr. Pease were going home from the mountain, they stopped at the hotel kept by Zadok Lyman, at Hockanum, and mentioned to Mr. Lyman that Mr. Pease was to take the lease of the house. He objected, on the ground that it would injure his hotel, and urged them to lease the house to him. They finally consented to, and gave him the lease. The next day Mr. Pease went to Northampton, but to find that he was too late.

THE PREMISES SOLD AND A NEW HOUSE BUILT.

The Mountain House stood on land owned by Thomas Moody, of Granby, and Mr. Pease having determined to get possession of it, purchased nine acres of land, including that part on which the house stood, for which he gave twenty-seven dollars. The purchase was made on the 28th day of August. The deed states "that it was common and undivided land, in South Hadley, situated in Thomas Hovey's second choice in the two thousand acre division, conveyed to Willis Pease by Thomas Moody." Mr. Pease, after he had purchased the land, finding that he was unable to get possession of the house without resorting to legal measures, concluded to build another, and about thanksgiving time went to Erving's Grant, now the town of Erving, and bargained for the necessary lumber. During the winter he hauled it home, and in March following took it to the top of the mountain and erected a house, twenty-four by twenty-eight feet, three rods north-east of the one previously built. There were two rooms on the south side of the building that were plastered and papered. It was completed and opened on the 5th of September, 1822. Mr. Pease occupied the house he erected that and the following year, for the sale of refreshments, when he sold,

February 21st, 1824, to Joel W. Smith, of Hadley, for $600. The original house was kept till that time by Mr. Smith and Samuel W. Lyman, son of Zadok Lyman, and they were the first ones to make a foot-path up the mountain on the west side. Mr. Smith moved the house built by Mr. Pease close to the one previously occupied by himself and Mr. Lyman, but in consequence of the insecurity of the foundation it finally fell down. February 29th, 1826, Mr. Smith sold to Isaac C. Bates, Thomas Shepherd, Isaac Damon, of Northampton, and Joseph Strong, of South Hadley, for $1,500. November 1st, 1828, Thomas Shepherd sold his fourth to William Swan, and in consequence of financial difficulties, Isaac Damon's interest passed into the hands of Eliphalet Williams, J. D. Whitney, and Lewis Strong, on the 10th of the same month. On the 9th of May, 1832, Daniel Stebbins purchased the fourth held by Mr. Williams, Mr. Whitney and Mr. Strong. August 4th, 1836, William Swan sold the fourth held by him to Daniel Stebbins, and on the 15th of the following November, Thomas Shepherd sold his interest to Daniel Stebbins. After the death of Isaac C. Bates, his widow, on the 17th of September, 1847, sold the fourth purchased by her husband to Daniel Stebbins. The original nine acres purchased by Willis Pease were now owned by Dr. Stebbins, who kept it till 1849, when it passed into the hands of John W. French and William P. Cooper.

A BOOK-BINDER AND PRINTER ENGAGE IN THE "HOTEL" BUSINESS.

That some one would ultimately build a house as a permanent establishment for the entertainment and accommodation of pleasure-seekers, was an idea long entertained by Mr. French; but that he should become the proprietor of it was not contemplated by him, and the ownership of it is the result of unforeseen and accidental circumstances. For some time he had been at work at his usual vocation—book-binding—in the eastern part of the

10*

state; but returning home in the spring of 1849, out of employment, in company with Mr. Cooper, a printer friend, the two happened to meet Dr. Stebbins in the street in Northampton. The Doctor, who had always taken much interest in the view from Mount Holyoke and the prosperity of the Mountain House, proposed to Mr. French that he should hire it. It appearing to be a feasible project, Mr. French declared his willingness to accede to Dr. Stebbins' request; but Mr. Cooper was adverse to the enterprise. He was, however, induced to visit the mountain, having never been there. When about half way up the mountain he was blindfolded and led to the summit by Mr. French. The summit reached, the covering was removed from his eyes, and such a prospect was there spread before him as he had little thought of. He was so pleased that he consented to enter into a business partnership with Mr. French, and they immediately made arrangements to occupy the premises. They found the house in a dilapidated condition, and then in possession of David Morse, who had leased it. His "refreshments" consisted of dried herrings, crackers, cigars, lemons, water, and a "toddy-stick." His stock in trade was purchased for ten dollars, and in about two weeks, after visiting the eastern part of the state, they returned and commenced to repair the house.

A NEW ROAD OPENED AND THE OLD ONE IMPROVED.

The road, which had only been a rough foot-path, was made wider and greatly improved, rendering the summit much easier of access. The number of visitors to the mountain rapidly increased, in consequence of the improved facilities for getting to and from it, and as there was no open road, except that over private land, the county commissioners were petitioned to lay out a public highway from Hockanum to within one-eighth of a mile or more of the summit. A bitter contest ensued, and a writer in one of the papers said that a certain portion of the opponents could see no use in any road, except that which was made to cart broom-corn and tobacco over. The commissioners, however, viewed the road and located it, and in 1850 it was built. A somewhat laughable incident occurred at the time the commissioners viewed the locality. An opponent, who was with the commissioners, set forth his reasons for not having the road located; and among others, said that the mountain was sometimes visited on Sunday, and the road ought not to be built. One of the commissioners turned to Deacon Cummings, of Ware, who was one of the commissioners at that time, and said, "Deacon, I am of the same opinion too. There's the town of Holyoke; it's a terrible wicked place, and I think all the roads leading to it ought to be discontinued." The deacon smiled complacently and proceeded with the work, while the aforesaid opponent thereafter held his peace.

THE PROSPECT HOUSE.—THE OLD RAILWAY.

On the summit of Mount Holyoke is a large and commodious hotel, 55 by 70 feet, known as the Prospect House, arranged with special reference to viewing the scenery around the mountain. Its history is told in the following paragraph:

Mr. Cooper sold his interest to Mr. French in the early part of 1851, and on the 25th of the following February, Edward H. Graves, of Northampton, son of Elisha Graves, became a joint owner with Mr. French. The old house being insufficient to meet the wants of visitors, it was decided to build a new one. The necessary lumber was provided, and on the 22d day of May, 1851, the frame was erected. Its size was 25 by 30 feet, two stories high, with an observatory in the center. It was located just north of the old one, which stood till June 5th, when it was demolished. The new house was completed and dedicated July 5th, and has since been known as the Prospect House.

The demand for sleeping accommodations and for permanent board during the summer season rendered it necessary to enlarge the Prospect House to meet the demand of pleasure-seekers, and in 1861 an addition, two stories high, was constructed, making the present size of the house 55 by 70 feet. There are sleeping accommodations for 20 or 30 persons, besides a hall in the second story, 20 by 55, that is well adapted for cotillion parties or prospect purposes. The first floor, which is occupied mainly as a prospect room, is remarkably pleasant, and well suited to the wants of visitors.

THE SEVERAL PROPRIETORS OF THE OLD MOUNTAIN HOUSE.

Among those who have sold refreshments on the mountain previous to Mr. French, in the original house, are, Willis Pease, Samuel W. Lyman, Joel W. Smith, Paul Strong, Alonzo Day, Almon Lyman, a Mr. Preston, Henry W. Prior, Thomas E. Elliott and David Morse. Paul Strong kept the house seven years. In an advertisement, dated Northampton, May 1, 1839, Henry W. Prior said: "A new and convenient avenue to the summit of Mount Holyoke will be opened this season, commencing near the house of Loren Pease, north of Mr. Lyman's hotel, in Hockanum. The subscriber will be in attendance from Monday morning till Saturday night, with such refreshments and personal attention as he hopes may be acceptable to the wants of the public. *No contraband* articles will be kept, and the house will be closed on the Sabbath."

A NEW SYSTEM ADOPTED.

Previous to 1853, it had been customary with those who kept the house, to charge a stipulated sum for the water that visitors drank, as it had to be carried to the top of the mountain by hand, and for refreshments, what would be exorbitant prices in other places. At the suggestion of those who were experienced, the proprietor concluded to furnish visitors gratuitously with all the water they wished, and give them the conveniences of the house, for which he would receive an admission fee; at the same time selling refreshments at prices usual in all public houses. This plan has produced good results in several ways. In the first place it has excluded that class who used to visit the mountain for no other purpose than to have a "spree," while the visitor does not now feel under the necessity of gorging himself with "refreshments" for the sake of compensating the proprietor of the house for the trouble he may make him. The first visitor to the Prospect House, after the new system was established, was Rev. E. Y. Swift, then of South Hadley.

THE STAIR CASE AND RAILWAY.

The rough and narrow foot-path, together with the steepness of the ascent, had deterred many, especially elderly people and invalids, from visiting the summit of the mountain. This difficulty, however, was in a measure obviated by the construction of a narrow and somewhat circuitous road from the old carriage road to the summit. A small horse cart and a Canadian pony were used for some time to convey to the top of the mountain, from the barn, or half-way house, such visitors as were unable to walk. But the great expense attending the repair of the road, and the increased travel, induced the proprietor to abandon the road and construct a stair case and railway to the summit, which were commenced and finished in 1854. The stair case contained 491 steps. To draw the car to the top of the mountain, a stationary horse-power at the summit was used till 1856, when a steam engine, procured for the purpose, was substituted, and found to work to greater satisfaction.

Mr. Graves and Mr. French continued together in the business till Feb. 5, 1856, when they dissolved partnership and Mr. French purchased Mr. Graves' interest. Since that time the property has remained in the hands of the present proprietor, who has done much to make Mount Holyoke a pleasant place of resort for tourists and the lovers of nature.

In 1857 a new road going north from the mountain, leading to Hadley, was opened, but it is not now used, another and more direct road having been opened to the river.

In 1860, a new and improved railway, 600 feet long, with double track, was built north of the old one and directly in front of the Prospect House. The old track was then given up to the use of foot passengers.

Mr. French, having purchased land and opened an avenue to the river in front of the Prospect House, a new covered railway and stair case was built in 1866 from the summit to the barn below, to connect with the horse railway to the river.

THE NEW TELESCOPE.

In 1866 a new and powerful telescope, made by J. B. Allen, of Springfield, was purchased for the house, and many objects that could not be seen with ordinary glasses previously used, are now discernable, which adds much to the interest of visitors.

WHERE THE WATER COMES FROM.

As there are no springs near the top of the mountain, the water used for drinking and cooking purposes has to be carried in kegs from the foot of the railway, 365 feet below the summit, to the Prospect House. Before the railway was constructed visitors were charged from three to five cents a glass for water, but the improved facilities afforded by the railway not only enables the proprietor to furnish water free, but to add to it, that desirable luxury in a warm day—ice. The spring water is remarkable for its purity and coldness, and there are but few springs in this region equal to it.

THE NEW BARN.

A new and commodious barn, 36 by 80 feet, was erected during the latter part of 1861, and is well adapted to the purpose for which it was built. It has been fitted up with stalls for the safe keeping of the horses of those who visit the mountain.

A PERMANENT RESIDENCE ON THE MOUNTAIN.

Previous to the time when Mr. French took possession of the mountain house, it had not been customary for the one who kept it to remain on the mountain over night, as the accommodations for that purpose were insufficient. Since the Prospect House was built, in 1851, Mr. French and family have remained there during the summer and autumn, and for ten years they resided on the summit the year round, and any one who has not, can form but a faint idea of the many beautiful scenes that have been witnessed, caused by the changes of season and the weather. Violent storms, terrific peals of thunder, vivid lightning, beautiful sun-sets, fogs, and rainbows; the glittering crystallizations of winter, the deep green foliage of mid-summer, and the golden tinted forest of autumn, have all formed scenes in which poet and artist would find abundant themes for song and picture.

THE MOUNTAIN GROVE.

The Grove, a short distance north-east of the Prospect House, where seats and tables have been provided for pic-nic parties, is a charming spot, and has become a popular place of resort for those who wish to enjoy out door amusements. It is only a few rods from the House, much secluded, while at the same time a beautiful view is obtained of the river, and old Hadley, with its broad streets, and waving elms.

THE MEADOWS.

The meadows which are so extensive on the West and North of the Mountain, remind the visitor of the Prairies of the West. It is supposed that the Valley was once a vast lake, and it is doubtful whether it was ever covered with forest trees. At the time of the purchase from the Indians, more than two hundred years ago, there were large patches of land that were free from trees, which the Indians used for cultivation, and were then called "meadows." In 1653, Nonotuck, a territory west of the Connecticut River, embracing the present towns of Northampton, Easthampton, Southampton, Westhampton, and part of Hatfield and Montgomery, was purchased of the Indians, for which was paid one hundred fathom of Wampum, (strings of beads, made of shells,) ten coats, some small gifts, and plowing up sixteen acres of land on the east side of the Quonnecticut River the ensuing summer." There are about 8000 acres in the Northampton Meadows, including Ox-Bow Island.

THE OX-BOW.

The serpentine course of the Connecticut river, forms a very attractive feature of the view from the mountain; but one of the greatest objects of interest is the old Ox-Bow, which receives its name from the peculiar course of the river, a mile below Hockanum Ferry. It formerly ran more westerly around a narrow strip of land, coming back directly opposite the place where the angle was made, and thence southerly, between Mounts Holyoke and Tom. The distance across the neck, from bank to bank, was only thirty rods, while the river in making the circuit, ran three and a half miles. The boatmen on the river had frequently endeavored to get permission to cut a channel through and change the course of the river; but the owners objected, as it would greatly discommode them. High water, however, accomplished what the boatmen failed to secure. On the 24th of February, 1840, the ice broke up and gorged in the river at the end of the "Bow," which caused the water to set back. It continued to rise till it run over the "neck." A few furrows had been plowed on the "neck" during the previous autumn, and as the frost was out of the ground a channel was soon cut through to the river below. A large number of acres were washed away, and the whole course of the river was changed. This made an island of the Ox-Bow, and it so remained till it was connected to the main land by the railroad embankment. There are 400 acres in Ox-Bow Island, as it is now called, although viewing it from the mountain with the naked eye, it does not have the appearance of containing upward of 100. Before the new channel was formed the Ox-Bow Meadows were within the limits of the town of Hadley, but by an act of the Legislature it became part of Northampton,

SHEPHERD'S ISLAND.

In the Connecticut River, northerly from the Prospect House, is a beautiful island covered with green grass, known to the old inhabitants as Shepherd's Island; but its peculiar shape, with the beautiful elm in the center, suggests to the mind of the visitor Captain Ericsson's famous Monitor, which so successfully fought the rebel ram, Merrimac. Strangers will be surprised to learn that there are twenty acres of the best of land on the island. It is never cultivated, but kept covered with grass to prevent it being washed away in freshet times. It is owned by L. N. Granger, of North Hadley. The large elm in the center of the island measures sixteen feet in circumference.

THE BIG ELM.

Half a mile west of the Hockanum Ferry is the Big Elm that Oliver Wendell Holmes alludes to in his "Autocrat of the Breakfast Table." It is thirty-one feet in circumference, and is one of the largest trees in New England. It is frequently visited by strangers, and can be seen from the Prospect House.

A NIGHT VIEW OF THE VALLEY.

It is thought by many that the view from the mountain by daylight is unsurpassed, but that obtained at night is, in some respects, much more beautiful. As the sun sinks behind the western hills and night comes softly on, the distant objects fade slowly from sight till nothing but the dim outline of the winding river remains, stretching far away, up and down the valley, like a silvery cord. The stillness of the night is only broken by the gentle rustling of the wind through the tree-tops and the plaintive notes of the whippowil as they come up from the valley below. In the morning, at the first approach of day, the visitor is awakened by the sweet music of the many birds that remain undisturbed in their native wilds.

THE GREAT FRESHET IN 1862.

The great freshet in the Connecticut valley, which reached its highest point on Sunday, April 20th—two feet higher at Northampton than any freshet since the settlement of the town—presented a beautiful appearance from Mount Holyoke. The Ox-Bow Island meadows, south and north Meadows in Northampton, and the Hadley meadows, were covered with water. It is estimated that nearly 10,000 acres were completely submerged. At the bridge over the Connecticut, between Hadley and Northampton, the water was within three or four feet of the floor-planks, and was much visited by Northampton people, where a good view of the vast body of water was obtained.

WHAT EVERY VISITOR DESIRES TO KNOW.

Distance from the Prospect House to

Northampton, - - -	3 miles.
Springfield, - - - -	20 "
Worcester, - - - -	76 "
Boston, - - - - -	120 "
Albany, - - - -	122 "
Hartford, - - - -	46 "
New Haven, - - - -	82 "
New York, - - - -	158 "
Greenfield, - - - -	22 "
Brattleboro, - - - -	45 "
Bellows Falls, - - -	70 "
White River Junction, - - -	109 "

Perpendicular elevation of Mount Holyoke, 1,000 feet.
Carriage road from base to feeding-stable, ¾ of a mile.
Railway from stable to summit, 600 feet.
Perpendicular ascent from stable, 365 feet.
First house built in 1821.
Second house built in 1851.
Enlarged to present size in 1861.
First railway in 1854.
Second railway in 1860.
Present track laid in 1866.
Number of passengers carried over its track to 1866, 125,000.
Number of acres in Ox-Bow Island, 400.
Number of acres in Shepherd Island, 20.
Number of acres in Northampton Meadows, 8,000.
Number of acres in Hadley Meadows, 2,700.
Number of trees in West Street, Hadley, 811.
Length of West Street, Hadley, one mile.

JAY PEAK.

FOURTEEN miles west of Newport, at the head of Lake Memphremagog, is Jay Peak. It is 4,018 feet in height, and from its summit is a magnificent view, said to be one of the finest in New England. From it can be seen Lake Champlain, the Adirondacks in Northern New York, St. Lawrence River, Montreal, Lakes Memphremagog and Willoughby, the White Mountains, &c., while the valley of Champlain and the country lying near, makes a beautiful and pleasing scene. A good carriage road leads from Newport to the cabin near the summit.

Mr. H. W. Baker, the mountain pioneer, has erected a spacious log cabin on the mountain, just below the summit, where guests are provided for. His "latch string" is always out, and as the streams abound with trout, old fishermen find this a pleasant stopping place.

THE WHITE MOUNTAINS.

A PRELIMINARY VIEW.

On the northern boundary of New Hampshire are the most elevated mountain summits of New England, the rocky boldness and grandeur of which justly entitle that region to the appellation of "the Switzerland of America." The lofty peaks, the deep and narrow passes, and sublime scenery, touches the poetic nature of man, and he wonders at the mighty power that has shaped such vastness and beauty. The fame of the White Mountains is almost world-wide, although hardly a half century has passed since they were looked upon only by neighboring primitive settlers, or the more daring lover of the sublime in nature. A period of about thirty years will cover the time since the Mountains were first visited by any considerable number. Small the number at first, the tide of sight-seekers has gradually increased, until now not less than ten thousand people annually visit all or some portions of the various mountains.

Darby Field of Pascataquack, accompanied by two Indians, ascended the highest peak of the White Mountains, in 1642, but the first mention of the mountains in print did not occur until 1672. The first rude public house for occasional visitors was erected upon the Giant's Grave, in 1803, by Eleazer Rosebrook, five miles west of the present Crawford House. In 1819 Abel Crawford and his son Ethan Allen Crawford were the first to clear a path through the woods to the rocky ridge, and in 1840 Abel Crawford, at the age of 75, rode the first horse that climbed the cone of Mt. Washington. The first house on that mouutain was built by his son Ethan.

No conception of the grandeur of the view from the summit of Mt. Washington can be formed without a visit to the mountain itself. The most faithful description when placed upon paper is spiritless in comparison with the mighty scene spread before you from an altitude of more than *six thousand feet!* While the tide of travel to this wonderful land is increasing year by year, there are thousands who have no realizing sense of the pleasure that they are depriving themselves of by remaining at home—toiling, perhaps, day after day in the never ceasing round of business, that a little more may be hoarded for a coming generation to squander. Oh! you man of toil! what will it profit you to wear your very life out in acquiring mere wealth while the finer instincts of your nature are blotted out or allowed to run to waste? The White Hills should be cherished by us all as the Mecca of America, to which it should be a *religious* duty to make at least one pilgrimage in our life time!

HOW TO REACH THE MOUNTAINS.

There are four routes to the White Mountains, but for tourists coming from New York and points farther south the nearest and most interesting is that through the Connecticut Valley. This is more than *seventy* miles shorter than any other. Many who have never visited the mountains and whose attention has not previously been called to them, set out to make their first trip with very little knowledge concerning them. To such a few words of explanation will not come amiss.

Littleton is the nearest point on the west side of the mountains that tourists can go to by railroad. From that place six-horse coaches are run in connection with all the trains to the

Profile and Crawford Houses. The former is situated 12 miles from Littleton in the Franconia Mountains, and the latter 22 miles distant, at the western entrance of the White Mountain Notch. In the vicinity of the Profile House are the Old Man of the Mountain, the Poole, the Flume, and various other points of interest. In the vicinity of the Crawford House are the White Mountain Notch, the Willey House, Mount Willard, Ammonoosuc Falls, the railroad to the summit of Mount Washington, &c. The bridle path to the summit of Mt. Washington commences near the Crawford House. The Glen House is on the east side of Mt. Washington, 8 miles from Gorham and the Grand Trunk Railroad. The carriage road to the summit of Mt. Washington commences at the Glen House.

In purchasing tickets for the mountains the tourist should call for one to the Profile House, if he wishes to go to that place first. If he goes to the Crawford House call for one to the White Mountains.

The Mt. Washington Railway, which is now in process of construction, is about 8 miles north of the Crawford House, on the west side of the mountain. A large hotel is to be erected near the Giant's Grave, (at the old Fabyan stand,) a few miles from the railway. With these brief explanations the reader is introduced to the details of the various routes:

ROUTE FIRST.

From New York by cars to New Haven, Hartford, Springfield, Northampton, Greenfield, Brattleboro, Bellows Falls, Windsor, White River Junction, Wells River and Littleton. Thence by stage direct to the Crawford House, 22 miles, or 12 miles to Profile House in the Franconia Mountains and thence to Crawford House, 27 miles. The tourist leaving New York by the 8 A. M. Morning Express can stop at any point between Springfield and Bellows Falls over night, and proceed to the White Mountain region the next day, arriving there in the evening,—the Profile House at 7½, and the Crawford House at 10½. Distance from New York to Crawford House, 324 miles, to Profile House, 314 miles.

ROUTE SECOND.

From New York to New London by steamer, and thence by cars to Worcester, Nashua, Manchester, Concord and Weirs, on Lake Winnipisseogee. From this point the tourist can continue by cars through Plymouth and Wells River to Littleton, and thence by stage to the Crawford or Profile House; or he can take the steamer 10 miles across the Lake to Center Harbor, and thence by stage 30 miles to Profile House through the Pemigewasset valley; or 35 miles to North Conway and thence 28 miles to Crawford House, through the Saco valley. By this route the tourist leaves New York in the afternoon, and, by traveling all night, reaches the White Mountains in the evening of the next day, providing he goes by cars to Littleton. If he goes by steamer to Center Harbor and thence by stage via North Conway to the Crawford House, he reaches there on the evening of the third day, having remained one night at North Conway. Distance from New York to Crawford House via New London, Nashua and Wells River, 424 miles; to Profile House, 414. To Crawford House via Weirs, Center Harbor and North Conway, 395; to Profile House via Plymouth and Pemigewasset valley, 370.

ROUTE THIRD.

From New York to Boston, either by steamboat or railroad; from Boston to Weirs and Plymouth, and thence continue to Littleton by railroad, or by steamer to Center Harbor from Weirs, and thence by stage to North Conway and Crawford House; or by stage from Plymouth to Profile House. Distance from New York by railroad to Boston, Concord, Wells River and Littleton to Profile House, 432 miles; to Crawford

House, 442 miles; by stage from Plymouth to Profile House, 388 miles; by steamboat and stage from Weirs to Crawford House, 413 miles.

ROUTE FOURTH.

From New York via Boston, Portland and Gorham to Glen House. Distance, 441 miles. The Glen House is on the East side of the White Mountains, and by this route there is only eight miles of stage travel before reaching the mountains —from Gorham to the Glen. To reach the Crawford House the tourist must either take the stage around the mountains or ascend Mt. Washington by the carriage road to the Tip Top House, and thence by ponies down the mountain to the Crawford House. Distance from Glen to Crawford House, *over* Mt. Washington, 17 miles, *around* it by stage, 36 miles.

LITTLETON—ENTRANCE TO THE WHITE MOUNTAIN REGION.

Having come through the Connecticut valley and enjoyed its delightful scenery, the tourist changes cars at Wells River and enters the valley of the Ammonoosuc, a stream which finds its source in the deep ravines of the White Mountains. A ride of twenty miles along the banks of the river and through small villages brings you to Littleton, a village of considerable trade and enterprise, where, from the neighboring hights, can be seen the distant summit of Mt. Washington. The village is situated principally on the north bank of the Ammonoosuc, and the river itself furnishes power for the various mills which give employment to the inhabitants. North of the village and upon a commanding spot is the building now being erected by the town at a cost of $25,000 for the graded schools.

THAYER'S HOTEL.

The tourist has the choice of proceeding immediately by stage, on the arrival of the cars, to the Profile House in the

Franconia Notch, or to the Crawford House at the White Mountain Notch, or remain over night at Littleton. If he remains he will find good meals and good rooms and a genial host at Thayer's Hotel. It is kept by Mr. H. L. Thayer, a veteran in the business and, withal, a gentleman. Summer guests find this an agreeable stopping place. Horses and carriages are furnished to those who desire them. The rides about Littleton are delightful, and a considerable number remain here during the summer.

FROM LITTLETON TO THE CRAWFORD HOUSE.

If the tourist proceeds to the Crawford House, which is 22 miles distant, immediately on his arrival at Littleton, and has come by the afternoon train, he will take supper at Sinclair's Hotel at Bethlehem, five miles from Littleton. Soon after leaving Littleton the various peaks of the White Mountains are first seen and are constantly in view until the darkness of night limits the vision. The ride is a pleasant one though taken at a late hour. The tourist will reach the Crawford House between ten and eleven o'clock.

FROM LITTLETON TO THE PROFILE HOUSE.

The six horse coaches will be in readiness on the arrival of the train at Littleton to convey the tourist to the Profile House, 12 miles distant. On leaving the village a southerly route is pursued and shortly you commence to ascend high table land. Within half an hour and after the ascent is made, you behold on your left the lofty White Mountain range, Mt. Washington standing sentinel over all the rest. Ahead of you is Mt. Lafayette, its deep furrowed sides in full view. Descending slowly you enter the village of Franconia, the name of which has become familiar to you if you have been an observer of the telegraphic weather reports in winter. This is one of the coldest places in the mountains and the thermometer sometimes registers in winter as low as 34 degrees below zero. The south branch of the Ammonoosuc, which rises in the Franconia Mountains, passes through the village. As you leave the valley of the Ammonoosuc and commence the mountain ascent the sun is nearing the western horizon. The golden shadows upon the dark forest trees which skirt the mountain side are singularly beautiful. Such a sunset as is sometimes witnessed here is rarely seen elsewhere. The long lines of light and shade give that brilliant coloring of purple and gold which is seen in perfection only in a Northern clime.

Soon after leaving Franconia a "slide," a long white line, will be noticed on the side of Mt. Lafayette extending downward. This is just to the right of the Profile House, and seems only a short distance to it; but an hour will be consumed before the hotel is reached. Slowly the coach ascends to the Notch, passing Bald Mountain on your left. As you reach the summit and commence to descend into the Notch the base of Mt. Lafayette and its great wall of green impresses you with its vastness and grandeur. In a few minutes you reach the border of Echo Lake, a clear and beautiful sheet, a half mile north of the Profile House. A few minutes later the coach is stopped in front of the hotel itself, as the evening twilight begins to deepen.

THE PROFILE HOUSE.

OBJECTS OF INTEREST.—The "Old Man of the Mountain," 100 rods south of the hotel —seen to best advantage early in the morning, or late in the afternoon; Echo Lake, half mile north; Mount Cannon—foot-path in rear of the hotel, one and a half miles to summit; Bald Mountain, 2 miles north; Mount Lafayette, carriage road north to base two miles, and bridle path to summit three and a half miles; Basin, 4 miles; Flume, 6 miles; Pool, five and a half miles. The Basin, Pool and Flume can be visited by taking the carriages from the hotel, at 8:30 a. m. and 3 p. m.

A welcome sight indeed is the Profile House to the weary traveler, as it greets his vision at the twilight hour. Fatigued by an all-day's ride he leaves the coach and enters this magnificent hotel, surprised at its extent and the strange wildness of the scene around it. Having satisfied the wants of an appetite that had been sharpened by the ride, he strolls down the carriage road, which is overshadowed by the dark walls above. All nature seems hushed in repose, and naught but the sighing of the wind in the tree tops far above disturbs his meditation. How vast and how mighty seem the everlasting mountains, whose summits are lost to him in the darkness of night! Retracing his steps he enters the hotel and joins, perhaps, in the merry-making in the parlor, where a gay and bewitching scene presents itself. Merry voices mingle with sweet music and joy seems unconfined.

The Profile House stands upon the highest ground in the Notch, and is nearly 2,000 feet above the sea. It is completely shut in by the mountains which rise almost from its doors to a great hight, Cannon Mountain on the West and Eagle Cliff on the East. Such wildness and grandeur the tourist has seldom if ever before seen, and he never tires in gazing upon the varied forms of beauty which on every hand fill his eye. The hotel, which is a model of neatness and comfort, is kept by Taft, Tyler & Greenleaf, long known to mountain tourists. It has several times been enlarged to meet the growing popularity of the place, until it will now accommodate 450 guests. The parlor is 84 by 50 feet, and 460 yards of carpeting are required to cover its floor. A band of music is always in attendance for the pleasure of guests, and dancing forms one of the attractions of the place during the evening hours. There is a telegraph office in the hotel, and the daily mails are received and made up there, so that guests, though away from the larger places, are not altogether outside of the comforts and luxuries of home.

Ponies and carriages are furnished on call at the office by Mr. R. M. Bishop for those who desire them.

There are several objects of interest near the hotel that can be reached on foot. First of all, and the great lion of the Notch, is

THE "OLD MAN OF THE MOUNTAIN."

There is no single object of so much general interest around the whole mountains, and thousands have looked upon the Titanic features of The "Old Man" in wonder and astonishment. If the tourist came by the evening coach he should rise the next morning at an early hour and walk down the carriage road towards the south a hundred rods from the hotel. Just as he reaches the path leading to the boat house on Profile Lake he should look upward, to the right, and there will greet his vision the unmistakable outlines of the human face projecting from the rugged side of Mt. Cannon, at least 1000 feet above him. So perfect and so wonderful he feels a thrill of half surprise and half fear creep over him. He starts back and exclaims, can it be possible that the great forces of nature by mere chance have carved such an exact image of the human features upon this great rocky mountain side? Thousands have been here to look upon this, Nature's greatest curiosity, and its fame is told in many a song and legend. The incredulous, however, before looking upon the "Great Stone Face," fancy it must require a wide stretch of imagination to witness that which is claimed, but a single glance sweeps away all unbelief. The profile is made up of three separate masses of rock some distance apart, and the whole length from forehead to chin is 80 feet. One piece forms the forehead, another the upper lip, and the third the chin. Passing farther down the road until coming in front the profile is entirely lost to view. The most favorable time for seeing it is either before the sun shines upon it, or late in the afternoon, after it has passed behind Mt. Cannon.

PROFILE LAKE.

While here upon the banks of this small, but beautiful lake, the tourist will notice something of its loveliness. It is here that the Pemigewasset takes its rise. Starr King in describing it very properly remarks: "How much joy it has fed in human hearts! Something of its bounty expended upon the infant Pemigewasset is borne down into the Merrimack and contributes to the power that moves the wheels of Nashua and Lowell, and supplies a thousand operatives with bread." The lake is filled with the best of trout and affords sport for old fishermen.

ECHO LAKE.

A half mile north of the Profile House, and a fitting companion of Profile Lake, is another beautiful sheet of water—Echo Lake. It is a quiet and beautiful spot and a ride upon its placid bosom is indeed refreshing after the fatigue of an all-day ramble upon the adjacent mountains. But its great charm is in the wonderful echoes that reverberate among the mountain-fastnesses, on loud shouting, blowing of a horn, or firing of a cannon.

BALD MOUNTAIN.

Two miles north of the Profile House is Bald Mountain. A carriage road has been constructed to its summit and is now easy of access. From it is a fine view of the Ammonoosuc valley to the north, and to the south you look down upon Echo Lake and the Notch, while beyond rises Mt. Lafayette. Carriages run regularly from the hotel to the summit.

EAGLE CLIFF.

On the east side of the road leading through the Notch, opposite the Profile House and completely overshadowing it, is

Eagle Cliff. It rises 1,200 feet perpendicularly and its peculiar formation makes it an object of interest to all. It derives its name from the fact that some years since a pair of eagles selected this for a home and there reared their young.

CANNON MOUNTAIN.

In rear and west of the Profile House, rising to the hight of 1,500 feet above the Notch, is Cannon Mountain. It received its name from a rock upon the summit resembling a cannon, which can be seen from the grounds in front of the hotel. A foot-path to the summit from the hotel renders it comparatively easy of access. The view down the valley of the Pemigewasset is beautiful and well repays the effort necessary to reach the summit. The view in other respects is fine, but not equal to that obtained from more elevated positions.

MT. LAFAYETTE.

Having visited the objects of general interest in the immediate vicinity of the Profile House, the tourist will now prepare to ascend Mt. Lafayette, which is 5,000 feet in hight, the view from which is hardly inferior and in some respects surpasses that from Mt. Washington. The distance to the summit from the hotel is five and a half miles. Careful guides and good ponies can be engaged at the hotel. On setting out for the trip you proceed down the road past the Old Man of the Mountain, and for two miles follow the Pemigewasset. Coming to the old stand of the Lafayette House, which was burnt some years since, you turn to the left and enter the forest. Winding through it you finally come out upon the bare rock from which you overlook the Profile House, down in the deep narrow glen. Further north is the valley of the Ammonoosuc. South, for twenty miles, you have full view of the lovely valley of the Pemigewasset and the river itself. After enjoying the view and resting your pony a few minutes you continue the ascent.

Finally coming out of the woods altogether the bare and still distant peak of Lafayette lies before you. The summit seems so far above you wonder how it is to be reached. Plodding on, zigzagging to right and left, the cone is finally gained. Such grandeur as is spread before you more than repays the toil necessary to reach the summit. Lofty mountain peaks without number lie before you on every hand. West, in the hazy distance, is the Green Mountain range—Mt. Mansfield, Camel's Hump and Jay Peak towering above their neighbors. Intervening are the valleys of the Ammonoosuc and Connecticut. North is the glorious and grand old peak, Mt. Washington—the Tip Top House, if not cloud-covered, in full view. Lying between are the summits of smaller mountains, while a trackless widerness stretches far away towards the east, where peak upon peak rises skyward. A little to the left is old Kearsearge, and to the right the sharp spur of Chocorua seems to pierce the very sky. South you look down upon the lovely valley of the Pemigewasset which has seemingly widened into broad meadows, and forty miles distant the eye rests upon Plymouth and the beautiful Lake Winnipiseogée, with its innumerable islands. You linger long in contemplating the scene, and wonder how it is possible that so much sublimity should remain so comparatively unknown to the great world of humanity within a day's ride, and yet so accessible.

The summit of Mt. Lafayette is void of vegetation, and formerly a rude house stood upon it for the protection of visitors. Time and the elements, however, have destroyed it. Ready to return you look carefully to your saddle girths and set out for the hotel, where you arrive in season for dinner, having accomplished the whole trip in five hours.

DOWN THE PEMIGEWASSET.

Having rested from the fatigue occasioned by the ascent of Mt. Lafayette, the tourist is prepared to take a trip down the

Pemigewasset to see some of the objects of interest that are found along this impetuous little stream, among which are the Basin, the Pool, the Flume, and Walker's and Georgianna Falls. The public carriages leave the hotel twice a day, at 8½ A. M. and 3 P. M.

THE BASIN.

Four miles south of the Profile House, and on the west side of the road, is the Basin. The Pemigewasset in its downward course, flowing over a rocky ledge, has worn a complete basin out of the solid granite, sixty feet in circumference and about twenty feet in depth. In the outer edge, nearest the road, is a peculiar formation of granite, worn by the water and resembling the human foot and leg.

THE POOL.

Further south and about five and a half miles from the Profile House, is the Pool. You leave the carriage road just north of the old Flume House, and turn towards the east. A walk of half a mile through the forest will bring you to the Pool, which lies in the deep gorge between the mountains. The Pool is about 40 feet deep and 150 in width, and the Pemigewasset, entering at the upper side, has worn this huge cavern in the solid rock. Its grandeur is not so fully realized until the tourist has passed down the rude stairway to the bottom, where, on either hand, the rocky sides rise above him, while the Pemigewasset itself rolls impetuously down from above and thence out over the broken bed below. Here, too, in years past has been found the "Philosopher," who is ready with his boat to take you, for a small stipend, around the pool, and give you *his* theory of its creation. Returning, you soon come to the

OLD FLUME HOUSE,

once a favorite place of resort, but now deserted. It is owned by the proprietors of the Profile House, and was closed several years since. From its piazzas are beautiful views of the mountains and the valley below.

THE FLUME.

Like the "Old Man of the Mountains," the Flume is one of the most important objects of interest, and no tourist should fail to visit it. The carriage leaves the road leading down the valley, just below the old Flume House, and turns to the east. It crosses the Pemigewasset and halts a short distance below the Flume. "Leaving the wagon," says Starr King, "we mount by a foot path that leads nearer and nearer to the sweet melody that gives a promise to the ear, which is not to be broken to the hope. Soon we reach the clean and sloping granite floors, over which the water slips in thin, wide, even sheets of crystal colorlessness. Above this, we meet those gentle ripples over rougher ledges that are embossed with green. Then, still higher up, where the rocks grow more uneven, we are held by the profuse beauty of the hues shown upon the bright stones at the bottom of the little translucent basins and pools. Still above, we come to the remarkable fissure in the mountain, more than fifty feet high and several hundred feet long, which narrows too, towards the upper end, till it becomes only twelve feet wide, and which doubtless an earthquake made for the passage of the stream which the visitors are now to ascend. We go up, stepping from rock to rock, now walking along a little plank pathway, now mounting by some rude steps, here and there crossing from side to side of the ravine by primitive little bridges, that bend under the feet and that are railed by birch poles, and then climbing the rocks again, while the spray breaks upon us from the dashing and roaring stream, until we arrive at a little bridge which spans the narrowest part of the ravine. How wild the spot is! which shall we admire most,—the glee of the little torrent that rushes beneath our feet, or the regularity and smoothness of the frowning walls through which it goes foaming out into the sunshine; or the splendor of the dripping emerald mosses; or the trees that overhang their edges; or the huge boulder, egg-shaped, that is lodged between the walls just over the bridge where we stand,—as unpleasant to look at, if the nerves are irresolute, as the sword of Damocles, and yet held by a grasp out of which it will not slip for centuries."

Leaving the Flume and following the foot-path above, along the northern side, you come to the rustic bridge which spans the chasm over the boulder. Here can be had an excellent view of the Flume from one end to the other. It is a pleasant spot for meditation, and all nature around you seems in harmony. You are lost in wonderment over the cause which produced such a remarkable scene. Whence came the power that rent these rocks asunder? and how long has this great granite boulder been suspended in its singular position?

THE RETURN.

The tourist has now seen the more important objects of interest in the Franconia Notch, but if he has time he will find pleasure in taking other rambles among the mountains. On leaving the Flume and reaching the old Flume House, he can proceed down the road for about two miles and then turn to the right, follow up a little stream into the mountains where he will come to Georgianna Falls, a series of beautiful cascades. Or, he can retrace his steps and when within about three miles of the Profile House, push into the woods to the right and come to Walker's Falls, where the little mountain stream makes a rapid descent over an irregularly rocky bed.

FOR THE CRAWFORD HOUSE.

At 8½ A. M. the coach is in readiness for the Crawford House, which is situated at the western entrance to the White

Mountain Notch. You go back nearly to Franconia village by the same route you reached the Profile House from Littleton, and then turn to the right and proceed to

BETHLEHEM.

At this place is the Sinclair Hotel, kept by E. R. Abbott, formerly connected with the Pemigewasset House at Plymouth. The scenery around Bethlehem is charming and beautiful. A distinct view can be had of Mt. Washington and other peaks farther to the north.

LOWER AMMONOOSUC FALLS.

Leaving Bethlehem, where the coach stops for a few minutes, a ride of about two miles brings you to Ammonoosuc Bridge. Here Capt. Rosebrook built a bridge in the early settlement of Bethlehem. It was afterward carried away by high water, and, in 1800, the town of Bethlehem voted to build another at a cost of $390. Provisions were so scarce that year, that the workmen were compelled to live on milk-porridge while building it.

A short ride from this place brings you to Lower Ammonoosuc Falls, on the south side of the road. The Ammonoosuc is one of the wildest rivers in the State, and it makes a fall of about one mile in a distance of 30 miles, from the White Mountains to the Connecticut.

WHITE MOUNTAIN HOUSE.

Within five miles of Crawford's you come to the White Mountain House, kept by Lindsey and Abbott, situated within full view of Mt. Washington.

THE GIANT'S GRAVE.

A half mile east of the White Mountain House you come to the Giant's Grave, a peculiar earth formation, sixty feet in hight, and from which there is a fine view of the valley and the mountains. In 1803 was erected on Giant's Grave the first public house built in the mountain region for the accommodation of visitors. In 1819, Ethan Allen Crawford, who lived at this place, marked and cleared a path, in connection with his father, Abel Crawford, who was then living 8 miles below the White Mountain Notch, to the side of Mt. Washington.

At the foot of Giant's Grave stood the old Fabyan House, which was burnt several years since, and here is to be erected a new Hotel, capable of accommodating 500 guests, by the proprietors of the railway to the summit of Mt. Washington.

No less than three public houses have been burnt at this place, while the meadows have been ravaged by freshets. There is a tradition that an Indian maniac once stood on Giant's Grave, and carrying a blazing pitch-pine torch, which he had kindled at a tree struck by lightning, shouted in the storm the prophecy—

The Great Spirit whispered in my ear,
No pale-face shall take deep root here.

ARRIVAL AT CRAWFORD'S.

An hour's ride from the Giant's Grave takes the tourist to the Crawford House. You are now in the heart of the White Mountains, close to the entrance of the White Mountain Notch, a sight of which alone is sufficiently interesting to well repay the cost of the whole trip. From here you can go to the summit of Mt. Washington by ponies, or make the complete circuit of the mountains by stage. But before introducing you to the wild scenery of this locality, we will give you some preliminaries concerning the mountains themselves.

WHO NAMED THE MOUNTAINS.

The several peaks of the White Mountain range were named

by a party from Lancaster, N. H., in 1820. Starr King, in his excellent book on the White Hills, who by the way, did much in his life-time, to make the public familiar with the beauty of the mountain region, very justly criticises the propriety of naming the mountains after the public men of the day. He says: "How absurd the order is! Beginning at 'The Notch,' at the Crawford House, and passing around to Gorham, there are the titles of the summits which are all seen from the village of Lancaster: Webster, Clinton, Pleasant, Franklin, Monroe, Washington, Clay, Jefferson, Adams, and Madison. What a wretched jumble! These are what we have taken in exchange for such Indian words as Agiochook, which is the baptismal title of Mt. Washington, Ammomoosuc, Moosehillock, Cantoocook, Pennocook and Pentucket. Think of putting Mount Monroe, or Peabody River, or Berlin Falls, or Israel's River, into poetry! The White Mountains have lost the privilege of being enshrined in such sonorous rythm and such melody as Longfellow has given to the Indian names in Hiawatha."

THE HIGHT OF THE DIFFERENT PEAKS.

Below is the hight, *above the sea*, of the several peaks of the White Mountain range, of which Mt. Washington is the highest:

Mt.	Webster,	4,000 ft.	Mt.	Washington,	6,285 ft.
"	Jackson,	4,100 "	"	Clay,	5,400 "
"	Clinton,	4,200 "	"	Jefferson,	5,700 "
"	Pleasant,	4,800 "	"	Adams,	5,800 "
"	Franklin,	4,900 "	"	Madison,	5,400 "
"	Monroe,	5,400 "			

THE CRAWFORD HOUSE.

PLACES OF INTEREST.—Mt. Washington, 9 miles to the summit; Mt. Willard, 2 miles; Willey House in White Mountain Notch, 3 miles; Ammonoosuc Falls, 5½ miles; Beecher's Cascade, ½ mile; Flume and Silver Cascades, ½ mile.

The Crawford House is situated on a broad plateau, 2,000 feet above the sea, at the western entrance to the White Mountain Notch, 22 miles from Littleton and 35 miles by stage route from the Glen House, on the eastern side of the mountains. The Hotel stands on the water-shed between the Saco and Connecticut—the water at the barn, just west of the Hotel, running west into the Ammonoosuc, and then into the Connecticut, while that, a little east of the Hotel, runs into the Saco.

The Hotel is spacious and is pleasantly furnished, and its proprietors, Messrs. Hartshorne, Wolcott & Doyle, spare no pains to provide for the wants of their guests. A band of music is kept at the Hotel during the season, and at night, after the return of visitors from their day's tramp among the mountains, the elegantly furnished parlor is the center of a gay scene. Fatigued though the tourist may be, a new life and vigor is at once infused, as the inspiring music falls upon the ear.

MT. WILLARD.

If the tourist came by the morning coach, after dinner he will have ample time to visit Mt. Willard and the Notch. The former is only two miles from the Hotel, and a good carriage road has been constructed to its summit. Frequently tourists who were never before here, thinking this to be of no especial interest, neglect to visit it. No where in the whole mountains is a finer and more striking view had, and no one should fail of seeing it. The Hotel carriage will be in readiness after dinner to make the trip. Leaving the Crawford House you go a short distance east, down the road towards the Notch, when you turn to the right and enter the woods. The road is generally good, and with few exceptions is not steep. Making a somewhat circuitous ascent you finally come out upon a plateau, where a most sublime scene bursts upon you. Two thousand feet below lies the famous White Mountain Notch, so narrow that there is only little more than room enough for the Saco river and the carriage road. The forest of spruce seem like low shrubs, while the famous Willey House half way down the Notch, is only discernable. On the right is Mt. Willard, and on the left Mt. Webster, their deep furrowed walls showing plainly the many slides that have taken place here in times past. You approach the edge of the precipice and sit down upon the bare rock and contemplate the scene. You look down the deep gorge and beyond to the distant mountain peaks, or note by the growth of the shrubbery the spot where the great avalanche swept down Mt. Willey and buried the Willeys beneath it. A visit to this place in the afternoon is preferable. The west side is covered with a deep shadow, while the golden sun-light, still clinging to Mt. Webster on the opposite side, gives the scene a picturesque appearance.

Leaving the place reluctantly you resume your seat in the coach, and return to the Hotel.

DOWN THE NOTCH.

There is still time left for a visit to the famous Willey house, 3 miles distant, in the White Mountain Notch. Leaving the Hotel and traveling eastward, you come to

THE SOURCE OF THE SACO,

a little pond just to the left of the road, and in view of the Crawford House. Here, this river which becomes a stream of considerable importance before reaching the ocean, is only a little trickling rivulet. Passing on and just before you reach the entrance to the Notch, you will notice on the left hand,

ELEPHANT'S HEAD,

a huge rock, so named from the fact that it resembles the head and trunk of a mammoth elephant. While viewing this as we pass, we are "reminded of a little story." Some time since, a very devout gentleman who had come to the mountains with the Good Book in one pocket and a Guide Book in the other, and like a good man, as he was, having that morning read both, names and places were a "little mixed." He accosted our jolly driver with: "Can you tell me, driver, where is Ephraim's Head?" "*Ephraim's* Head? You have the start of me now, sir. Guess there's no such place about *these* mountains." "Yes, there must be, I read about it this morning." "Don't you mean *Elephant's* Head?" The good man drew forth his guide book to make sure that he was right, and was afterwards seen quietly replacing it in his pocket, remarking as he did so, something about poor "specs" and bad eyesight.

THE GATEWAY.

Passing on you enter the Gateway to the Notch. The Saco finds its way through the rocks at your side, while almost perpendicularly rise above you, in curious forms, great masses of rocks in almost every conceivable shape. The driver, who is not deficient in imagination, will point out various profiles, from the little infant to the old maid. A little further on you come to

FLUME AND SILVER CASCADES,

both of which come dashing down over the irregular and rocky surface of Mt. Webster, on your left. The Flume Cascade, which you first reach, is more regular and less interesting than Silver Cascade. The latter makes a descent of more than four hundred feet, and as it leaps from rock to rock, it presents an extremely enchanting appearance. It seems like a silver cord stretching up towards the very clouds.

THE DEVIL'S DEN.

As you pass down the Notch the driver will point out to your view the summit of Mt. Willard, and on its broken face an aperture in the rock. This is the Devil's Den, though we have some doubts concerning its occupancy by his satanic majesty. This cavern is only accessible by means of ropes from the summit of Mt. Willard. Dr. Ball of Boston explored it in 1856, and found it to be 20 feet wide, 15 high and 20 feet deep. A better view can be had of it as you come up the Notch.

THE WILLEY HOUSE,—SCENE OF THE TERRIBLE DISASTER.

Continuing down the Notch, you at last come to the Willey House, made famous by that terrible calamity that happened here more than 40 years ago. It stands on the west side of the road, Mt. Willey rising from its rear to the hight of 2000 feet. The original house (an addition has since been erected, adjoining it on the south) was built for a public house by a Mr. Hill, about the year 1820, who occupied it for one year. Before it was built there was no house for 13 miles, from the old Crawford place, south of the Willey House, to Rosebrook's, near the Giant's Grave. In the Autumn of 1825, Mr. James Willey, Jr., moved into the house, and on the night of August 28, 1826, a terrible storm raged in the Notch, masses of rocks, trees and earth, covering a space of nearly a mile in length, were precipitated from the side of Mt. Willey into the valley below, burying the whole family, consisting of nine persons, Mr. Willey and wife, five children and two hired men. Mr. Willey apprehending that a slide might take place had constructed a rude hut below the house to which he thought his family might retreat with safety, in case of necessity. It appears that some time during the night his family set out to reach the hut, and were overtaken and buried in the advancing avalanche. A huge rock 30 feet high, stood in rear of the house, which parted the sliding mass and saved the building from destruction. Had the family remained in it, their lives would have been saved.

Starr King has told the story of this terrible tragedy so admirably in his White Hills, that we transfer it to these pages. He says:

"In the Spring of 1826, Mr. Willey began to enlarge the conveniences of the little inn for entertaining guests. And in the early summer the spot looked very attractive. There was a beautiful meadow in front, stretching to the foot of the frowning wall of Mount Webster, and garrisoned with tall rock maples. To be sure, Mount Willey rose at a rather threatening angle some two thousand feet behind the house but it was not so savage in appearance as Mount Webster opposite, and pretty much the whole of its broad steep wall was draped in green. In a bright June morning the little meadow farm, flecked with the nibbling sheep, and cooled by the patches of shadow flung far out over the grass from the thick maple foliage, must have seemed to a traveler passing there, and hearing the pleasant murmur of the Saco and the shrill sweetness of the Canada whistler, as romantic a spot as one could fly to, to escape the fever and the perils of the world."

Late in June Mr. Willey and his wife, looking from the back windows of their house in the afternoon of a misty day, saw a large mass of the mountain above them sliding through the fog towards their meadows, and almost in a line of the house itself. Rocks and earth came plunging down, sweeping whole trees before them that would stand erect in the swift slide for rods before they fell. The slide moved under their eye to the very foot of the mountain and hurled its frightful burden across the road. At first they were greatly terrified and resolved t move from the Notch. But Mr. Willey, on reflection, felt confident that such an event was not likely to occur again; and was satisfied with building a strong hut or cave a little below the house in the Notch, which would certainly be secure, and to which the family might fly for shelter.

Later in the summer there was a long hot drought. By the middle of August, the earth, to a great depth in the mountain region, was dried to powder. There came several days of south wind, betokening copious rain. On Sunday, the 27th of August, the rain began to fall. On Monday, the 28th, the storm was very severe, and the rain was a deluge. Towards evening the clouds around the White Mountain range and over the Notch, to those who saw them from a distance, were very heavy, black and awful. Later in the night they poured their burden in streams. Between nine o'clock in the evening and the dawn of Tuesday, the Saco rose twenty-five feet, and swept the whole interval between the Notch and Conway.

On the morning of Tuesday the sun rose into a cloudless sky and the air was remarkably transparent. The North Conway farmers, busy in saving what they could from the raging flood of the Saco, saw clearly how terrible the storm had been upon the Mount Washington range. The whole line was devastated by land-slides. Great grooves could be distinctly seen where the torrents had torn all the loose earth and stones and left the solid ledge of the mountain bare.

What had been the fate of the little house in the Notch and of the Willey family during the deluge? All communication with them on Tuesday morning was cut off by the flood of the Saco. But at four o'clock Tuesday afternoon, a traveler passing Ethan Crawford's, seven miles west of the Willey House, desired if possible to get through the Notch that night. By swimming his horse across the wildest part of the flood, he was put on the track. In the narrowest part of the road within the Notch, the water had torn out huge rocks and left holes twenty feet deep, and had opened trenches also ten feet deep and twenty feet long. But the traveler, while daylight lasted, could make his way on foot over the torn and obstructed road, and he managed to reach the lower part of the Notch just before dark. The little house was standing, but there were no human inmates to greet him. And what desolation around! The mountain behind it once robed in beautiful green, was striped for two or three miles with ravines, deep and freshly torn. The lovely little meadow in front was covered with wet sand and rocks, intermingled with branches of green trees, with shivered trunks whose splintered ends looked similar to an old peeled birchbroom, and with dead logs, which had evidenly long been buried beneath the mountain soil. Not even any of the bushes that grew up on the meadow in front of the house were to be seen. The slide from the mountain had evidently divided, not many rods above the house, against a sharp ledge of rock. It had then joined the frightful mass in front of the house, and pushed along to the bed of the Saco, covering the meadow, in some places thirty feet, with the frightful debris and mire.

The traveler entered the house and went through it. The doors were all open ; the beds and their clothing showed that they had been hurriedly left ; a Bible was lying open on a table, as if it had been read just before the family had departed. The traveler consoled himself, at last, with the feeling that the inmates had escaped to Abel Crawford's below, and then tried to sleep in one of the deserted beds. But in the night he heard moanings which frightened him so much that he lay sleepless till dawn. Then he found that they were the groans of an ox in the stable, that was partly crushed under broken timbers which had fallen in. The two horses were killed. He released the ox and went on his way towards Bartlett.

Before any news of the disaster had reached Conway, the faithful dog came down to Mr. Lovejoy's, and, by moanings, tried to make the family understand what had taken place.

Not succeeding, he left, and after being seen frequently on the road, sometimes heading north and then south, running almost at the top of his speed, as though bent on some absorbing errand, he soon disappeared from the region, and has never since been seen.

On Wednesday evening suspicions of the safety of the family were carried down to Bartlett and North Conway, where Mr. Willey's father and brothers lived. But they were not credited. The terrible certainty was to be communicated to the father in the most thrilling way. At midnight on Wednesday a messenger reached the bank of the river opposite his house in Lower Bartlett, but could not cross. He blew a trumpet, blast after blast. The noise and the mountain echoes startled the family and the neighborhood from their repose. They soon gathered on the river bank and heard the sad message shouted to them through the darkness.

On Thursday, the 31st of August, the family and many neighbors were able to reach the Notch. Search was commenced at once for the buried bodies. The first that was exhumed was one of the hired men, David Allen, a man of powerful frame and remarkable strength. He was but slightly disfigured. He was found near the top of a pile of earth and shattered timbers, with hands clenched and full of broken sticks and small limbs of trees. Soon the bodies of Mrs. Willey and her husband were discovered—the latter not so crushed that it could not be recognized.

No more could be found that day. Rude coffins were prepared, and the next day, Friday, about sunset, the simple burial service was offered. Elder Samuel Hasaltine, standing amidst the company of strong, manly forms, where faces were wet with tears, commenced the service with the words of Isaiah: "Who hath measured the waters in the hollow of his hand, and meted out heaven with a span, and comprehended the dust of the earth in a measure, and weighed the mountains in scales, and the hills in a balance?" How fitting this language in that solemn pass, and how unspeakably more impressive must the words have seemed, when the mountains themselves took them up, and literally responded them, joining as mourners in the burial liturgy! For the minister stood so that each one of these sublime words was given back by the echo, in a tone as clear and reverent as that in which they were uttered.

The next day the body of the youngest child, about three years old, was found, and also that of the other hired man. On Sunday, the eldest daughter was discovered, at a distance from the others, across the river. A bed was found on the ruins near her body. It was supposed that she was drowned, as no bruise or mark was found upon her. She was twelve years old, and Ethan Crawford tells us she had acquired a good education, and seemed more like a gentleman's daughter of fashion and affluence, than a daughter of one who had located himself in the midst of the mountains. These were buried without any religious service. Three children—a daughter and two sons—were never found.

The relatives who studied the ground closely after the disaster, were unable to conjecture why the family could not have outrun the landslide, or crossed its track, if they left the house as soon as they heard its descent up the mountain. Some of them, at least, they thought, should thus have been able to escape its devastation. Mr. James Willey informs us that the *spirit of his brother* appeared to him in a dream, and told him that the family left the house sometime *before* the avalanche, fearing to be drowned, or floated off by the Saco, which had risen to the door. They fled back, he said, further up the mountain to be safe against the peril of water, and thus, when the landslide moved towards them, were compelled to run a greater distance to escape it than would have been required if they had stayed in their home; while they would have been swept off by the flood, if they had kept the line of the road which could have conducted them out of the Notch. It is a singular fact, Mr. Benjamin Willey tells us, that this explanation accounts for more known features of the catastrophe than any other which has been found. It explains why the eldest daughter was found without a bruise as though she had been drowned; and also the fact that a bed was found near her body, with which certainly the family would not have encumbered themselves, if they had rushed from the house with the single hope of escaping destruction when the avalanche was near. It accounts for the appearance of the body of the hired man, who was first discovered. And by connecting the terror of a sudden flood with the other horrors of the night, it brings the picture into harmony with what we know of the ravage and disaster along the Saco below.

The Bible was open on the table in the Willey House when it was entered the next day. The family were then secure from the wrath of elements that desolate the earth. At what place could the book have been found open more fitting than the sixteenth Psalm, to express the horrors of the tempest and the deliverance which the spirit finds? "The Lord also thundered in the heavens, and the Highest gave his voice; hailstones and coals of fire. Then the channels of waters were seen, and the foundations of the world were discovered at thy rebuke, O Lord, at the blast of the breath of thy nostrils. He sent from above, he took me, he drew me out of many waters. He brought me forth also into a large place; he delivered me, because he delighted in me."

South of the Willey House, upon the spot where a portion of the family were buried by the avalanche, it was a custom during several years for each visitor to cast a stone, and thus a large monument was reared out of the ruins of the slide.

RETURN TO THE CRAWFORD HOUSE,—THE NOTCH IN FORMER DAYS.

After the carriage has taken the tourist to the monument south of the Willey House, it returns to the Hotel. The view as you pass up the Notch is more interesting than the one you get while going down. The bare and broken rocks on the side of Mt. Willard stand before you like a great wall.

In the early settlement of New Hampshire a turnpike was constructed through the Notch at a cost of $40,000, and until the railroads were built, there was a great deal of travel through it, to and from Portsmouth. The Notch was discovered in 1772, by a hunter named Nash, who climbed a tree on Cherry Mountain, west of the Crawford House. It was, however, with great difficulty that teams could pass through it. Horses were pulled up the narrowest portions between Mt. Willey and Mt. Webster, and let down by ropes. "The primitive method," says Starr King, "of transporting any commodities, was to cut two poles some fifteen feet in length, nail a couple of bars across the middle, on which a bag or barrel could be fastened, then harness the horse into the smaller ends, which served as thills, and let the larger ends, which had no wheels under them, drag on the ground. The first article of commerce that was carried in this way from the sea-shore, through the solemn walls and over the splintered outlet of the Notch, was a barrel of rum. It was taxed heavily in its own substance, however, to ensure its passage, and reached the Ammonoosuc Meadows, west of the Notch, in a very reduced condition."

BEECHER'S CASCADE.

In rear of the Crawford House is Beecher's Cascade. Formerly this was known as Gibbs' Falls, named after a former proprietor of the Hotel. Mr. Gibbs' name has been attached to another, in the woods on the opposite side of the road. Leaving the Hotel you turn to the right and enter the foot-path along side of the small mountain stream. In a few minutes you come to the first cascade. Here Henry Ward Beecher took an involuntary bath, and since his name has been given to the pretty little water-fall. For nearly half a mile up the mountain you will find a series of cascades quite pretty to look upon. Cross the stream and follow the foot-path near it until you come at last to the guide-board pointing north. Here upon this rock a beautiful view is to be had. Looking out through the opening in the forest, you have a good view of Mt. Washington and the Tip Top House on its summit. This is the only place near the Crawford House, accessible by foot-path, where a view of Mt. Washington can be had. It is a quiet, charming place, and all will enjoy the walk to it as well as the view.

THE MT. WILLEY CASCADES.

There are several cascades on Mt. Willey, seldom visited by tourists, that are said to be quite equal to any in the mountain region. They were first discovered in 1858. To reach them you go down the Notch until you come to Cow Brook, the second stream below the Willey House. Following this for nearly two miles into the mountains you come to Sylvan Glade Cataract. Here the little stream leaps down a rocky stairway and then glides down a solid bed of granite, 150 feet at an angle of 45 degrees. A mile higher is Sparkling Cascade, quite equal in beauty to the first. Some labor is necessary to reach these water-falls, but if one has the leisure he will find himself well repaid.

AMMONOOSUC FALLS.

Five and a half miles north of the Crawford House are Ammonoosuc Falls. The Hotel carriage makes regular trips to them, and you should by no means neglect to avail yourself of the opportunity of seeing one of the most remarkable sights of the mountain region. The river itself is one of the wildest in New England. Rising in the ravines of Mt. Washington, it makes a fall of not less than 5000 feet before it reaches the Connecticut. The ride to it from the Crawford House is very pleasant. You keep along the road leading to Littleton, for several miles, when you turn to the right and soon enter the forest. On coming to the river you leave the carriage and walk up and down the bank for several rods, from which a better view is had. A deep and narrow channel has been worn in the gray granite, and the appearance of the rock is singular in the extreme. Great pot-holes, worn out by the water, and some of them more than ten feet above its usual summer hight, suggest the long ages that must have past since it commenced to drain this region. The tourist should pass down the river after viewing it at the rustic bridge.

THE MT. WASHINGTON RAILWAY AND NEW FABYAN HOTEL.

Sylvester Marsh, Esq., of Littleton, New Hampshire, having invented an engine for ascending and descending steep grades, a railroad was commenced to be built in 1866, from the base to the summit of Mt. Washington. It is located on the west side of the mountain, commencing at a point above Ammonoosuc Falls, and 6¼ miles from the Littleton road. The distance from the commencement of the railroad to the Tip Top House is nearly three miles. Nearly a mile of the track was laid in 1866, and the engine and car ascended and descended a grade of 1760 feet to the mile, with perfect ease and safety. The remainder of the road will be completed during 1867–8. Passengers will be carried this year over the road as far as completed, and horses will be kept at the terminus to convey them to the Tip Top House.

This invention was suggested to Mr. Marsh several years since, and when he applied for a charter in the New Hampshire Legislature for a road to the summit of Mt. Washington, a member suggested that the bill be so amended that the road extend to the moon. Mr. Marsh thanked the gentleman for his suggestion, but for the present he only contemplated ascending to the cone of Mt. Washington. The idea was scouted at first, and it was some time before he could get his invention tested. A third rail is laid between the two upon which the outside wheels rest, consisting of a series of cogs. In this runs a cog-wheel, and at each revolution the engine is propelled up the mountain at a slow but regular speed. The boiler is so arranged that it keps a perpendicular position whatever the grade. It is calculated that the ascent will be made in an hour, and those who have examined it, claim with entire safety.

A new Hotel, capable of accommodating five hundred guests, is to be built near where the old Fabyan House stood, by the Railroad Company, who also have contracted for the building of a turnpike from the Hotel to the Railroad. The Hotel will be completed in season for the summer travel of 1868.

Visitors at the Crawford House can go to the railroad by taking the road leading to Ammonoosuc Falls. The distance is about eight miles.

ASCENT OF MOUNT WASHINGTON FROM THE CRAWFORD HOUSE.

The tourist having seen the places of note near the Crawford House, he will now prepare to ascend Mount Washington, the crowning glory of the visit to the mountains. It is said of the dwellers in our modern Athens that when they die they expect to go to Paris. If Mount Washington was substituted we should be inclined to regard the arrangement as complete. It is evident that they would receive a heavenly experience at the summit. There is nothing more grand and elevating than the view from Mount Washington, and if it is possible to get a foretaste of heaven in the material world, one is sure of it there. The mighty space that comes within the vision, impresses one with his own insignificance, and the greatness of the Cause of all this vastness and sublimity.

There is usually from twenty to thirty degrees difference in the temperature at the summit of Mount Washington, in comparison with that at the Crawford House. If possible select a clear day just following a storm, but if your time is limited take the best you can get, if not too cold, for you should by no means fail to make the trip. The cone is quite frequently cloud-capped. This in a great measure detracts from the view, but don't stop for that. Your experience will be worth the effort, and it will be an event that you will always treasure. Dress warmly at all events. Thick gloves, an overcoat or shawl will not come amiss before you have reached the summit. The sharp winds are no where more searching.

The ponies are brought out and stand in a group in front of the Crawford House. The names of the party who have registered themselves for the trip are called, and each steps forward and mounts the trusty animal which is to bear him upon his back to the regions above. Passing across the road he waits until all are ready. The band appear and strike up a familiar air, and the word "go" is given, the guide, who has the party in charge, falling in rear at first and then following closely up to urge the animals forward. You enter the forest and press on, the sweet strains of music falling pleasantly upon the ear, until you pass beyond its sound.

The bridle path follows closely the summit of the White Mountain range, which you travel in a northerly direction until you reach Mount Washington. Each peak of the range has a separate name, and that which you commence to ascend at the Crawford House is Mount Clinton ; then comes Mount Pleasant, Mount Franklin, Mount Monroe, and Mount Washington.

As soon as you are out of the forest you are on the summit of Mount Clinton, 4,200 feet above the sea. Following the ridge you descend a little, and soon mount the rounded summit of Mount Pleasant, 500 feet above Mount Clinton. Descending to the narrow ridge you come to Mount Franklin, which is only a little more than a hundred feet above Mount Pleasant. Still beyond and 500 feet higher, are the double peaks of Mount Monroe. Winding down and to the east of Monroe, you come in full view of Mount Washington, which is more than a thousand feet above you. Here on your left is the Lake of the Clouds, from which the Ammonoosuc takes its rise. If not cloud-capped the Tip-Top House is in full view. It seems only a short distance to it, but your path is exceedingly circuitous, and it will take nearly an hour before the summit is gained.

The view all the way has been full of interest, and from each peak you have had a new grandeur unfolded. The horizon, at the Crawford House close around you, recedes at every step towards the summit, and at last it seems hardly defined, so wide the extent over which the eye wanders.

Onward and upward being the motto, you strike for the summit. After passing the Lake of the Clouds, all around you there is nothing but a broken mass of rocks, through which a narrow path has with great difficulty been made. Bearing around to the north-westerly side, you finally come to the enclosure of rocks, where you dismount. Leaving your ponies here, you pick your way over the loose rocks to the Tip-Top House, which is only a few rods distant. If the wind is blowing a gale from the north-west, as it frequently does, you are glad to enter the House before stopping to get a realizing sense of the scene before you. The cheerful fire within has too many attractions.

THE SUMMIT OF MT. WASHINGTON—THE VIEW.

The goal is reached. You stand on the summit of Mt. Washington. Sixty-three hundred feet above old ocean! The grandeur and sublimity of all New England at your feet! Oh! Heavens! is there another such a view? You have read, you have dreamed of grand old mountains, but not even the rose-coloring of boyhood ever pictured to your imagination such vastness and sublimity. Words fail to give adequate expression to the feeling that has come over you and you stand in mute silence before this awe-inspiring scene. If there be one place more holy than another you are sure that it has at last been reached, for here is a grand temple not reared with hands, and it seems too sacred a place to be profaned by the coarse and vulgar, who never read sermons in towering mountains, trackless forests and mighty rocks.

The scene is so vast that the effect of first standing upon the summit is bewildering. Below you are huge mountain peaks, the earth's surface seemingly having been tossed into a tempest, and you are sure that this must be chaos itself. A great white cloud, perhaps, sweeps by, enveloping you in its mist. Then again it is sunlight above, while below only here and there a mountain peak protrudes through the thick clouds, resembling islands in a vast lake.

The summit upon which you stand, covering about an acre and a half, is comparatively level, and is made up of a broken mass of dark mica slate, so rough that it is with great difficulty that you walk over it. Here are the Tip Top and Summit Houses, built of the loose rocks, the roofs of which are made secure by long chain cables passing over them and then fastened to the rocks below. They are owned by Mr. John R. Hitchcock of the Alpine House at Gorham. Lodging accommodations are provided, so that those who wish may remain over night and witness the setting and rising of the sun. Just east of the house is the stable, where the horses are kept that come to the summit by the carriage road from the Glen House.

North of the Tip Top House, and a part of the White Mountain range, are Mts. Clay, Jefferson, Adams and Madison.

Easterly, seemingly not far from the base of Mt. Washington, is the Androscoggin valley, while in the distance, rising from the central forests of Maine, is Mt. Katahdin.

South-east, and directly below you, are Carter and Pinkham Notches. Further beyond are ponds in Maine and the harbor at Portland, the latter 76 miles distant. Lovewell's pond, where an Indian tragedy once occured, can also be seen. Mt. Kearsarge also stands prominently before you.

South the sharp peak of Chocorua is seen, touching the very sky, while a little to the right of it is Lake Winnipisoegee. Still beyond the dim outlines of Monadnock are seen.

South-west are Mts. Carrigan and Lafayette.

West lies the beautiful valley of the Ammonoosuc. Beyond are the Green Mountains, Camel's Hump, Mount Mansfield and Jay Peak, standing prominently in the distant view. With favorable light it is claimed that one of the highest peaks of the Adirondacks can be seen.

These are only some of the more prominent objects that can be seen from thn summit of Mt. Washington. The minor details that fill the eye on every hand have a thousand beauties peculiar to themselves, and you want time to carefully study them. Light and shade as they alternate reveal the hidden loveliness of this great expanse, and so great and so many are the changes you never grow weary in tracing the deep valleys or long mountain ranges.

THE MISS BOURNE MONUMENT.

A few rods northerly of the Tip Top House, and just below it, is the rude pile of stones thrown up in memory of Miss Bourne, of Kennebunk, Maine, who perished here in a September night in 1855. She, together with an uncle and cousin, left the Glen House in the afternoon of a lovely September day to walk on the carriage road, and tempted by the favorable weather they concluded to make the ascent of the mountain. Sunset and a deep fog settled over them, and the wind became fierce and cutting, and finally Miss Bourne sank exhausted, about ten o'clock, within hailing distance of the summit. A wall of stone was thrown up to protect her against the wind, but she soon expired. They remained by her until morning, which revealed to them the nearness of the Tip Top House.

Not far from this place Mr. Benjamin Chandler, of Delaware, was lost, and his remains were not found for more than a year. Still farther below Dr. Hall, of Boston, passed two nights in an October snow storm, without food or covering. His feet were frozen, but he was saved from death.

TUCKERMAN'S RAVINE.

East of the Tip Top House is Tuckerman's Ravine, named after Prof. Edward Tuckerman, of Amherst College, who used to explore it years ago to complete his knowledge of the lichens and flora of the White Mountain region. The distance from the Tip Top House to the bottom is about a mile. Here, sheltered from the sun, the snow remains nearly through the year, only disappearing in August, a few weeks before it falls again. By the melting of the snow underneath, a beautiful arch is formed, which can be seen usually as late as August. It is a wild and interesting place, and if time will permit it should be visited.

THE RETURN.

Having enjoyed the beautiful view at the summit, and refreshed by an excellent dinner at the Tip Top House, you are now ready to return. If you prefer you can go down by carriage to the Glen House, which usually reaches the summit at noon. If you go back to the Crawford House you will find your pony in the enclosure where left, and a ride of about three hours will take you back to the hotel.

FROM CRAWFORD'S TO THE GLEN HOUSE.

From Crawford's to the Glen House you have the choice of two routes, over Cherry Mountain, to the Waumbeek House, and thence to the Glen; or south through the White Mountain Notch, down the valley of the Saco, and thence through Pinkham Notch. The distance either way is about the same, 35 miles, and involves an all day ride.

THE CHERRY MOUNTAIN ROUTE.

The coach leaves the hotel about 8 o'clock, soon after breakfast, and follows the Littleton route until it reaches the White Mountain House. Here it turns to the right and passes over Cherry Mountain. The ride over the mountain is very uninteresting, but you no sooner emerge from the forest than a lovely view greets the vision. Beyond is the Waumbeek House, at the foot of the Jefferson Hills, and to the left are mountains in Vermont. Reaching the Waumbeek at noon you stop for dinner. The hotel is kept by Mr. B. H. Plaisted. In rear of the hotel is Starr King Mountain, from which a good view is had. The view of Mt. Washington and the entire range from the Waumbeek House adds much to the interest of the place. From the Waumbeek to the Glen House the ride is exceedingly interesting, and from no where around the base do you get so good a view of the mountains.

THE WHITE MOUNTAIN NOTCH ROUTE.

In going to the Glen House from Crawford's by this route, you enter the Notch east of the Crawford House and pass the

Willey House. A half mile below is where lived old Abel Crawford, the pioneer of this mountain region. Continuing down the valley you come to

NANCY'S BROOK.

A poor girl who lived with a family at Jefferson, was found frozen to death here in 1778. She was engaged to be married to a man who lived in the same family, and to whom she had entrusted all her earnings. They were to leave for Portsmouth in a few days, to be married, and while she was absent in Lancaster, the faithless lover started for Portsmouth with his employer, without leaving any explanation for her. She learned the fact the day he left, and at once walked nine miles to Jefferson, where she tied up a small bundle, and started in pursuit. Snow had fallen, and only a hunter's path, marked by spotted trees, indicated the way through the wilderness. It was thirty miles to the Notch, but nothing daunted she set out at nightfall, hoping to overtake her lover in camp at the Notch, before the party left the next morning. When she reached the spot, they had left, though the ashes of the camp fire were still warm. Continuing down through the Notch, where only one woman had passed before her, cold, wet and hungry, she sank exhausted by the side of a tree near "Nancy's Brook." Alarmed for her safety, a party left Jefferson in pursuit, and they found her chilled and stiff in the snow, her head resting upon her staff, not a long time after she had ceased to breathe. The lover of the poor girl, on hearing the story of her faithfulness, her suffering and death, became insane and died a raving maniac.

SAWYER'S ROCK.

Below Nancy's Brook you come to Sawyer's Rock, which the driver will point out to you. The discovery of the Notch by a hunter named Nash, who climbed a tree on Cherry Mountain, was made known to Governor Wentworth. The Governor promised Nash a large tract of land if he would demonstrate the feasibility of the pass by bringing a horse through it to Portsmouth. Aided by a fellow hunter named Sawyer, the horse was let down the rocks at various places until they had passed over all. Draining his rum bottle and dashing it on the rock, Sawyer exclaimed, "This shall hereafter be called Sawyer's Rock!"

Just below the Rock you come to Upper Bartlett House, kept by Mr. N. F. Stillings. Passengers from the Glen House, stop here for dinner, and a good one they are always sure of. From here to Ellis River, the Saco valley is more broad and fertile. On reaching Ellis River you turn to the left and pursue a more northerly route. At Jackson you stop for dinner. From Jackson to the Glen House, you pass through Pinkham Notch. The scenery is quite interesting, the mountains rising to great height. Glen Ellis Falls, Crystal Cascade, and other places of note, a short distance from the road, are passed before reaching the Glen House, at the close of the day.

GLEN HOUSE.

OBJECTS OF INTEREST.—Thompson's Falls, two miles; Crystal Cascade, three miles; Glen Ellis Falls, four miles; Emerald and Garnet Pools, and Tuckerman's Ravine.

Down in the narrow valley, which lies between Mount Washington and Mount Carter, is the Glen House, of which Mr. J. M. Thompson is landlord and proprietor. It is a charming spot indeed. Back and east of the Hotel is the Mount Carter range, 3,000 feet high, while before it on the west are Mounts Washington, Clay, Jefferson, Adams, and Madison. The Hotel is only eight miles from Gorham, on the Grand Trunk Railroad, which makes it easy of access. It is 414 feet in length, a very large addition having been made to it in 1866; and it will now accommodate between four and five hundred people. Its nearness to the Railroad, and the ease with which the ascent of Mount Washington can be made from the Glen House, has always made this a place of great resort. While no where about the mountains are the water falls so grand and beautiful, the mountain scenery is in no respect inferior.

THE MOUNT WASHINGTON CARRIAGE ROAD.

One of the greatest triumphs of engineering skill, was the construction of the carriage road to the summit of Mount Washington. Commencing in front of the Glen House, it was made over a circuitous route to the Tip-Top House, on the cone of Mount Washington. Its entire length is eight miles, and no where does its grade exceed sixteen feet in one hundred, while its average is only twelve. It is broad and well built, and no where is there a better road in New England. A charter was procured, and in 1855 its construction was commenced, under the management of Mr. D. O. Macomber. In the following year it was finished to the Ledge, four miles from the Glen House. Five years afterward, in 1861, it was completed to the summit, and opened for travel. The surveys were made and the road laid out by Mr. Charles H. V. Cavis, who continued to be Superintendent of construction until 1857, when work was suspended on account of financial difficulties.

For half the way up the mountain the road winds through the forest, coming out at the Ledge. From here it continues along the edge of the deep ravine, which separate Mount Washington from Jefferson and Adams. Then it curves to the eastern side of the mountain, where it overlooks Peabody and Ellis Rivers. The scenery here is perhaps superior to that on any part of the road. Above and below you can see the carriages moving slowly along the road, while the distant view is grand in the extreme. Just before reaching the summit you will notice, on your left, the rude monument which marks the spot where Miss Bourne died of exhaustion, in September, 1855.

The ascent is made in four hours, by the carriages, from the Glen House.

Below are the rates of toll charged for passing over the road:

Foot passenger,	32 cents.
On horseback,	80 "
In carriage,	80 "
Sulky, with one horse,	64 "
Carriage with four wheels, each person,	64 "
Carriage with two horses,	94 "
Carriage with four horses,	$1.28 "

The charge for riding each way, up or down the mountain, is $4 for each person, which includes toll.

GARNET POOL.

A half mile north of the Glen House is Garnet Pool. The Peabody River in its descent over the granite rocks, has worn out singular looking places, some fifteen or twenty feet in circumference.

The most interesting cascades and water falls are south of the Glen House. First you come to

EMERALD POOL,

about two miles below the Glen House. The water in Ellis River passes over broken rocks, and then flows into a quiet stream.

THOMPSON'S FALLS,

are also about two miles from the Hotel, near the road leading to Jackson. You turn to the left and enter the woods at the guide board. A walk of a few minutes takes you to a series of beautiful cascades in a small brook coming down the mountain side, which extend more than half a mile. From the upper cascade you get a fine view of Tuckerman's Ravine and Mount Washington.

CRYSTAL CASCADE.

Continuing down the Glen till you come to the guide board on your right, three miles from the hotel, you leave the carriage and follow the foot path for nearly half an hour, when you come to Crystal Cascade. Part of its water comes from the summit of Mt. Washington, through Tuckerman's Ravine. Stopping for a moment at the bottom to view the cascade, you climb to the top of the high bank opposite, that overhangs it, where a better view is had. Is there anything more beautiful? At the top the water issues from among the rocks in a single narrow stream, and its descent broadens until it reaches the pool below. Eastman very happily compares it " to an inverted liquid plume—the rill above, where the water is one stream, being the stem, and the widening, fleecy flow its nodding, graceful, feathery spray."

GLEN ELLIS FALLS.

Four miles south of the Glen House is Glen Ellis Falls. You leave the carriage and enter the woods on the left, and a walk of a few minutes brings you to the grandest cataract in the White Mountain region. The Ellis River in its southward course is here compressed into a narrow channel, and at this point makes almost a perpendicular descent of 60 feet at a single bound. You should pass down the stair-way to the bottom of the fall to get its greatest beauty. An hour spent here in studying the wildness of the scenery will always be a pleasing recollection of your visit to the White Mountains.

HOTEL AND STAGE FARES.

Board at all of the first class hotels in the White Mountains this year will be from $4.00 to $4.50 per day.

Stage fares between the different points will be as follows:

Littleton to Profile House,	$2 00
Littleton to Crawford House,	3 50
Profile House to Crawford House,	4 00
Crawford House to Glen House, by Cherry Mountain, or White Mountain Notch,	4 00
Glen House to Gorham,	1 00
Glen House to Tip Top House,	4 00
Pony from Crawford House to Tip Top House and return,	4 00
Pony from Profile House to Summit of Mt. Lafayette,	3 50

BRANDON, VERMONT.

Brandon is situated on the Rutland and Bulington Railroad, 17 miles north of Rutland, and 50 south of Burlington. It is noted for being the birth-place of Stephen A. Douglas, its extensive marble quarries, most of which have just been discovered, and for the manufacture of

HOWE'S SCALES,

which are extensively carried on. The Howe Scale Company commenced manufacturing in 1857. Almost every variety is made, from the capacity of 100 tons, to the small post-office balance, and they are getting a wide celebrity for their neatness, accuracy and durability. The proprietors have never shrunk from exhibiting at all important State fairs, in the face of veteran performers, and have never failed to obtain first class premiums. The proprietors have several patents which secure to them advantages not possessed by other scale makers. By introducing Chilled Iron Balls between the platforms and the knife edges, and by making all the bearings *self-adjusting*, they take nearly all the wear from the pivots, upon the sharpness of which the accuracy and durability of all scales very largely depends. All the large scales which are designed mainly for out door use, have their bearings so protected from the snow and ice, as to render them very easily kept in order during the winter. They require but little and often no Pit, and although the most simple scales ever made, are so constructed as to secure the greatest strength at all points where strength is needed. These, as well as the Hopper Scales, for Elevators and Grain Depots, Rolling Mill Scales, for weighing Iron in its various forms, Dormant Scales, for large stores and warehouses, and the large variety of Portable Scales, are made in the most thorough manner by the best mechanics and most experienced scale makers that can be obtained. None but the *best* materials are used. All the pivots are made of the best refined steel.

Tourists who may stop at Brandon will find the Scale works well worth visiting.

J. ESTEY & COMPANY.
J. ESTE

Green Mountain Scenery.
500 Stereoscopic Views
From all parts of Vermont.
Published By
A. F. Styles,
Burlington
Vermont
Catalogues Sent
To Any Address
Freedom
Vermont.
Unity.
Kilburn
Boston

AMONG the thousands of Tourists who annually pass over the Railroads or through the Lakes of Vermont, there are very many who would gladly avail themselves of the opportunity of obtaining views of some of the beautiful scenes which are constantly presented to their notice. In view of this demand, the subscriber has made a series of twelve stereoscopic pictures, on each of the principal routes in the State, selecting points of the greatest beauty and interest, which can all be seen by the traveler passing over the line. Specimens of the views can be seen on all the boats and cars, and the set obtained from the newsboys.

LAKE CHAMPLAIN.

Views at Whitehall, the ruins of the old Forts at Ticonderoga and Crown Point, Split Rock, the Adirondacks, Juniper Island, Rock Point, Burlington and Plattsburgh, make up a series which every lover of Lake Scenery should possess.

Vermont Central Railroad,

Commencing at White River Junction, several views in the lovely valley of the White River, have been taken in Hartford, Sharon and Royalton, which for the beauty of the combination of hill and stream, are unsurpassed in the State. At Ridley's, on the Winooski, is No. 154, which, in addition to its beauty as a picture, has a large number of heads and faces pictured in the rocks, some of them almost as perfect as though carved from the stone. The High Bridge at Burlington, the valley of the Lamoille River, and the new and magnificent Depot at St. Albans, complete the series.

Rutland & Burlington R. R.

From Brattleboro to Burlington, on the line of this Road there is the greatest possible variety of scenery. The beautiful valley of the Connecticut, the hills and mountains before reaching Rutland, and Lake Champlain, with the Adirondacks in the distance, near Burlington, makes the most difficult part of the Artist's task to limit the number of views to a single dozen.

Passumpsic River R. R.

The first of the views upon this line is taken from an eminence above the Depot, at White River Junction, showing the Railroad Bridges and Buildings, together with the wide-spreading meadows of the Connecticut Valley, with a long reach of hills and mountains in the distance. Views on the Connecticut and Passumpsic Rivers, in the Valleys and by the Falls, Bell Water Pond at Barton, with several views of the unsurpassed scenery of Memphremagog Lake, complete the series.

The subscriber has also a large collection of Stereoscopic Views of the Hills, Valleys and Mountains in other parts of Vermont; a catalogue of which, each purchaser will find in the box with the picture. Selections from this Catalogue will be sent by mail, post paid, at the prices named.

A. F. STYLES, Burlington, Vt.

AMONG the thousands of Tourists who annually pass over the Railroads or through the Lakes of Vermont, there are very many who would gladly avail themselves of the opportunity of obtaining views of some of the beautiful scenes which are constantly presented to their notice. In view of this demand, the subscriber has made a series of twelve stereoscopic pictures, on each of the principal routes in the State, selecting points of the greatest beauty and interest, which can all be seen by the traveler passing over the line. Specimens of the views can be seen on all the boats and cars, and the set obtained from the newsboys.

LAKE CHAMPLAIN.

Views at Whitehall, the ruins of the old Forts at Ticonderoga and Crown Point, Split Rock, the Adirondacks, Juniper Island, Rock Point, Burlington and Plattsburgh, make up a series which every lover of Lake Scenery should possess.

Vermont Central Railroad,

Commencing at White River Junetion, several views in the lovely valley of the White River, have been taken in Hartford, Sharon and Royalton, which for the beauty of the combination of hill and stream, are unsurpassed in the State. At Ridley's, on the Winooski, is No. 154, which, in addition to its beauty as a picture, has a large number of heads and faces pictured in the rocks, some of them almost as perfect as though carved from the stone. The High Bridge at Burlington, the valley of the Lamoille River, and the new and magnificent Depot at St. Albans, complete the series.

Rutland & Burlington R. R.

From Brattleboro to Burlington, on the line of this Road there is the greatest possible variety of scenery. The beautiful valley of the Connecticut, the hills and mountains before reaching Rutland, and Lake Champlain, with the Adirondacks in the distance, near Burlington, makes the most difficult part of the Artist's task to limit the number of views to a single dozen.

Passumpsic River R. R.

The first of the views upon this line is taken from an eminence above the Depot, at White River Junction, showing the Railroad Bridges and Buildings, together with the wide-spreading meadows of the Connecticut Valley, with a long reach of hills and mountains in the distance. Views on the Connecticut and Passumpsic Rivers, in the Valleys and by the Falls, Bell Water Pond at Barton, with several views of the unsurpassed scenery of Memphremagog Lake, complete the series.

The subscriber has also a large collection of Stereoscopic Views of the Hills, Valleys and Mountains in other parts of Vermont; a catalogue of which, each purchaser will find in the box with the picture. Selections from this Catalogue will be sent by mail, post paid, at the prices named.

A. F. STYLES, Burlington, Vt

www.ingramcontent.com/pod-product-compliance
Lightning Source LLC
LaVergne TN
LVHW010216110826
845151LV00004B/1096

* 9 7 8 1 4 2 5 5 2 7 2 7 3 *